THE PARENTING BOOK

First published 2009
Reprinted 2009

ISBN: 978-1-905887-36-1

Published by Alpha International
Holy Trinity Brompton
Brompton Road
London SW7 1JA
publications@alpha.org

Cover and text illustration by Charlie Mackesy
Cover design by Sascha Green

THE PARENTING BOOK

NICKY & SILA LEE

ILLUSTRATED BY CHARLIE MACKESY

Alpha

It ought to come naturally but it doesn't always. Parenting is something which for practically everyone brings quite unsuspected challenges and these can produce either a degree of panic or a sense of failure. This wonderfully clear and practical book shows how a deep conviction about the unconditional love of God and the value this gives to everyone can shape a whole approach to parenting that is at one and the same time affirming, realistic about boundaries, patient and grateful.

As we recognise more and more clearly how necessary it is to offer accessible and honest guidance about being a parent in a society that's as muddled as ours is where children's welfare is concerned, Nicky and Sila's book is a real gift.

Rowan Williams
Archbishop of Canterbury

'The Parenting Book' is practical and full of wise advice. I believe it will help give parents a vital ingredient in the task of bringing up children – confidence! It's just what parents need today.

Rob Parsons
Care for the Family

Hugely practical, endlessly inspiring, packed full of humorous stories and insights – this book is a must for all parents. As a father, I know already that I'll be reading and re-reading this book over the years!

Tim Hughes
Worship leader

This is one of the best parenting resources I have seen. It is bursting with wise practical parenting insights. We owe it to our children to be the best parents we can be. 'The Parenting Book' is essential reading.

J John
Author and evangelist

A sensitive, practical book that provides real insight into how to be a good parent – a role we all try to fulfil as best we can.

Bear Grylls
International speaker and author

I heartily endorse this book as an extremely helpful and practical aid to those parents seeking to find reassurance in the process of raising their children.

Tom McMahon
Bishop of Brentwood

Parents need the support and the skills to bring up their children well more than ever. Too many people lack good parental role models which is why I commend this book so warmly.

Andrew Selous
MP

'The Parenting Book' is interesting, practical and easy to read, and I would recommend it to any parent wanting to do the best they can for their child.

Natasha Kaplinsky
TV newsreader

"I'm afraid your C.Vs are inadequate"

Contents

roughly the same ages, and though Nicky and Sila and Pippa and I work together and live round the corner from each other, our families have often holidayed together.

Watching Nicky and Sila parent their children over the past thirty years, it is clear to me that they have something very valuable to pass on. Their marriage and family life have given us a model to follow and we are constantly thankful for their wisdom and support in helping us to parent our own children.

Few things have such a positive impact on people's lives as good parenting, while bad parenting can be devastating, not just for the individuals involved, but for wider society as well. In our culture today there is almost unanimous support for the idea that children need a strong, positive parental role model. However, many parents often feel that they are failing in their role and are frustrated by their inability to cope with their children's behaviour and attitudes.

What is the answer? Does good parenting come instinctively to some but not to others? Or is it possible to learn how to be a good parent?

In this book, Nicky and Sila show how good parenting can be learned. Family life can become fulfilling and positive for both parents and children. *The Parenting Book* helps parents think intentionally and creatively about how to foster a healthy family life.

I am convinced that every parent will find a very constructive point of learning in this book. Many will find that it helps them to avoid or solve the problems they encounter in raising their children. While others will find that the book helps to make their good parenting even better.

Nicky Gumbel

Acknowledgements

This book has been a longer project than we had anticipated! Without the encouragement and help of a number of people it would never have been finished. As a result we want to say thank you to those who have stuck with us through the writing and rewriting and urged us not to give up. Most especially we want to thank Nicky and Pippa Gumbel for encouraging us that we had something to offer other parents. The friendship between our two families over so many years has been a huge support for us and our children as well as great fun, such as when we were snowbound in Chicago Airport for six hours with seven children and a rugby ball.

The help of our two editors has been tireless: first, Jo Glen, who had to hand over as she took up the position of Head Teacher, and then Ali Briston, who has carried us through to the end. Thank you for your skill, enthusiasm and creativity, but most of all for the fun of working on this together.

We want to thank Charlie Mackesy, who got to know our family well through living with us for several years. We are so grateful for his humour and the artistic skill he has brought to the cartoons and the cover.

Then there are a host of other people who have contributed to this book in different ways. A huge thank you to all the children (whether still children or now adults) who gave us wonderful quotes from their own experiences of family life. (In some cases we have changed their names to save them being embarrassed in years to come.) Thank you to all the parents who have shared their own personal stories of the ups and downs of bringing up their children – you will be an inspiration to many others doing the same thing.

Thank you too to the many people who have helped by reading the manuscript and suggesting changes and additions. We are particularly grateful to John and Diana Collins for the large amount of precious time given to a detailed reading of the manuscript and adding their insights and wisdom.

We also want to express our gratitude to Katherine Boulter and Linda Van Tinteren for typing and retyping so many drafts with enormous skill and patience – and who, in the time this book took to be written, have become engaged, married and parents themselves!

Two final words of thanks: first to our own parents, who gave us loving, fun and secure upbringings, and a model of parenthood that was so helpful to us for when we became parents ourselves. And finally to Kirsty, Benj, Barny and Josh – we most certainly could not have written this book without you. Thank you for turning out to be such lovely people (in spite of all our mistakes and all the sleepless nights you caused us when you were babies and then when you were teenagers). The two extra people in the family photograph at the back of this book are Rick and Tamsin, who became members of our family through marrying Kirsty and Benj. It has been like gaining a new son and daughter without any of the hard work of bringing you up – we are thrilled with the good job your parents did!

Nicky and Sila Lee

Introduction

Before I got married I had six theories about bringing up children; now I have six children and no theories.

John Wilmot
Earl of Rochester

All of us have moments in our lives that test our courage. Taking children into a house with a white carpet is one of them.

Erma Bombechk
Columnist

Wrinkles are hereditary. Parents get them from their children.

Doris Day
Actress

We turn up for this job unprepared. There are no degrees or diplomas in parenting. Most of us have had no training at all. The pay? Child benefit paid by the government to every parent in the UK is around £20 a week.

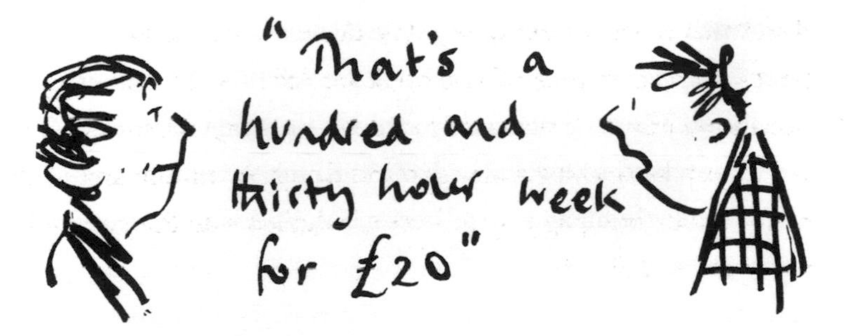

But when we bring our newborn baby home from hospital, for many of us, the realisation dawns: this is the most important job in the world and we have not got a clue what we are doing.

Children bring an awesome responsibility. We are entrusted with the task of shaping the lives of real people, with all their potential to do good or harm. At times, it is highly inconvenient. They disturb our sleep; they interfere with our plans; they stir up dormant and unresolved passions. And yet, as we seek to teach them, they are teaching us. They teach us what sacrifice is all about. The total dependence of a baby upon us, their powerlessness to reciprocate what we do for them, their inability to say thank you, all lead us to become less selfish. We are forced to change, to grow up, to look at the needs of another, to raise our boredom threshold, to develop patience, to deal with our insecurities, to become more whole. We are learning to love.

Parenting is a higher calling than the pursuit of our own happiness. It carries a big cost – tiredness, worry, and for some, the terrible pain of losing a child. But it can also bring the highest of rewards: the depth of love a parent feels and the privilege of knowing that we have helped shape a life.

Nothing really prepares us for the impact of our first child's arrival, although some parents are more ready than others. We were definitely among the 'others'.

Nicky Sila and I were living in Japan when we found out that we were expecting our first child. With two weeks to go until the due date, Sila woke me to say that she thought her waters had broken. Neither of us knew how long we had, but it fell to me to pack 'the bag of essentials' to take with us to hospital. Sila shouted to me from the shower that there was a useful list in the back of a book she had been sent by a friend in England. I found the book and madly started packing, not daring to leave anything out.

'Towel, nightie, dressing gown' all seemed straightforward enough. Then came: 'a tennis ball in a sock'. I found myself hunting around our flat for a tennis ball at 2.15 am, realising that there was more to having a baby than I had previously thought. Only some weeks later did I discover that this could relieve backache if placed in the small of the back during labour.

'Lemon and honey as a drink to quench thirst and restore energy during labour'. Running short of time by now, I hastily squeezed a lemon and poured the juice into a jam jar with generous spoonfuls of honey. When I later unpacked and put this concoction by Sila's bed, it looked just like a urine sample. (I had overlooked the instruction to dilute it.) And when I suggested Sila took a sip of it, I noticed one of the Japanese women, also in labour and resting between contractions, wince at what she probably took to be a strange Western remedy to ease the pain.

Sila I had read up on the 'natural childbirth' approach to having a baby, and had naively imagined I would be allowed to do pretty much what I wanted. The delivery room was about as far removed from a natural childbirth environment as could be imagined. It looked more like a medieval torture chamber! I was hurried towards an uncomfortable looking metal bed with a bar across one end and two elevated stirrups at the other, designed for women a lot shorter than me. I had neither the energy nor the language with which to protest. I squeezed onto it and my feet were strapped into the stirrups. My horror was, however, short-lived as the arrival of our baby overshadowed everything else.

Nicky If the mothers-to-be were surprised by my presence in the labour ward, the midwife in the delivery room was even more disconcerted. Having the father present (and a foreigner at that) was as new an experience for her as childbirth was for me. Only when it became clear to her that I might be required to translate her instructions, did she start to soften. Twenty-six years after leaving Japan I do not remember many Japanese words. However, two phrases will always stay with me: 'Ha-ha shté kudasai!' meaning, 'Please pant!' and, 'Ikinde shité kudasai!' meaning, 'Please push!' Shortly after the midwife's third, 'Ikinde kudasai!' our daughter emerged, with a strong cry of protest at her rather sudden arrival.

Kirsty was born six days before Easter. I returned home under a clear blue sky between trees laden with cherry blossom, thinking the world was more beautiful than I had ever known it. The roads were still deserted but I drove more carefully than I had ever driven before, suddenly feeling this huge new sense of responsibility. For the

> first time in my life someone was totally dependent on me, and I did not want to let her down.
>
> For any parent to try to describe the complex surge of different emotions at the moment of their first (or indeed subsequent) child's birth is not easy. I felt a sudden, overwhelming rush of joy and pride mixed with relief and, to be honest, astonishment. Here was a real, living and breathing person in whose creation we had played a part.

So began the journey of parenthood and, four children later, we have experienced more excitement, more challenges, more heartache, more joy and more exhilaration than we could ever have imagined.

Parenting has much in common with white water rafting. We are swept along, sometimes out of control, without the option of stopping and getting out. At times we feel overwhelmed by the forces that hurtle us forward, expecting to overturn at any moment. There are dangers for which we feel untrained and ill-equipped: exhilarating rapids that cause us to catch our breath, or rocks and whirlpools that require decisive action. Sometimes there are disasters – we tip over and have to swim to dry land before setting off again. Sometimes we are all enjoying the ride together. Then there are other periods of slow progress and unchanging scenery until the pace quickens again. And there is no expert on board. It is up to us to call the shots – we are at the helm, in charge of steering the family through each stretch of the river. Sometimes we carry trusting passengers, at other times a mutinous crew.

As we have been writing, we have reflected on some of the highs and lows of parenting, the more difficult times and the most rewarding.

The hardest aspect of parenting

Sila My greatest challenge has been coming face-to-face with my weaknesses – being too judgmental, jumping to conclusions, being impatient, over-reacting when under pressure, failing to listen when one of our children is upset and angry and being too bossy. In short, parenting has meant holding a mirror up to myself and seeing all of the work that needs to be done on me!

Nicky For me, the most demanding part of becoming a father has been making time for our children on a regular basis. I regret all those days when I allowed work to squeeze out the opportunity of an hour or so to be with our children, sitting around the table together, playing with them or reading stories.

The most fulfilling aspect of parenting

Sila The most rewarding part of parenthood has been seeing each of our children develop into a unique person with their own character, gifts and interests, while at the same time having a strong sense of identity within our family. I have also loved seeing strong and close relationships develop between them as siblings, though of course it wasn't always like that!

Despite the fact that bringing up children is hard work, I've always enjoyed the full-on nature of family. Mealtimes were often chaotic and I found myself endlessly trying to teach them basic table manners, but these times day by day also helped to build the relationships between us. Holidays – including the barbecues on the beach in the rain, because we've had them there every year – required energy and creativity, but the rewards far outweighed the costs.

Nicky Leaving aside for a moment the tiredness, the worry and the self-questioning that are part of the job, I have found huge fulfilment in being a parent. But I often anticipated that the next stage – when the children went to school, were allowed out on their own or became teenagers – would be harder and less enjoyable.

My experience, however, has been the reverse. We loved having teenagers in our home, often accompanied by hordes of their friends. I found that as each child has grown up my relationship with them has matured. I have enjoyed helping them face the next stage in life, talking through different options with them, encouraging them when they have been under pressure or known they have got it wrong.

Now, as adults, they keep coming back and the relationships keep growing.

Our children's perspective

Every family has a unique dynamic. No two families are the same. We will tell you a little about ours to give you more of the context from which we write.

After Kirsty we had three boys: Benj, Barny and Josh. The age gap between Kirsty and Josh is seven years. We have lived in Japan, the North-East of England (where Benj and Barny were born) and, for the last twenty-four years, in a flat without a garden in Central London – often feeling on top of each other for lack of space. Both our wider families live in rural parts of Scotland, so our children have had the opportunity during holidays to experience life in the countryside as well.

Our home has been more male-dominated than female, and all three boys are very keen on sport. The house has always been very busy, with people coming and going, often dropping in unannounced. Family mealtimes are a central feature – the tempo fast and the volume noisy – with everyone competing to get a word in.

We do not pretend we have done everything right in our parenting. Far from it! We can think of things we would do differently if we had our time again. We asked our children, all now in their twenties and Kirsty and Benj both married, to recount a few of the times and ways where they remember us getting it wrong.

Kirsty Growing up with three sports-mad brothers, conversations at supper would often be about surfing or a rugby match one of the boys had played, and sometimes I felt that there was not much space for anything 'girly'. The boys would naturally think any talk about clothes, shopping and make-up was boring. Even though I wasn't much into all of that, I still wanted the space to find out for myself and I didn't feel that Mum, as the only other female in the house, really supported me. It was one of the reasons I was keen to stay for weekends with a friend who only had a sister, as they talked about stuff that I found interesting. As I got older, I think Mum realised my need of this and I loved being able to talk to her about all my feelings.

Benj I remember one time on holiday when Dad completely lost it with me. And for once it was totally unjustified. Josh had been winding us all up in the car as we were sitting waiting for Dad to take us surfing. Barny and I had managed to restrain ourselves but, when Dad got in the car and Josh subtly carried on annoying us, I finally lost it and punched him. At which point Dad exploded and said, 'Benjamin – get out! You are not going to the beach,' and dragged me out of the car.

He was as angry as I have ever seen him. Normally he was very controlled in situations where he was justified to have shouted at us. Later Josh owned up and I remember Dad apologising.

Josh It was thirteen years ago, and I was only eight, but I remember feeling really bad when Dad pulled Benj out of the car. I knew it was my fault and I would be in trouble from Dad, Benj *and* Barny

Barny Mum and I are very similar – physically and in character. Tough, volatile and Scottish! We can give as good as we get. I often caused trouble but then I was often picked on. Victimised! I remember one time we were all supposed to be tidying up the house and we all started messing around. Mum came in and said, 'Barnabas, stop that immediately!' But it wasn't just me. All three of us boys were larking about.

Benj I did feel sorry for Barny sometimes. He gave a lot of grief, but he took a lot of the flak too.

Barny Once Mum virtually threw me downstairs. She certainly didn't mean to. I can't remember what I did – probably deliberately hacking her off. I used to love winding her up. Anyway, she came to get me and I leapt out of the way and ran off to my room. She followed and by this time she was mad! Mum's strong so I was trying to dodge her. I was holding on to my bedroom door while she was trying to pull me out so she could tell me off.

At this point, I let go of the door handle and the force of her pulling sent me flying down the stairs. It was definitely to my advantage as it didn't hurt me, but Mum was so shocked, she forgot her fury and we all ended up apologising.

Kirsty I remember a time when Dad had some big work stresses but he never talked to us about them at all. He wanted to protect us and so at home none of this was ever mentioned. We all knew it was a tough time. I was in my teens and old enough to understand – and yet nothing was communicated. That was not good for Dad's and my relationship at the time. It made me withdraw. Of course, now we have talked all about it, but it would have been better to have done so at the time.

Josh I think maybe they were too lax with me; it was definitely 'fourth-child syndrome'. They should have made me work harder. They got very lax about my exams and didn't say much about me working. Probably, after Kirsty got over-anxious about her exams, they didn't want to see that again. It would have annoyed me but it would have been better for me if they had made me do more work. I was not mature enough to know how much to do, even for my 'A' levels.

Thankfully children are remarkably resilient! As you read this book and parent your children, we hope you will be encouraged by the knowledge that love covers up a multitude of parental failings. Our aim with our own children has been to love them as individuals as well as encouraging them that they are a vital and valued member of our family. Strong family identity builds close relationships between us, despite the inevitable turbulence. Ours has been a unique journey; so is yours.

The aims of this book

Parenting has never been easy. Even in the time we have been parents we have seen our culture become more complex, more demanding and, for some, more scary. This is an exciting, stimulating and sometimes bewildering time in which to grow up. But despite all the new technology, globalisation and the internet, there are certain truths on parenting that withstand the test of time. There are many books on the market offering a staggering array of approaches. In this book we aim to pass on simple insights and time-tested values, which can easily be incorporated into your family life, even if it looks and feels very different from ours. Our experience from running our courses – *The Parenting Course* and *The Parenting Teenagers Course* – and from talking to thousands of parents, as well as many professionals, is that, whatever our situation, there are things we can do that will change our family life for the better. The advice we give is based on our own experience and valuable, practical tips we have learnt from others.

We have not experienced the extraordinary and painful challenges some parents go through, whether suffering the illness or death of a child, being rejected by an adopted child, facing behavioural disorders or handling drug addiction. These challenges are not within the aims of this book. We have, however, recommended other books and organisations that we hope will be helpful at the end of the book. For those who are parenting on their own, we appreciate that the job can be doubly hard and we hope the ideas we offer will be helpful and encouraging to you.

Family life is rarely (if ever) as tidy as we would like it to be. We have high aspirations and make neat little plans for our children but they often refuse to co-operate with them. They are not impressed by our ideas regarding their homework, bedtime or potential career in medicine. There are days when they exhaust us: their behaviour, their continual arguing, the mess they make, their unreasonable demands, their ridiculous fashion sense and their relentless needs can wear us down. We may at times look longingly back to our days without children and wonder how we filled our time or found anything to worry about.

'Whose idea was it to become parents anyway?' we ask. Our best intentions about parenting go out of the window and we find ourselves becoming as unreasonable as our children.

Occasionally we struggle simply to get through the day, castigating ourselves for letting everyone down, including ourselves. But at the same time we need ideals to aim for, without beating ourselves up each time we fail.

For us, our Christian faith has made a difference to everything in our lives, and not least to the way we have tried to parent our children. Your perspective may be different and you do not need to have a Christian faith to benefit from this book.

Wherever you are in your journey of parenting – right at the beginning waiting for your baby to be born, navigating the ups and downs with young children, or further down the line with teenagers – and whatever challenges you are currently facing, we hope this book will offer some useful ideas and practical tools that you can adapt to your own situation. Most of all, rather than make you feel guilty, inadequate or plain tired at the thought of what is involved, we hope to inspire you, encourage you and give you a vision for what lies ahead.

Section 1

Understanding how families work

Chapter 1

Knowing what the family is for

Family is having music on and Mummy, Daddy, Bart and Fergus dancing.

Fergus, aged 3

Family is a place where I feel totally safe and able to show my weaknesses, knowing they will still love me afterwards.

Kirsty, aged 28

Family. What family? They were never around for me.

Rupak, aged 22

Our family is the mould for what we become.

Simon Walker
Lecturer and author

The family is both the fundamental unit of society as well as the root of culture. It represents a child's initial source of unconditional love and acceptance and provides lifelong connectedness with others. The family is the first setting in which socialisation takes place and where children learn to live with mutual respect for one another. A family is where a child learns to display affection, control his temper and pick up his toys.

Professor Marianne E. Neifert
Paediatrician

Everyone needs a family. Our family is our home; the place where we know we belong, where we turn when we need comfort, support, advice, or help. It is where we can be ourselves, where we do not need to pretend, where we are accepted and

"I come from a large family...... mammals"

loved, where we can relax, where we can grow, where no-one is allowed to take themselves too seriously and where we can laugh. Or at least it should be. And our family is where we learn the balance between looking after ourselves and looking out for each other.

Nicky One Friday evening, we were driving out of London in rush-hour traffic with our four children aged between four and eleven. It had been a hectic day and I was opening my mail at the red traffic lights. One envelope was marked 'private and confidential' and Benj, looking over my shoulder, asked me what 'confidential' meant. I tried to think of a way to explain that he would understand. The best I could manage was 'only for you'.

Half an hour or so later, in order to survive the traffic jams, we bought a McDonald's meal to eat in the car. Sila was taking orders from the children and asked Josh, our four-year-old, what he would like. He replied emphatically, 'A Big Mac and confidential chips, please.' With three siblings and the frequent need to share, this new word was a useful addition to his vocabulary!

Creating a family

Family life has had to survive all sorts of pressures through the ages. Today in the West, the threat comes mainly from heightened social and economic expectations, broken relationships and a pressure on our time. For many children, the TV and the Internet have become surrogate parents, providing generally poor, if alluring, role models.

Many of us are stretched in one way or another, some to breaking point. Feelings of anxiety and inadequacy are universal among parents. Rob Parsons, Director of the UK charity *Care for the Family*, started a talk to 200 parents with the words: 'You are almost certainly doing a better job than you think you are.' There was an almost audible sigh of relief.

As parents we can easily compare ourselves with others – perhaps making us critical of other families, whilst trying madly to present the perfect front. But comparisons are unhelpful for us and our children: some children are more compliant and are easier to parent than others who are more strong-willed or complex. Your family will be different to our family and any other family. We can take tips from our friends, but we will not parent in the same way. We must decide on our own approach and have confidence in the uniqueness of our own family.

A friend of ours found herself having to bring up three children on her own after her husband left. She told us, 'As a single parent I have to work hard at building a sense of family for my children – that means being very careful what we do at weekends. We can spend time with other family units and they can see how a family with both parents works but I also need to show them that we *are* a family.'

It is worth taking a long term view of what we want to achieve. We can easily be caught up in the immediate crisis: trying to persuade a baby to sleep through the night, repeatedly disciplining a child for hitting a brother or sister, or arguing with a teenager who wants to pierce every available body part. The result can be that we miss the bigger picture – our desire to see our children grow up to be confident, secure adults who fulfil their potential and build strong relationships with us and with others.

Before you read on, pause for a minute or two to take stock of where you are and how you feel about the way you are parenting your child or children. (Throughout *The Parenting Book* we will refer to 'children' while being aware that you may have only one child, a step-child or step-children.)

However you feel you are doing in your parenting, we hope this book will encourage you that there are changes you can easily make to strengthen your family life. We can choose the type of family we create. You will probably want to do some things differently to the way you were brought up. We do not have to repeat the past. In the middle of a blazing argument, a teenager said to his father, 'You have never told me that you loved me.' To which his dad replied, 'Well, it was never said to me.'

Our family life

Have a look at the statements below, decide which are relevant to your situation and ask yourself how true they are for your family life now. Try to be honest!

- We set aside special time to be together as a family at least once a week.
- I spend some time each week doing something with each child that they think is fun.
- We sit down around a table to eat together as a family (with the TV off) several times a week.
- I regularly tell my children I love them and give them more praise than criticism.
- I know what makes my children feel loved.
- I limit the amount of time my children watch TV or play computer games.
- My children feel they can talk to me and that I listen to their concerns.
- I know who my children's friends are, what they enjoy doing at school and their favourite food.
- My children feel they can tell me if and when I have upset them.
- I am in control of myself when disciplining my children.
- I am able to discuss key parenting issues with my partner and we work on a joint approach.
- My children, as appropriate for their age, know my beliefs and values.
- I pray regularly for my children and am passing on spiritual values.
- I have friends or family members I can turn to when I feel overwhelmed in my role as a parent.

All parents need goals to aim for. Without them, we drift. We have highlighted four that have helped give our family life direction over the years. Admittedly, we have not always acted in line with them, but they have been a helpful yardstick. You may well choose others.

1. The family provides support

> *If I was feeling unhappy, Mum or Dad would have a little chat before bed – pretty cringy – but it always made me feel much better.*
> **Josh, aged 21**

Family is the first reference point of who we are. The old saying, 'Blood is thicker than water,' remains true whether we have had a smooth or bumpy ride through our upbringing.

All children will experience hardship and disappointment in some form or another. Young children can be very cruel to each other. They may not be invited to a friend's party or be picked for a playground game. As teenagers or young adults, they may be excluded by their classmates or let down by a friend.

Most children will face failure sooner or later: whether failing an exam or getting themselves into trouble. All teenagers will experience times when they know that they have let their parents and themselves down.

Former prisoner Sam Huddleston described how he started drinking heavily in his early teens. He fathered his first child at sixteen and began to make a living selling drugs. Throughout this time, he ignored his father's advice and 'God-talk', as he described it. On one occasion he was drunk and tried to steal alcohol from a shop with his cousin. They got into a fight with the shopkeeper. The cousin stabbed the shopkeeper, who subsequently died. Sam was arrested and later sentenced to life in prison.

On his first day in prison his father came to see him in the 'visiting tank'.

He described what happened:

> I picked up the phone. 'Hello, Dad.' I looked down; I couldn't look at his face. 'Sammy,' came the voice through the receiver, 'we're in trouble, and I don't know what we're gonna do. But we're gonna make it …' He said a lot more, but I kept hearing those first words. 'We're in trouble …' 'We.' Dad and I. The family and I. Not Sam alone, no matter how many times I'd turned my back on everything Dad stood for. I hoped I wasn't going to cry.[1]

Our children need to know that, whatever happens, their family will keep loving them and will pick them up and encourage them to keep going. They need to know their family values them, accepts them for who they are, misses them when they are not there and forgives them when, like Sam Huddleston, they mess up.

2. The family provides fun

> *Family has always been a place where we have laughed a lot. The boys, I think, are all genuinely funny and Mum and I never really minded being laughed at.*
>
> **Kirsty, aged 28**

Laughter is healing – psychologists tell us that laughter releases endorphins into the brain, reduces stress and improves our mood. Laughter helps us to keep life in balance. As we laugh together, we feel like a unit. Laughter dissolves tension – it draws us together in a shared understanding. Laughter stops us taking ourselves too seriously, and the family is a great place to learn to laugh at ourselves. Family teasing can be a way of conveying affection, though we have to tread carefully. Teasing can say, 'I know you intimately and I love your funny quirks.' But we must never laugh unkindly at our children and we must be prepared for them to laugh at us. We asked our eldest son, Benj, what he and his siblings thought about having us as their parents, to which he immediately replied, 'We laugh at you guys the whole time!' We decided not to press him for anything more specific.

A sense of humour provides fun and draws us closer together as a family. Fun does not need to be expensive – it might just be jumping in puddles, playing games, recounting stories at mealtimes or going out for the day together.

Sila When I was growing up, we were great friends with a family who had children of a similar age to my sister, my brother and myself. They were always fun to be with. The dad in particular had a wonderful sense of humour.

I remember the shock I felt as a teenager when I heard that he had left his wife and children to set up home with another woman. I had always thought they were a very close family. However, I heard later from the children that, when there were no visitors, there was no sense of fun or laughter in their home. When they were alone as a family, the father made no effort.

Children want to be where the fun is and, as parents, we may need to lighten up. That involves stepping back at times and asking ourselves what really counts. A pattern of having mealtimes with talk and laughter might be more important than children eating every last pea with their mouths shut. A mother with three children commented on the change of mindset required to make her home a place of enjoyment:

> Many parents are under a lot of pressure, particularly at the end of the school day. The idea of having fun – while doing the school run, serving supper, doing homework, practising a sport or music, organising bath time, reading them bedtime stories – seems rather remote to the conscientious parent. But any efforts to lighten the gruelling routine will reap rewards. My son Max is pretty allergic to doing his homework. As adults we are so used to pressing on and getting jobs done that it's a real effort for me to lighten up enough so that we all survive. But I've realised even a few minutes of distraction helps dramatically – a tickling session, a few judo moves, chopping carrots together, anything to help us relax and connect.

Family life needs to be punctuated with times of fun and celebration, occasionally holding parties for no reason other than that we are all at home together. Children can then learn the important art of celebrating each other.

If we do not spend time having fun together as a family, we can drive our children into themselves and, when they are old enough to vote with their feet, away from us altogether. If we set a high premium on doing activities with them that *they* enjoy rather than always what we like, on developing a shared sense of humour and on laughing with them and their friends, we will make our home a place they will want to come back to, now and when they are grown up.

In Chapter 3 we suggest practical ways to have fun together as a family.

3. The family provides a moral compass

> *I have appreciated being taught to look for the best in everyone and everything, and to value 'people' and 'relationships' in preference to 'things'.*
>
> **Sam, aged 31**

The family is the place where children learn about good and bad behaviour. It is where they are taught values for living well: that honesty matters; that kindness is a virtue; that anger should be controlled appropriately; that generosity is better than selfishness; that forgiveness and faithfulness are essential to friendships; that respect for authority is good and that self-control is important.

These values do not come naturally. Children learn through seeing them lived out, particularly by their parents; through hearing stories where good prevails over evil; through being taught to distinguish between right and wrong and through practising them in the safety of their home. When children see honesty modelled by their parents, and when they are taught that telling the truth is sometimes difficult but is always better in the long run, they are more likely to grow up to be honest and trustworthy. Without boundaries and guidance, children will flounder.

4. The family provides a model for relating to others

> *My parents always encouraged me to speak about things and be open with them. They created a home that was fun and welcoming to others.*
>
> **Milly, aged 23**

Above all, the family is where we learn to love, which is why it plays such a crucial role in the structure of every society. Children grow in their ability to relate through watching, experiencing and participating in the different ways family members relate to one another and to others.

For parents who lacked close family relationships in their own childhood, talking about what they missed, forgiving those who let them down and getting professional advice, if necessary, will help them not to replicate the same pattern of behaviour with their children.

Here, we focus on three relationships in particular. Not every family will have all three, but each one can help to teach children how close, loving relationships are built and sustained.

1. Parent – Child

Our ability to love others is based on the knowledge that we ourselves are loved. Knowing that we are loved regardless of our looks, our gifts, our abilities or our achievements gives us the confidence to open up to other people. We are prepared to let others in to the inner world of our thoughts and feelings, our hopes and fears, to make ourselves vulnerable and to risk rejection.

Parents' unconditional love gives their children a sense of security, self-worth and significance, each vital to their development. Ross Campbell, a professor of paediatrics and psychiatry and father of four, writes about the importance of not making our love conditional upon our children's behaviour:

> If I only love my children and convey my love when they please me, they will not feel genuinely loved, they will be insecure; it will damage their self-image and actually prevent them from moving on to better self-control and more mature behaviour.[2]

From the earliest months of our lives, we construct a picture of ourselves based on what we think our parents think of us. As we give that unconditional love to our children, they will have the confidence to let others get to know them and build good relationships.

2. Mother – Father

A strong, loving relationship between us as parents is one of the greatest gifts we can give to our children. The knowledge that we will stay together through thick and thin, working through difficulties and resolving disagreements, gives our children a deep sense of security. Parents who stay together just for the sake of their children often make significant sacrifices. But even this is not enough. Whether our children are two, or twenty-two, they want us to love each other, not simply be together. They will see through any pretence.

They observe how we speak to each other: whether we listen or make demands, whether we are rude or show respect, whether we are appreciative or critical of each other. They notice the physical contact, or lack of it, between us. They see how we express our anger and they watch how we resolve conflict. They take in whether we apologise or never admit to being wrong, whether we hold grudges or forgive each other.

Our marriage acts as a role model for our children and for their relationships. The impression we give to our neighbours, our work colleagues or our friends matters far less than what our children see when no one else is around. What they see in our relationship influences their ability to trust others. If our relationship with each other is critical and destructive, it will be harder for them to build close friendships and they will be more inclined to keep people at a distance.

On our *Parenting Course* and *Parenting Teenagers Course* we encourage couples who are parenting together (whether or not they are married) to do *The Marriage Course*[3] to invest in their relationship. One husband said to us, 'I have suddenly realised the truth of the saying: The best way to love my children is by loving my wife.'

Children whose parents are separated or divorced still have a deep longing to see their parents getting on with each other. It can make a huge difference to a child's happiness and well-being if they are able to work at their relationship with each other. One fourteen-year-old boy, whose parents split up four years ago, told us what it meant for him when his parents came to his school together: 'A couple of months ago it was my birthday and I was playing in a football match. All I wanted was for my parents to be there. It was one of the best days of my life just to see them together.'

If you are parenting on your own, spending time with two-parent families can be invaluable in helping your children to experience a healthy marriage relationship close up. A mother, who brought up her children on her own without any contact with their father, told us recently: 'As a single mum, I used to look for role model families so my children could see how the parents related to each other and how fathers got involved in playing with their children. Another great example for them has been their grandparents' marriages.'

3. Sibling – Sibling

We recently watched a nature programme featuring a family of bear cubs growing up. When they were not sleeping or eating, they generally spent their time fighting with each other. But it was the playful kind – provoking each other, chasing, wrestling, biting an ear – and, curiously, it reminded us of our own children.

Siblings build relationships with each other through playing, fighting, squabbling, sharing toys and adventures, settling arguments, teasing and learning to take care of each other. Brothers and sisters are not the only source of lessons in socialising, but they are a great help.

Dealing with sibling clashes is one of the most common and challenging of all tasks in parenting. Most brothers and sisters do not always enjoy each other's company, and learning to live together will include plenty of bickering and fights. The clashes may stretch the whole family, but learning to get on is good for our children's characters! While they can choose their friends, they cannot choose their brothers and sisters. Siblings who have learnt to appreciate each other as children will often be a source of great strength and friendship to each other as adults.

Conclusion

Of course no family is perfect, or even anywhere near! But whatever our circumstances, our family can be a place of unconditional love where our children have the opportunity to experience what relating to others is all about. In the rough and tumble of family life, they learn what love looks and feels like.

Families have the potential to build bonds that support each member through both the good times and bad. An American mother recounted an incident with her daughter, Amy, who was desperate to join the cheerleading team in her high school:

> It really meant a lot to her. She wanted to be on that team. She practised really hard. She went to all of the rehearsals. The day came. She went and she had a great try out. I was really proud of her. But she didn't make the team. She was devastated. All the way home I drove this sobbing, inconsolable girl. There was nothing I could say that would comfort her. She ran upstairs, into her room – into the walk-in cupboard and slammed the door. I didn't know what to do. We decided we'd go and get into the cupboard. So, the four of us, Rick (my husband) and I and the two boys, went into the cupboard with her. And we were all crying and sobbing.
>
> After we'd been in there a while, wiping our noses on our sleeves, I said to one of the boys, 'Go and get some Kleenex.' A few moments later he came back with one Kleenex and he was blowing his nose. We laughed and the mood was broken. What had been a tragedy in her life turned into something that became a shared family experience.
>
> When she and I were talking about it yesterday, she said, 'That event, almost more than anything else in my life, cemented for me what our family is.

> You guys were there for me. You didn't tell me to buck up. You didn't tell me, 'In the scheme of things, this is not that important. You'll get over it.' You just got in there and cried with me.[4]

Pause and consider

- What do you want 'family' to mean for your children?
- If you could make one change to your parenting, what would it be?
- Do your children feel supported by you when they are upset?
- Do you regularly laugh together as a family?
- What are the most important values you want to model to your children?
- What else could you do to nurture your relationship with your partner?
- If you have more than one child, are there other things you could do to help your children grow up as friends?

Chapter 2

Building a healthy family life

I feel whole. My parents have given me the greatest gift any parent can give, the knowledge that I am loved.

Thea, aged 16

There's no such thing as a perfect family, but I seem to love mine more and more as the world becomes less and less rosy.

Tara, aged 20

The way I want to parent our one-year-old daughter is totally different from my own experience of growing up. As that's my only reference point, I am trying to learn as much as I can, watch others and think hard about what we want to create as a family.

Mother, aged 30

Like all parents, my husband and I do the best we can, hold our breath and hope we've set aside enough money for our kids' therapy.

Michelle Pfeiffer
Actress

Creating close family relationships is a long-term endeavour. There is no quick gimmick that sorts it all out, rather it is a steady investment at many levels. Building a home that is a healthy and nurturing environment to shape new lives requires vision, planning and hard work.

It is not unlike creating a garden. This, too, requires long-term vision (regardless of what the TV makeover programmes suggest). You need to hold a picture in your mind's eye of what the uncultivated plot might look like in twenty years.

The gardener must create the right conditions: the soil must be cultivated and fed with compost; the seedlings must be protected and the weeds controlled. Those first few years are particularly critical in establishing the garden. Once the plants have good roots they become more resilient to bad weather. So it is in creating a family.

Nicky When our children were all still under seven, I vividly remember us meeting and spending a weekend with a family with four children aged between fifteen and twenty-two. What struck Sila and me was the way the children related so naturally to their parents, to each other and to us. The children were clearly friends. In fact, at first we assumed that they could not possibly all belong to the same family, as they all got on so well. They showed an interest in us and, over supper, all of them were involved in the conversation and the frequent laughter.

That weekend gave us a vision of the sort of family life we wanted to create and inspired us because we saw that it was possible. We were witnessing the fruit of the healthy environment these parents had provided for their children over many years. We knew it had involved a lot of time, sacrifice, considerable heartache and persistent prayers, but we knew we wanted to achieve something similar in our own family.

In this chapter we want to look at three ingredients for building a healthy family life.

1. Finding a healthy work-life balance

Giving children 'quantity' time

For children, love is spelt T-I-M-E. For new parents, the greatest pressure and the biggest shock is that we have the same amount of time that we always had, but the demands on it have multiplied overnight. Children do not fit neatly into the space we used to reserve for pursuing our own interests and relaxation. They do not readily agree to 'play quietly' in their bedroom to enable us to have a lie-in, read the paper, go through the post, cook meals, have a bath or even go to the bathroom.

Our time is also theirs, and for several years they will have little understanding that we might need some space. Even in their teens, they are likely to assume that we are on hand to provide a laundry service, chauffeuring service and one-to-one counselling twenty-four hours a day!

It is not just *quality* time our children want; they also want and need *quantity* time. One mother spoke to us of the cost and rewards of parenthood:

> I had no idea how utterly selfless one had to be to look after a baby. My purposeful life came to an abrupt halt. Suddenly I couldn't achieve the simplest task without interruption. I longed just to be able to do some boring housework, if I could only work in peace. I badly missed the recognition and acknowledgement that work gives, so different from the unnoticed life of the mother. But along with this frustration came the overwhelming love for my baby son Alex, who I thought was the most beautiful thing ever to be born.

Cherie Blair is a barrister who has four children. During the time her husband was Prime Minister she spoke about the difficulty of achieving a healthy work-life balance:

> My husband was told by a senior colleague that he would not get anywhere if he insisted on leaving work in the early evening. That warning, as history shows, was completely wrong. And thank goodness for that.
>
> This work-life balance issue is crucial, and it is, of course, a particularly important issue for women … I feel like those jugglers, like so many other parents, desperately trying to keep everything up in the air. And pretty well every day something will fall to the ground.[1]

Our children will be with us for a few short years. Those years may seem interminable at the time. But the moment when they are no longer living at home will arrive suddenly, at which point it will be too late to turn back the clock, as one father discovered:

> I don't know if the price I've paid to get where I am has been worth it ... What I missed most was the childhood of my kids. I just wasn't there for them, and even when I was there, I wasn't really '*there*'. My mind and my heart were focused on other things. I have climbed the ladder of success, and as I'm getting near the top rung, I realise that the ladder is leaning against the wrong wall.[2]

The actor Martin Clunes was interviewed by Michael Parkinson, who asked him whether he had enjoyed taking the lead role in Molière's *L'Avare* at the National Theatre. He said he had loved it. When Clunes was asked if he was looking for another similar role, he replied: 'I'd love one but theatre happens at the wrong time of day.' He told Parkinson that he hated missing bath and bedtime with his two-year-old daughter. 'Some things have to be sacred. Our work is supposed to serve us, not the other way round.'

It is not just work that takes parents away from their children. Some parents, who do not need to work, can all too easily find their time is filled up with other people and other activities, such as shopping or keeping fit, rather than being with their pre-school children. It can be easier to let someone else give the children their supper, oversee bath time and carry out the rest of the daily routine. Yet these are the valuable hours when we do our parenting. A mother we know admitted her struggle: 'I have realised I don't really enjoy playing with babies, so each day I pray I can give Cara what she needs despite myself. It's a daily battle to stop myself handing her over to someone else to look after her.'

To work or not to work?

Today in the West, the full-time, stay-at-home mother is often perceived as the alternative to the full-time working mother. Yet this polarisation can obscure the much more complex situation in which most mothers find themselves. A mother earning a living is not a modern phenomenon. Over two thousand years ago a highly-esteemed wife and mother in the biblical book of Proverbs was described as doing both unpaid and paid work to look after her family's needs:

> … she provides food for her family … she considers a field and buys it; out of her earnings she plants a vineyard … She sees that her trading is profitable … She makes linen garments and sells them … She is clothed with strength and dignity.[3]

The question with which many parents wrestle today is how much time they should leave their child in the care of someone else, whether it be a child-minder, day-care centre, au pair, nanny, grandmother, other relative or friend. In writing her book, *Toxic Childhood*, educationalist Sue Palmer researched what kind of childcare is best for the child:

> For the first year or so of a child's life, familiar faces and settings are of paramount importance.

> This is when attachment is critical, when calming, sleeping and eating habits are established, and when the process of learning to communicate begins. The opinion of all the developmental and childcare experts I met was that – if at all possible – parental care in the family home is the best option, at least for the first eighteen months. The work of developmental psychologist John Bowlby suggests that a child's 'internal map' is largely determined by the relationships formed during this period.[4]

A couple may not be able to survive on one income alone. They may both be involved in careers they love, or careers for which they have trained hard over a number of years. They may have pressure from inflexible employers. A single parent may have to work full-time to support a child. Or a mother may struggle with the emotional shock of full-time parenting and become depressed. In each situation the best possible solution between parental care and supplementary care has to be worked out carefully.

Parenting involves sacrifice. We know many parents who have made extraordinary sacrifices for their children. Some have given up a career, foregone bigger houses or their own personal fulfilment to put family life as a higher priority than their work. Others have chosen less demanding roles, or started part-time work to be their child's principal carer.

Whatever sacrifices they have made, they will not share the regrets of those who find that the time to be there with their children has suddenly passed. Of course childcare varies tremendously in quality but few do it better than the parents of the child. And children benefit enormously from consistency in who cares for them.

If the primary carer changes by the day, the week or the month, children are required to attach to, and then detach from each new person they have bonded with, to the detriment of their emotional development. Where both parents work full-time, organising the most stable childcare possible will provide more security for a child.

When people ask us what we think is best for children, we recommend that wherever possible, one of the parents should be the *main* caregiver (ie, the person with whom the child spends the most time) in the first eighteen months, and ideally until their child begins primary school. Sometimes this can be achieved by both husband and wife arranging to work flexible hours so that one of them can be at home for their young child.

A disincentive to a parent spending more time at home with a child is that parenthood is grossly undervalued. Sue Palmer writes:

> The hugely important lesson the developed world has to learn from the great sociological experiment of the last quarter-century is that bringing up children is not some sort of part-time hobby. It's a real job: skilled, full-time and personally demanding. Owing to women's low status in the past, this traditional aspect of 'women's work' has never been properly valued – and much of the developed world still finds it difficult to grasp its significance.[5]

Sila Looking back I am so grateful that I was able to be at home until all of our children started school, although I didn't always appreciate it at the time! As they grew older I gradually increased the hours I worked. Being able to work part-time and flexible hours was a huge bonus in terms of our family life. Nicky and I decided that I would be the consistent presence for our children on a daily basis, especially for the early evening routine of tea, bath time, stories and bedtime when they were little. When they became teenagers, I tried if at all possible to be at home by 4.30 pm when they got back from school.

Being at home wasn't always fun or easy when our children were little. There were times when I felt desperate to be involved in anything other than parenting. Sometimes that led to resentment; at other times the daily routine of boring chores, shopping, cooking, feeding and washing got me down. I was exhausted a lot of the time, but the underlying knowledge that I was investing my time in our children's lives kept me going.

Finding support as a parent

In the past, support often came from the wider family who helped with childcare, passed down tried and tested advice and provided a break for stressed parents. Today that help is less likely to be available. Families live further apart, and grandparents may be out at work themselves. But stay-at-home parents benefit hugely from other adult company and a change in routine.

Suggestions for finding support

The following ideas, where applicable, will help relieve the pressures involved in looking after young children.

- Accept offers of help from those you trust.
- Find a local parent and toddler group. Many churches run them weekly. If there is not one in your area, consider getting together with one or two other parents and starting one in a church hall or community centre. The effort will be rewarded by the mutual support that the group provides. *The National Association of Parents and Toddlers* can provide useful advice on how to go about it.[6]
- Make friends with another parent who has a child (or children) the same age as yours. Take it in turns to look after each other's child for a morning or an afternoon so that you can do something different once a week.
- Discuss with your husband, wife or partner regularly (but not constantly, or your relationship will suffer) how to cope with the latest parenting challenge.
- Plan your weekends carefully so that everyone in the family will have activities they enjoy – avoid being totally child or adult-centred. If one parent works outside the home and the other is the main carer, try to work out a way of giving each other a decent break. One couple with two children under six take it in turns to lie in on a Saturday morning and sometimes give the other a half day 'off duty' over the weekend.
- Nurture the relationship between your children and their grandparents. You may be able to leave the children in their care and go away for a whole weekend once or twice a year.
- Nurture relationships with the rest of your wider family. Aunts, uncles and cousins can all be a great support.
- Do not worry about mess unless it reaches health hazard levels, and take any domestic help on offer. Remind yourself that spending time with a child is more productive in the long run than continually tidying up the house – even if there is nothing to show for it immediately.
- Remember you will never be a perfect parent – and tomorrow is a new day.

2. Encouraging healthy play

The value of play

In the words of the celebrated developmental psychologist, Jean Piaget, 'Play is the work of children.' Play is fundamental for children's health and well-being. Playing comes naturally to them. It starts as exploration – they are discovering the shape, the feel, the texture, the properties of the world around them.

Soon they begin to play games with other children that involve pretending, sharing, inventing and competing. They are learning to socialise and to identify with other people through role-play. Through playing they develop physical skills – running, climbing, making things. They use their imagination and exercise their creativity. And in the process they have fun – vital, whatever our age.

Imaginative play

Today, technology often threatens creative play. Of course children benefit from a time of less frenetic activity each day, perhaps by watching TV or a DVD, or, better still, by reading or listening to story-tapes that cause them to conjure up the scenes in their minds. But sitting passively for long periods is no substitute for actively creating their own fun.

The child's mantra, 'I'm bored,' well-known to most parents, is often a gateway to imaginative play. Every parental suggestion is likely to be dismissed, but children dislike doing nothing. Children are amazingly creative and in times of free, unsupervised play, will make use of whatever is available to them.

Nicky Our own children's favourite games when they were young did not usually require much expense. A dressing-up box of old clothes kept them entertained for hours. On many occasions their bedroom was transformed into a world of tents and secret passageways with the aid of a few blankets and some brooms. And I remember how a large discarded cardboard box, in which the washing machine had been delivered, became the best playhouse. They just needed me to help them cut three openings to make a door and two windows. It lasted almost as long as the washing machine.

This kind of play is threatened by consumerism. Ever more sophisticated and expensive toys are marketed aggressively. Not only are our children subtly wooed by the adverts but we, as parents, all too easily fall prey to the attitude that, unless our children have the latest fashionable toy, they will be emotionally and educationally deprived. It takes confidence to believe in the benefits of creative play with simple toys.

The great outdoors

Children benefit hugely from playing outside. Farley Nursery School in Wiltshire, England, was founded in reaction to the trend for children to be indoors and sedentary. It allows three to five-year-olds to be outdoors most of the day, whatever the weather. The children can roam, make dens and mud pies, and are encouraged to explore. They choose to stay outside ninety per cent of the time. The official school inspectors, Ofsted, have called the school 'outstanding'. The school's founder said: 'Today's world is too sterile. Children are wrapped up in cotton wool. My children know stinging nettles sting and that fire is dangerous. Some nurseries say, "Let's stay indoors, it's raining." But we say, "Come on, let's go and splash in the puddles." '[7]

We will not help our children if we are over-protective. According to the Mental Health Foundation, reasonable levels of risk in unsupervised outdoor play – such as tree climbing, den building, skateboarding or using the climbing frame –

help children build self-confidence and resilience.[8] In addition, tension between children is greatly reduced through participating in outdoor activities together. The head teacher of a primary school said to us recently, 'Relational issues in a class? Go camping! We did just that with some of our children. Wellies and mud work wonders for relationships.'

For us, bringing up our children in central London meant regular trips to a park with bikes, balls or roller-blades to get them outdoors when they were young. As they got older, they graduated from swings and roundabouts to the more dangerous adventure playground. Getting there was an effort and could be fraught if one child was dawdling or the football had gone missing. But these outings were invaluable for their social and physical development. Children who sit indoors all day are much more prone to obesity.

Teenagers, too, benefit from outdoor activities, not only for their health and to socialise in an unpressurised setting, but also to burn off excess energy. A woman with three siblings told us, 'My mum made us all bike miles to school to use up teenage energy and aggro. We were too exhausted to scrap by the time we got home!' For parents bringing up teenagers in a town, a holiday in the countryside or by the sea can make a big difference.

Safe play

The issue of safety is a source of anxiety for many parents. We need to teach them about 'stranger-danger' and where to play. Ponds in gardens are very dangerous to little children, and we cannot be too careful. Encouraging our children to explore, while guarding them from hurting themselves, is part of the parental juggling act. Children need to be protected but not stifled.

Sila When one of our sons, Barny, was six he spent hours one summer whittling pieces of wood with a penknife he was given by a godfather. I was constantly terrified the knife would slip and stick into his leg or take a gouge out of his hand.

Nicky, however, was much more relaxed about it, having done exactly the same as a child. He gave Barny a few basic safety rules, like keeping the blade pointing away, watched him for a few minutes and then left him to it. I frequently had to bite my tongue not to stop this pastime. I am glad I did as he now makes his living working with wood (though he does cut himself from time to time).

Some of the activities teenagers engage in are likely to provoke even greater feelings of alarm. But again it is a balance between helping them understand (and minimise) risks while allowing them to pursue a sport or hobby that may hold no attraction for us.

Sila A favourite activity for all three of our sons is surfing. I had heard of horrendous surfing accidents and seen pictures of gigantic waves in their magazines. I was happy enough when the sea was calm and, ever-hopeful, they sat on their boards waiting for bigger waves with one of us keeping an eye on them. As they became more experienced, they wanted to go out on stormier days, when there was no way we could help them if they were 'rumbled' by a big wave or hit on the head by their board.

Slowly I came to realise that having done all we could to drill them on safety, I had to trust them. Obviously they enjoyed the adrenaline rush of bigger waves, but they were more safety-conscious than I had given them credit for. I recognise now

> that my own anxiety was making me very negative towards this activity. I am glad that with Nicky's encouragement I was able to let go. We have seen how surfing has provided them with greater independence as teenagers, as well as many days of good, healthy exercise and huge fun.

Making a mess

The issue for other parents is tidiness and control. The desire to guide our children can so easily turn into an unhealthy and humourless drive to organise and direct their behaviour twenty-four hours a day. A friend of ours, who was expecting her first child, realised that she needed to face her fears. Her obsessive desire to keep everything at home perfectly in place was not going to work with a young child. Unchecked, this controlling behaviour can stifle a family's ability to enjoy each other's company and play together.

A newspaper article on the dangers of over-tidying cited one household: 'The children's toys were all tidied away before their father came home because he would fly into a rage if he saw so much as a piece of Lego lying on the floor. Most weekends they were allowed to play with their toys only one at a time in their playroom.'[9]

Healthy play often involves making a mess. Allowing our child to get covered in paint or turn their bedroom into a set for a battle scene can be challenging for us, but extraordinarily liberating for them.

One question we learnt to ask ourselves was, 'Why not?' to check if our reactions were reasonable. 'Why not create a toy mountain?' if that's what a three-year-old wants one day. 'Why not let them get soaking wet?' if they are having their best fun of the holidays. 'Why not bring snails into the kitchen?' (We may be able to think of several reasons, but it is worth asking ourselves the question!)

Tips for tidying up

- Do not tidy up more often than you have to. Once a day is generally quite enough. Fight any 'perfectionist' tendencies.
- Do not do it all yourself. If the children are too young to tidy up toys on their own, do it with them. Try making it into a game. Challenge yourselves to beat the egg timer, for example.
- Give warning of how much longer they have to play before needing to tidy up, and stick to it. Otherwise they will use delaying tactics every day.
- Break the job down into more manageable tasks. For example, tell your child, if they are old enough, first to tidy up all the pens, then all the Lego, then the cars, etc. This makes the job seem less overwhelming for them.
- Establish, early on, a 'clean-up time' before moving on to the next activity.
- Make tidying up as easy as possible by giving away old toys they no longer play with and, if necessary, reorganising the space where toys are kept.

3. Establishing healthy routines

The benefits to children

Routine, order and stability are deeply comforting to children as they thrive on knowing what to expect. Routines bring a sense of security. If we are erratic and have no consistency, our children can become anxious or nervous. Familiar patterns give a feeling of safety and, for young children, are a good preparation for school.

Mealtimes

Sitting around a table on a regular basis is one of the most beneficial activities for children. This may be the only time a family is together. Eating together at least once a day has been part of family life in almost every culture, until the second half of the twentieth century in the West. Longer working hours have meant one or both parents may not be at home to eat with their children during the week. With the advent of the TV, families began to sit passively in a semi-circle, being entertained rather than attempting to make conversation with each other. Fast food and microwaves mean family members can eat separately at different times. Now in the UK, with eighty per cent of children aged five to sixteen having a TV in their own room, arguing about which channel to watch is a thing of the past.

Homes today are being built without a space for a family dining table. But healthy family life thrives on eating together. Children learn (eventually!) to eat what is put in front of them, rather than each choosing their own food, and are more likely to have a balanced diet. They learn table manners. When they are old enough, they are expected to take a share in the preparation and the clearing up. All of these routines, reinforced day by day, teach them that they are part of a family; that they are a valued member, but not the centre; that their views will be heard, just as they are expected to listen to others; that they have a contribution to make, and so does everyone else.

Of course children will grumble, refuse to eat the food, or throw it on the floor. They will forget to say thank you, or seem incapable of staying on their chair for more than thirty seconds – in some cases, well into their teenage years! We may feel we have reminded them every day for years to offer the tomato ketchup before helping themselves, and they still forget. Mealtimes can be a battleground and sometimes we feel as if we are losing the war. But they are a vital, regular social activity that prepares children for just about every other type of social activity. We neglect family meals at the risk of failing to socialise our children effectively. And, if we persevere, eventually we will see the benefits of eating regularly together.

For some families, the weekends are the only time for regular family meals. One father we know, who could not be home early enough during the week to eat with the children, made lunch at the weekend fun by initiating games at the table, such as challenging each family member to talk on a favourite topic for one minute without hesitation or repetition. With a sullen teenager, encouraging conversation might involve asking each person to describe their best and worst moments of the day or week.

The chef and restaurateur, Raymond Blanc, wrote of the value of family mealtimes in a newspaper article, called 'Let's eat en famille!':

> To cook for family and friends is an act of love that binds together all who share it. But in Britain, we are cooking and eating together less – and this frightens me. A family that eats together is more likely to be a kind, close family whose children will grow up to be kind and considerate …
>
> But the child, who grows up knowing nothing of these mealtime disciplines, will grow up respecting neither good food nor other people, and will almost certainly have limited communication skills.[10]

Providing a healthy diet

Life in an image-conscious, diet-obsessed culture has put a new kind of pressure on what we look like. But our children's attitudes will be influenced first and foremost by *our* attitudes. Just as parents who communicate their dread of the dentist are likely to have children who are afraid of going to the dentist too, so, if we are hung up about our own appearance, they will take that on. And if we are obsessive or neurotic about what we eat, they probably will be too.

We would suggest that dieting, as a concept, is not right for children (unless advised by a doctor). However, thinking about what and how much we eat is quite a different matter. Eating three balanced meals a day, including vegetables and fruit and avoiding excessive 'E' numbered ingredients, will give children a healthy attitude to food. Nutritionist Susan Jebb stresses the value of establishing good patterns early on: 'They are not called "eating habits" for nothing – habits are ways of behaving which have become very deep-seated and are therefore difficult to change. Habits acquired in childhood tend to stay with you life-long.'[11]

Nicky One rule we established was not to have fizzy drinks (except on special occasions) and our children simply didn't miss them. Another routine was to have a snack the moment they arrived home from school to keep them going until teatime.

If the cupboards are full of cakes, chocolates, biscuits and crisps, our children are likely to develop a sweet tooth. But there is a big difference between having those sorts of things all the time and putting a chocolate brownie in their packed lunch. If we only give our children carrots, sunflower seeds and yoghurt, we may have a revolution on our hands.

One family we know has a 'sweet tin' that only comes out on Friday nights. Another mother with two children aged fourteen and eleven told us: 'We've always allowed one thing a day from the treat box, and now they often don't want one. Sometimes other children, who are never allowed sweets or chocolate, come to stay and want about ten!' Forbidden fruit can be dangerous. Our advice is not to make it a big issue.

A bedtime routine

The regularity of a bedtime routine with children provides a positive ending to the day; it helps a child who is over-tired or over-excited to calm down; it establishes a pattern so that our children get enough sleep; it serves as an opportunity to read stories that pass on to them values we believe to be important; and it gives an opportunity to talk about their day and any worries they may have.

Sila For me, this was generally the hardest time of the day, and juggling bath time and story time with two to four young children was a daily challenge. Often I was putting them to bed on my own. We were usually all overtired and the temptation was just to get it over as quickly as possible. The bedtime routine often felt more like a battle than a family time.

To prevent it becoming purely functional, I had to keep reminding myself of the benefit a consistent, enjoyable routine can have in the life of a child. I knew that if I made the effort yet again at this less-than-scintillating part of the day, it would be the stories, the conversations and the sense of security that would stay with them.

Patterns established at a young age can continue to be a natural and valuable parent-child time in the teenage years. A couple with two teenagers said to us recently: 'Our children still insist one parent says goodnight and chats at bedtime as a consequence of their early childhood routines, and these provide our best times to talk with them.'

Sleeping patterns

The amount of sleep children have affects their mood, their behaviour and their ability to learn. Children need enough sleep in order to function in a healthy, happy way. Primary school teachers are facing an epidemic of 'sleep deprivation' amongst children in the UK.

The table below is a guide drawn up by professionals in children's health on the amount of sleep children need:

Recommended hours of sleep[12]

	Age group	Recommended hours of sleep (daily)
Babies	3 to 11 months	14 to 15 hours
Toddlers	12 to 35 months	12 to 14 hours
Pre-school children	3 to 6 years	11 to 13 hours
School age	7 to 11 years	10 to 11 hours
Adolescents	12 to 18 years	8 to 9.5 hours

The problem is that good sleeping habits do not just happen; we have to insist our children go to bed and then consistently enforce those patterns. Insisting on a routine 'rest' or 'quiet time' during the day for pre-school children is very beneficial. Make it non-negotiable. A four-year-old will try everything to convince us they do not need it but, if it becomes part of everyday life, they will accept it as the norm.

The regularity of a bath helps signal bedtime and the end of the day. Cutting down the amount of TV or DVDs they watch before going to bed (as these cause over-stimulation) and increasing the amount of active play during the day (which tires them out physically) will help them get to sleep.

Getting children to bed at a reasonable time is a particular challenge for working parents who want to see their child when they get home. A father we know always phones his young children if he is not going to see them in the evening, and this is a pattern they know and enjoy.

Storytime

Reading stories is one of the most enjoyable ways to bond with our children and we can start when they are very young. Hearing stories widens a child's world and helps to develop their thought processes. They learn to understand life from other people's points of view. As we read stories about anger, love, kindness and sadness, we are helping our children to identify different emotions and to talk about their own feelings.

Bedtime stories have other benefits. Reading and re-reading stories many times over with young children builds a sense of security. That is why it is worth finding good books that can withstand frequent repetition, though a young child's taste in literature may well differ from our own. There are strong links between children being read to and learning to read. They can also be a good regular opportunity for five to nine-year-olds to do their 'homework' reading.

Prayer time

The final part of our bedtime routine was to pray with and for our children each night.

Sila Each child had to get into their own bed (once they were past being put to bed) and one of us would go in, turn the light out, then get down beside the bed and pray with each one individually for a couple of minutes, finishing with a hug and a kiss and a clear goodnight as we left the room. It became for them a cosy, intimate one-to-one moment, which brought an end to their day in a regular and special way.

Other routines

Weekly and annual traditions also contribute to a healthy family life. For many families that includes making Sunday, or the whole weekend, different by stopping work and relaxing together, with longer mealtimes, playing sport or doing some other activity together, and, for some, attending a place of worship as a family. Others establish rituals on holidays, or mark the seasons with different activities, such as picking strawberries in the summer, having conker fights in the autumn, going ice-skating in the winter, picking wild flowers in the spring, and so on. (We write further about the power of traditions for children in Chapter 19.)

Of course life should not only consist of routine. Moments of spontaneity, when we grab the opportunity to do something new and different, can also be a wonderful part of family life. But routines give a strong sense of rhythm to the days, the weeks and the years, which build deep security for children.

Conclusion

Spending time with our children, encouraging healthy play and creating routines are invaluable. Sue Palmer puts the need for these aspects of parenting into a wider context:

> Society has conditioned us all to believe that money, hard work and consumer durables can solve most problems. But the problems of babies who bite, pre-schoolers struggling to write before they can talk, and children corralled for several hours with unqualified minders round the edges of every school day will not be assuaged by the purchase of the latest technological gadgets. As the twenty-first century progresses, the problem of who's looking after the children isn't going to go away.[13]

The day to day experience of looking after children can easily make parents feel that they are not achieving anything significant, sometimes in sharp contrast to paid work. Working out what is best can be complex and invariably involves compromise and sacrifice. Parenting requires seeing the big picture. And every day makes a difference to our child's development and wellbeing.

Pause and consider

- What do you consider most important for a healthy family life?
- In five or ten years' time, how are you going to feel looking back at your current work-life balance? If you could change one thing about your family life, what would it be? Even small changes can make a big difference.
- Do your children have enough opportunities for healthy play?
- How much time do they spend outdoors?
- Do you eat together as a family on a regular basis? How could you use mealtimes more effectively to build the relationships between you?
- Have you established a bedtime routine that results in healthy sleeping patterns for your children? If not, what could you do?

Chapter 3

Creating special family time

One would be in less danger
From the wiles of the stranger
If one's own kin and kith
Were more fun to be with.

Ogden Nash
Poet

I can't remember seeing much of my father – he was always busy doing something else.

Jim, aged 26

If Mum said, 'Let's do a family outing,' we'd all groan and say, 'Do we have to?' And then find we really enjoyed ourselves – even if we didn't admit it.

Mary
Writer

For me the most special times were holidays in Ireland when we were just family. We still talk about things we did together when we were children.

Kirsty, aged 28

A philosophy professor stood before his class. When the class began, he picked up a very large Perspex jar and proceeded to fill it with stones, each about two inches in diameter.

He then asked the students if the jar was full. They said that it was. The professor then picked up a box of small pebbles and poured them into the jar, shaking it so that the pebbles rolled into the open areas between the stones. He asked the students again if the jar was full. They said it was.

The professor then poured sand into the jar. The sand filled up the tiny spaces. He asked once more if the jar was full. The students responded with a unanimous, 'Yes.'

'Now,' said the professor, 'This jar represents your life. The stones are the important things – your faith, your family, your health, your friends – things that if everything else was lost and only they remained, your life would still be full.

'The pebbles are the other things that matter like your job, your house, your car. The sand is everything else – the small stuff.

'If you put the sand into the jar first,' he continued, 'there is no room for the pebbles or the stones. The same goes for your life. If you spend all your time and energy on the small stuff, you will never have room for the things that are important to you.

'Pay attention to the things that are critical to your happiness. Play with your children. Take time to stay healthy. Take your partner out dancing. There will always be time to go to work, clean the house, give a dinner party and mend the door handle.

'Take care of the stones first – the things that really matter. Set your priorities. The rest is just sand.'

Spending time with the people we love the most does not just happen. This dawned on us when our three eldest children were five, three and one. We always seemed to be busy in the evenings and our weekends filled up rapidly with all those activities that clamoured for our attention: doing jobs around the house or garden, catching up with friends and paperwork, shopping, fitting in some extra work, pursuing a hobby, going to parties and attending other special events. We realised, unless we made some changes, we would continue to experience frustration and regret as other aspects of our lives crowded out spending time together as a family.

We talked with an older couple who helped us find a solution. We decided to put two regular commitments in our diaries each week.

One we call our 'marriage time' – a weekly date, time to enjoy being alone together, doing something fun. The other was 'family time' – the same concept, with the emphasis on a meal and an activity the whole family could enjoy.

Looking back over the past twenty-five years, these times have probably been the best commitments we have ever made. Most weeks, keeping them was a challenge. Some weeks, we did not succeed. But we never regretted it when we managed to stick to them.

Our 'marriage time' has given us the opportunity to communicate regularly at a meaningful level and to keep romance alive in our marriage.[1] Neglecting our relationship was an easy trap to fall into, particularly with the huge and often overwhelming responsibilities that came with being parents. But we realised that the strength and well-being of our marriage had far-reaching implications for our children, not least safeguarding the presence and involvement of both of us in their lives.

Owing to the nature of our work, with weekends often busy, we generally had our family time midweek around a meal in the early evening. Over the years these 'family nights' (as they became known) enabled us to relate to each other beyond the nuts and bolts of daily life and they built a reservoir of shared memories for our children and for us.

Of course there were other occasions in the week when we were all together, but planning at least one weekly time, when we would stop everything else to have fun as a family, has helped to communicate to our children more loudly and clearly than we ever could with our words: 'You are our priority. We love you. We want to spend time with you.'

Sila To help to make it different and special, we allowed our children to take turns to choose what we ate. It was often something that I might not otherwise make or buy for them. Pizza was a hot favourite when they were younger; stir-fry with noodles became the top choice later on. I sometimes used these evenings to show them how to make their particular choice – cooking and tossing pancakes, making spaghetti bolognese, preparing a fondue.

We also took turns to choose the activity. The only constraint was that it had to be something everyone could join in with. In the summer it might be cricket, football, playing frisbee, roller-blading, going on a bike ride, a barbecue, a picnic, a drink in a café or a trip to the cinema. In the winter their favourites were playing indoor games like hide and seek, sardines, hunt the thimble, a board game, or a game that involved acting and dressing up. These may sound old-fashioned, but children love them. Your choice of activities may be different to ours. The point is they need to be inclusive, and they do not need to cost anything to be fun.

It is the interaction with other family members that provides the amusement. We found that, when we as adults were prepared to be laughed at, to get down to their level and to do things that might be considered silly, they loved it. We connected as a family.

Once our children had all become teenagers and more independent, we continued our family night as one occasion each week when we knew we would be together. The games stopped and the meal became longer, while the conversation remained as loud as ever.

We chose the evening to fit in with our children's and our own commitments. No child or family should be under such pressure that they cannot find an hour or two each week to relax and have fun together. Homework, music and sports practice could usually be planned around family time. One mother said, 'There's only one night in the week when my husband is home in time for us all to eat together – and so I tell the kids, "No late clubs that night," and we have a family supper.'

If possible, we kept to the same night each week, although we retained flexibility so that this was a mutually agreed time rather than inflicted on our children. Sometimes our family night included a godparent or some other close friend, who understood that conversations would be geared around the children. As they progressed through their teenage years, a boyfriend or girlfriend might join us.

Other families we know have chosen part of the weekend for their regular family time – going out together for the day, playing in the park, Sunday lunch, going for a walk in the country, watching a favourite TV programme or finding a sport that they can all enjoy together.

Prioritising family time

Parenting changes everything: our hobbies, our social life, our weekends and our holidays. Keeping some time for ourselves is likely to make us better parents, but it may not be possible to play golf for a while, go to the gym three times a week, or read every page of the Sunday papers. We may not be able to volunteer for every need at church or in the community. In fact, it might be a good idea to curtail our activities drastically while our children are young enough to want to be around us.

For some families, it is the children's schedule that pushes out time together. Clubs after school, extra activities or playing at friends' houses can easily mean that the children's days become frenetic. Parents rush to take their children from one activity to the next, frantically trying to fit in meals, pushing for homework to be finished before bedtime, then collapsing exhausted into bed for a few short hours before the next action-packed day begins. Time to relax together can easily be lost in an over-busy schedule.

Despite pressure from other parents, we do not have to live like this. That might mean telling our children they have to make a choice. So we say to them, 'You can choose to do swimming *or* ballet *or* football *or* gym.' In the long term, making some family time will be more beneficial than any number of extra-curricular activities.

Protecting family time

Even when carefully planned and prioritised, many things can intrude on our family time. In our home the telephone has been the main interruption. Each call could potentially take twenty minutes. After a number of ruined family nights we turned on the answering machine. Some members of the family were keener to answer the phone than others, so we came to an agreement that during a family night, bar emergencies, the answering machine would take all the calls and mobiles were switched to silent.

In his book, *The Sixty Minute Father*, Rob Parsons helped us to realise what can happen if we are there for our children physically but not emotionally:

> I remember well coming home from work and sitting at the meal table. My wife had long since given up trying to communicate with me at that hour of the day but two small children hadn't. 'Dad, I'm in the football team on Saturday,' one would say. Or, 'Susan pulled my hair again today!' But I was distant, my mind still with a client or planning the evening's strategy. I would mumble a reply. And then the telephone would ring and a small boy would say, 'Dad – it's for you.' And suddenly I would come alive – animated as I talked. And two young children would be watching me. They weren't stamping or kicking; it would have been better for me if they

> had been. But the message they were getting loud and clear was, 'This matters to him. This brings him alive.' Changing that kind of lifestyle is, for me, an ongoing battle.[2]

The struggle must be fought and won more often than it is lost. Family time that is protected from interruptions tells our children at a deep level that we love them and that they matter to us.

Persevering with family time

In the short-term it is all too easy to measure the impact of our family time by whether a particular event seemed to be a success or a disaster. We often felt that we were fighting an uphill battle. A game sometimes ended in tears and the whole evening was ruined. A video night degenerated into arguments and sulks as we tried to find a film that everyone was happy with. We wondered if it was worth bothering with at all.

Having spoken to other families trying to maintain family time, their experience has been the same as ours. A mother told us, 'I would say that one in three of our family nights ends in a row, or it all goes pear-shaped before we've even started. But it's worth all the aggro for the two that go well.' Another family said, 'There's a lot of compromise that goes on. We have four children between the ages of five and fourteen, and finding something we would all like to do at a time that works is a challenge. But well worth the effort. I save up special offer vouchers from the newspapers and we all go out for a pizza. Or we play tennis and our youngest acts as ball boy.'

Activities for family time

We have included below a list of ideas that could be used to plan a family time with your children or to create a surprise for them. Choose the ones that will work with the ages of your children.

- Go to the park: play football, cricket, Frisbee, etc.
- Have a card, draughts or chess tournament.
- Play charades.
- Go to the cinema and out for a milkshake or quick meal before or afterwards.
- Draw or paint together. (Try doing some portraits of each other.)
- Play with bricks, cars or soldiers.
- Play 'houses' or dressing up.
- Try cooking a new recipe together.
- Make something together such as Christmas cards or decorations.
- Watch a DVD the children will enjoy.
- Play hide-and-seek or a similar game.
- Go for a walk or a bike ride.

⇨

- Go jogging.
- Hire a rowing boat or a pedalo on a local pond.
- Go on a picnic (even in the rain).
- Make pancakes or pizzas together.
- Go roller-blading.
- Go swimming.
- Explore a park you do not normally visit.
- Plan a scavenger hunt. Try to find something in the house beginning with each letter of the alphabet.
- Read a book aloud. (Books like C.S. Lewis' *Chronicles of Narnia* appeal to children and adults.)
- Look through family photo albums or look at old family videos/DVDs.
- Make a recording of your most recent family news and send it to a friend or relative whom you do not see very often.
- Play a board game that the children all enjoy – *Monopoly*, *Scrabble*, *Balderdash*, *Pictionary*, *Sorry* and *Trivial Pursuit* have been our family favourites at different times.
- Sing favourite songs or nursery rhymes (perhaps with home-made musical instruments).
- Make a collage using anything from old buttons and scrap material to pictures out of a magazine.
- Make a family website with photos and news.
- Make a simple bird feeder for the winter and hang it where the whole family can see it.
- Act out a favourite story (eg, *Goldilocks and the Three Bears* or *Cinderella*) with each person taking a different part. Use props and costumes.
- Make puppets and put on a puppet show.
- Have a barbecue and try bananas in their skins – cut lengthways and stuffed with smarties.
- Listen to a story CD or tape – some come with read-along books.
- Encourage younger children to draw and colour a picture to send to a grandparent. Older children could send a home-made card.
- Play tennis, basketball, golf or whatever sport they enjoy.
- Take the children on a tour of a parent's workplace.

⇨

- Draw a family tree on paper and complete it as a family – add photographs if you have them.
- Give each person a large piece of paper and take turns tracing the outline of each other's bodies. Colour in each outline to look like the person.
- Gather a variety of leaves in the autumn and press them in a book.
- Plan how you could help a child in a developing country as a family.
- Go for a walk near your house to get to know your neighbourhood better.
- Put together a scrapbook describing a favourite holiday or a special event (with pictures, photos and other souvenirs).
- Play charades or 'the adverb game' (which involves one member of the family doing an action on command and the rest of the family trying to guess the adverb. For example, someone might have to act out eating their supper 'jerkily' or playing tennis 'clumsily').
- Go out together for an ice-cream or hot chocolate.
- All pile into the same bed at the weekend for a breakfast-in-bed lie-in.
- Have a 'lock-in day' – all stay in pyjamas and do not answer the door or phone.

Family holidays

Some people get excited about family holidays; others dread them. Usually the younger members of the family will be in the former group, which says a lot about their benefit. For many children this is the time when their parents are most relaxed and when they have time to do enjoyable activities as a family.

Successful holidays usually need careful planning. With young children they also require a lot of energy. We might want to sunbathe – they want us to help them build yet another sandcastle. We might enjoy educational tours of ancient Mycean ruins – they would become bored and resentful. We might want to spend most of the day reading – they want us to play with them.

Nicky One of my favourite pastimes on holiday is dinghy sailing. Over ten days of the summer I would take part in daily races organised by the local sailing club. I continued this when we got married – with Sila as my crew. Children, however, made that impossible. After a fraught summer when Sila had watched one too many races with restless children wanting to go to the beach, I realised that the racing would need to be put on hold for a time so that we could go to the beach together as a family. Similarly my golf clubs went into semi-retirement for eight years until the children were old enough to want to start playing with me.

We also need to think carefully about who we are with on holiday.

Sila When our children were young, we made sure some of our holiday time was just us as a family so that we were not always with other adults. When our children became teenagers, family holidays continued to be very special, although by this stage they would usually invite one or more of their friends to come with us.

For parents who did not have positive experiences of holidays in their own childhood, family holidays may not be appealing. Planning, being willing to be flexible and learning from previous years what worked and what did not are usually the keys to success. One family who struggled to get their family holiday right said, 'The last few years we have found something that really works for us. A lot of it before that was experimenting until we found a place to go with something for everyone to enjoy.'

We may find holidays easier when we go away with others, but family life also benefits when we have time with our children on our own. Some parents may feel they would not be able to manage that. The only thing to do is to try. A couple with two children told us, 'Getting away from home is all about getting them away from distractions – often we see the results in terms of family dynamics after the event. The children play better and are closer. We love holidays with other families, but actually we have come to see it's better when the bulk of them are just us.'

The most expensive holidays are not necessarily the best. The main consideration is what will draw us together as a family.

Nicky I remember several years as a young teenager when we went camping as a family in Cornwall, in Devon and then in France. I loved it. I'm not sure it was the most comfortable holiday for my parents and the weather was not always ideal, but it was a bonding experience for our family. Everyone was involved when we arrived at a campsite. We had a tent that attached to a camper van and my father, my brother and I would time ourselves to see whether we could break our record in how quickly we put it up.

I loved surfing, playing beach cricket, exploring new places and having time to play cards or board games in the evening by the light of a gas lamp. These were some of the best family times as I was growing up.

Conclusion

In almost every other role we undertake in life, others can take our place. But as a parent we are indispensable for the relatively short time we have our children around us. We have often heard parents, whose children have left home, say words like, 'I wish I'd made more of the times when they were around and needed me.' The only way to be sure that we do not live with regret is to say to ourselves now, 'Family is non-negotiable.' That may take a change of mindset, but building up a bank of shared special memories will benefit everyone – and build the family unit.

Pause and consider

- Could you book in 'family time' this week?
- How could you make it a fun event for your family?
- Plan a game or an activity that everyone will enjoy – for an evening or at the weekend.
- Ask your children what they would like to do next time.
- Plan your next family holiday. Have a discussion with the whole family about where you might go and ask your children what they most enjoy about holidays.

Chapter 4

Helping sibling relationships

> *They may drive me up the wall, but I know my brothers and sister are always there for me – and vice versa.*
>
> **Salma, aged 16**

> *When you are small you just beat each other up – you can't expect young boys to say, 'I'm angry but I respect you.' You need to have a good fight with your brother.*
>
> **Barny, aged 23**

> *Having one child makes you a parent; having two, you are a referee.*
>
> **Sir David Frost**
> **Broadcaster**

Brothers and sisters. What associations do these words conjure up from your experiences, first as a child and now as a parent? An ally? A rival? Endless squabbling? Chalk and cheese? Close friends? Frustration? Common bonds? Odd one out? Shared laughter?

The concept of siblings will evoke different responses from different people. However, what almost all parents with more than one child have in common is a deep longing for their children to get on with each other and to become friends. Few things are more rewarding for parents, who have put up with years of squabbles and fights, than to see their grown up children enjoying each other's company.

Family life in our society has changed radically over the last sixty years. There are many more families with an only child, and a huge increase in the number of families with step or half-brothers and sisters. The principles we will look at for helping sibling relationships are relevant to every family, regardless of their situation, although the challenges are usually much greater in a 'blended' family.

For an only child the principles will be worked out mainly through their peer group friendships and cousins of their own age.

The benefits of having siblings

Through having brothers and sisters, children learn tough but important lessons for life. Siblings provide a natural training ground for building relationships. The inevitable clashes are an important part of the learning process.

Enjoyment of having a sibling:

- Someone to play with
- Someone to share jokes with
- Someone to tease
- Someone to talk to
- Someone who looks out for you and looks after you
- A role model
- A great friend
- A lifelong connection
- Someone who knows you closely
- Mutual appreciation of each other's qualities

Lessons for life provided by siblings:

- Learning to take turns
- Learning to wait
- Not always being listened to
- Not always being the centre of attention
- Having your possessions moved or broken
- Being left out
- Having to live with someone who regularly annoys you
- Having to alter or abandon your plans
- Learning to get on together

Sibling clashes

Dealing with sibling clashes is one of the most common and challenging of all parenting tasks. Children will squabble. They will annoy each other, fight, wind each other up and compete. Hopefully not all the time, but almost certainly for some of it.

Allowing them to resolve their own squabbles

Teasing, name-calling and shouting between brothers and sisters is normal. The older ones boss the younger ones about and occasionally bully. The younger ones may whine, cry and frequently complain: 'She hit me!' 'He's calling me names!' 'She's picking on me!' 'He took my toy/pencil/book/bicycle/clothes/trainers!' The list is endless.

In *The Parentalk Guide to Brothers and Sisters*, Pat Spungin and Victoria Richardson write, 'As brothers and sisters jostle for position and before they work out ways of living together, there are the wars that precede the settlements. These are arguments about sharing, about fairness, about privacy, about possessions and about absolutely nothing at all. There are scraps and hitting, pushing and pulling and just getting in the way.'[1]

While squabbling is irritating, it has a purpose. Children are discovering how to resolve problems in relationships. While parents may try to keep the noise down and stop them hurting each other, they do their children a disservice if they shut down every quarrel. Siblings need space to sort out their own arguments. It is through these quarrels that they learn how to interact in a conflict, how to handle their anger, how to negotiate, how to compromise and how to make up afterwards. Squabbling is much healthier than no communication at all. And, if possible, keeping out of most of the arguments when children are playing on their own, is generally the best course of action. Two of our sons commented:

Barny You need to sort it out without anyone around. We all had our own court cases before it got to Mum. Often we sorted it out due to self preservation.

Benj We had a healthy fear of Mum's wrath when we were young. We knew there were consequences.

Barny Also, if you were playing and had an argument, you needed to sort it so you could carry on playing together.

Penny Palmano, author of *Yes, Please, Whatever!* advises: 'Always try and encourage your children to sort out their problems, otherwise parents just become judge and jury over their disagreements. And in a few years they won't have you to do their negotiating and compromising for them, so it's best they get in as much practice as possible.'[2]

Sila I gradually learnt not to get involved in the children's squabbling unless I absolutely had to, not least because it was incredibly difficult to adjudicate in situations where I was not on the spot.

Many a time I imagined it was an older child who had hurt or said something unkind to a younger one because the younger child was crying and making a big scene. But I had no way of knowing for sure and insisting on a blow-by-blow account usually made matters worse.

If the bickering and arguing turn into unkind name-calling or physical aggression and one of them might get hurt, we do need to step in.

Nicky We would always take action if we saw one child was hurting or making life miserable for another one. If tempers flared out of control, rather than trying to work out who was in the right or the wrong, we generally sent them to different rooms to cool down. (Sometimes that required pulling two boys apart first!)

Staying calm and being in control of ourselves is important. Becoming loud or aggressive will not help the situation.

Sila Not flaring up and shouting at them when they got cross with each other was hardest of all. My general policy when they were little, if they were fighting over a toy or a game, was to take it away and tell them they couldn't have it back until they had worked out how to play together peacefully. Although it took a lot of encouragement to get them to say the words, 'I'm sorry,' and, 'I forgive you,' the effect was invariably powerful in restoring their friendships. (We talk more about this in Chapter 14.)

Teaching them to share

Arguments and fights over sharing are normal. Children say the same things over and over again: 'That's mine!' 'It's my turn to choose.' 'No, you can't look at it.' 'Let go! You're going to break it.' 'We don't want you to play with us.'

Most of the time sibling spats over their possessions, the TV remote control, whose turn it is and so on, do not last long and the feelings do not run deep. Our aim is to create situations in which they learn that sharing will be best for them all in the long run. So, if they fight loudly and repeatedly over which TV channel to watch, we might say, 'No TV at all if you're going to fight over it,' and switch it off. That means they have to work out for themselves a solution that is fair.

Learning to share their own possessions and to respect each other's is important, but takes time. We can teach them not to take each other's things without asking first, even if it is 'just borrowing'. Precious and fragile property does not have to be shared. We may need to put such things out of sight or out of reach of a younger sibling.

Nicky Each of our own children had a home made wooden box for special things, which they called their 'treasure box' and kept beside their bed. They all knew each other's boxes were out of bounds.

Taking pre-emptive action

Three common reasons for fighting are tiredness, low blood sugar levels and seeking the attention of a parent. So, if our children are hungry when we pick them up from school, taking a snack for them to eat on the way home can make for greater harmony between them and a much happier journey. If they get irritable with each other at the same time each day, having the next meal earlier or making sure they get more sleep can cut down the amount of bickering. If they are regularly picking a fight with a brother or sister in an attempt to get our attention, giving each child some one-to-one time may be the solution.

It may be that they are taking out their frustrations from the school day on their siblings, and the argument itself is nothing to do with why they are bad tempered. A friend recalled, 'I remember my brother was foul to us when he played badly in a rugby match. Just knowing that meant we didn't take his remarks too personally.' Being sensitive to the reasons for sibling clashes helps parents to read the situation rather than 'crisis manage'.

Teaching children how to express negative emotions

To get angry with a sibling is normal, but children must be taught that hitting, punching, pinching, screaming, shouting, pulling hair, making unkind, cutting remarks and throwing things are unacceptable ways of expressing their frustration or annoyance. As we teach our children to express negative feelings – disappointment, hurt, anger and so on – without losing control and becoming aggressive, they are learning one of the best lessons for building healthy relationships: that they can work through conflict without falling out with each other.

If we stop them voicing their anger and simply get cross with them for hitting a sibling, we are not allowing any outlet for these negative emotions. We may well need to teach them to express *why* they are annoyed. It is fine for an upset child to say angrily to a sibling, 'You broke my toy,' or, 'You knocked down my castle.' This is much better than, 'I hate you,' or, 'You're an idiot.' We are helping them to label the action rather than attack the person. This kind of learning, of course, does not happen overnight.

Sibling rivalry

Parents who have more than one child must do all they can to help their children feel equally loved and important. This may be challenging for some, but unhealthy competition, whether or not the result of a parent's favouritism, can easily cause our children to become jealous and resentful of a sibling. If this continues, it will be damaging to their relationships with one another and with us.

As parents, we know our children best and we will usually be able to judge when the normal bickering turns into more serious sibling rivalry. Pat Spungin and Victoria Richardson offer some tests: 'Is the competition persistent and determined? Do they dislike spending time together? Perhaps play fights are becoming more violent. Maybe you can see an intention to cause bodily harm, or perhaps someone is being truly malicious. When everyday teasing becomes spiteful, or when one child is being bullied by the other, things are getting out of hand. You have a case of sibling rivalry.'[3]

Comparing themselves with a brother or sister is the root of sibling rivalry and turns children into competitors rather than allies. A child can start to think:

- Why do they love him more than they love me?
- Why does she get more attention?
- Why do they think he is cleverer/funnier/nicer/more lovable than me?
- Why do they give her bigger and better presents than me?
- Why do they always pick on me?
- Why do I always get left out?

These questions can become the springboard in a child for jealousy, a lack of self-esteem and, sadly, if these feelings continue over a long period, a real dislike for a brother or sister. We must ask ourselves if we are, perhaps unconsciously, inviting comparisons. Telling one he is much better at making friends than his sister, or telling the other she is better behaved than her brother, is likely to build barriers between them.

If we say, 'He's the sporty one in our family,' 'She's the brightest,' or, 'He's the good-looking one,' the others will tend to think, 'I'm no good at sport,' 'I'm not intelligent,' or, 'I haven't got good looks,' and may feel resentful or give up trying to do their best. Equally, if we say, 'He's the naughty one,' the child in question can take that on as his identity within the family. As one child said, 'If I can't be good, I'll be the best at being bad.'

Avoiding favouritism

We will build deep resentment in a child if as parents we show a preference for one child over another. Favouritism leaves emotional wounds in children that can adversely affect the rest of their lives. We may think we are being unbiased, but if we continually hear a child saying, 'It's not fair,' 'I always get the blame,' 'He gets away with everything,' we need to pay attention and ask ourselves whether there is some truth in their complaints.

Many parents find they get on with one child more easily than another. One child may be more compliant; a father may find he has more interests in common with one of his children; or a mother may find one child is easier to talk to than another. Parents cannot change these feelings overnight and should not blame themselves for what they feel. In an article entitled, 'Can you love one child more than another?' psychologist Linda Blair writes, 'It is important to realise that dislike isn't the opposite of love. You can simultaneously love and dislike your children at times. The opposite of love is indifference. If you don't care about your children at all, that would be a cause for concern. So take heart when they irritate you.'[4]

Whatever our feelings, we must choose not to show a preference. Even our body language can betray a bias. We may find ourselves always frowning at one child and smiling at another. The way to counter favouritism is by regularly assuring our children with our words and our actions that they are each special. One child may need to be told off more frequently than another, but we can still make sure that we do not give that child less one-to-one attention, smaller presents, or fewer hugs because of our annoyance.

One mother told us, 'Children are jealous of parental love. So I try to be even-handed in compliments and embraces. Whilst hugging one, even a wink or a kind look at the other supports them as well. I found this policy to be very important and it cannot be started too early.'

As we make a point of treating our children equally, we will usually find that over time our biased feelings change. We start to appreciate aspects of the harder-to-get-on-with child's personality and notice skills and traits that may have been masked by his lack of co-operation. As we value each child's uniqueness, rather than comparing them with each other, they will become more confident, more loveable and less competitive with a sibling.

Tips for building sibling relationships

1. Give each child space and some privacy

Some children need more time on their own than others and this is likely to increase in their teenage years.

Nicky One of our sons used to lock himself in the loo and read comic books for up to an hour when he got home from school. This was the only way he could guarantee some solitude. After spending all day in the company of others, he needed his own space and that was the best way to secure it. Sibling relationships were the better for this time he had on his own (even if there were long queues for the loo).

When two or more children have to share a bedroom, they may benefit from a clear demarcation of some space to call their own.

Sila When our two younger boys were sharing a bedroom, Barny became increasingly upset by the way his own things, which he kept very neatly, got absorbed into his younger brother's mess. The solution we came up with (which sounds rather dramatic now, but it worked like a dream) was a pole with a curtain on it dividing the room in half at just above head height. Barny was able to disappear behind the drawn curtain when in need of his own space and the two brothers' relationship definitely improved.

As children grow older, it is courteous and right to expect that others (including their parents) knock before entering their room. If the door is open and they are happy for free and easy coming and going, that is great – but be sure it is what they want.

2. Do fun things together as a family

Eating together, going on holiday together, finding activities that everyone enjoys, watching TV together and playing games together all contribute to a pool of shared experiences and build a sense of belonging. Few things are more important for building sibling friendships and stopping one child feeling left out. Doing chores together, with or without a parent, builds a strong sense of teamwork, particularly if they want to get through them quickly.

3. Allow them to play childish games together

Often our children's activities will not seem to us to be either purposeful or 'improving'. We may be keener for them to practise their skills at football, tennis or swimming, while they would rather have fun messing around, making up games, or building yet another den in their bedroom. Childish games may look like time wasted, but activities like these exercise their imagination and build their friendship.

A mother said to us, 'My young children love to chase each other naked around the house after their bath, roaring with laughter. I long for them to be great friends, so I have to bite my tongue hard if they're having their best fun of the day just when I desperately want them in bed and quiet.'

4. Allow play fighting

Many children spend a lot of time playing rough and tumble. Children benefit from play fighting. Usually after a certain amount of wrestling, chasing and crashing into each other, one of them will shout 'Ouch!' or, 'Stop it,' but as long as no one is getting seriously hurt, they need to be allowed to get on with it. Our three boys still rag around together. And it still helps them bond again when they have been apart for a while.

Having space outside, or a room in the house without precious things that could get broken, is a great help to parental nerves! If it looks as if they are hurting each other, ask, 'Is this play fighting or real fighting?' If one child says it is real, separate them.

5. Affirm each child

Aim to value each child's different qualities. Make sure they know they each have a special place in the family, whether they are the oldest, the youngest or in the middle; whether they are one of three girls or the only boy. This is the opposite of labelling one of them as 'a typical middle child' or 'acting like an oldest girl'. If your younger child has more obvious social, academic or sporting abilities, find ways to affirm the older child's own gifts. If they each feel loved for being themselves, they are less likely to feel threatened by a brother or sister.

6. Build a sense of love and understanding between them

From a young age we can help our children to articulate their affection and respect for their siblings rather than always trying to get the upper hand. If we say to them when they are little, 'You are really great as a big brother,' or, 'Your sister loves the way you play with her,' we are not only reinforcing positive attitudes and behaviour now, but also encouraging positive feelings about each other for the future.

We can give them a sense of mutual care and responsibility by saying, 'Can you go and cheer your brother up? He's feeling sad,' or, 'Could you get a plaster for your sister? She's cut her knee,' or, 'Will you look out for Emily at the party tonight? She'll be the youngest one there.' If we expect them to show a reasonable level of courtesy and kindness towards each other, they will probably live up to it.

7. Be fair

Brothers and sisters watch very carefully to see who gets what and whether they are getting their fair share. We should be as impartial as we can be without becoming obsessive about it. Sometimes life cannot be fair. One child may need more help from a parent with homework. Another may need new trainers. That does not mean we have to spend the same amount of time helping each child or that everyone has to have new trainers. We can explain this to them if necessary.

Celebrate each child's birthday and successes, but do not buy presents for everybody on every occasion. Help them to make or buy presents for the one whose birthday or achievement is being celebrated. Allow the spotlight to be on the relevant child (or parent) on the basis that the others will have their turn. In this way, we are teaching them to celebrate each other.

8. Allow them to express their concerns

A toddler may be angry at the arrival of a new baby who has stolen the limelight. A younger brother or sister may be bullied by an older sibling when we are out of earshot. A teenager may feel resentful of the responsibility we have put on them or of the extra attention given to a sibling with special needs. If they are upset, it is important to allow them to express their feelings and to try to get to the bottom of their concerns. These scenarios require our understanding, even if we cannot change the situation.

9. Encourage laughter

Being able to laugh together as siblings builds strong bonds. Our son, Barny, commenting on the sense of humour that has developed between him and his two brothers over the years of them playing together, said recently: 'My brothers are my best friends – I often think of jokes that will crack them up.'

Allowing them to laugh at some of our quirky ways, funny ideas, or old-fashioned taste in music helps them to enjoy being brothers and sisters as part of our family. A woman who grew up with three siblings told us, 'We used to find that some of the things my father did made us cry with laughter and it drew us closer together.'

10. Praise in private

Children in the same family often have very different characteristics and giftings. Telling a child in private, rather than when everyone else is around, is sometimes a better way to praise one without another feeling put down.

11. Appreciatc the differences

It would be so dull if our children were the same and reacted similarly in every situation. Help them to see that the differences between them are good, and not just sources of irritation.

We might be able to point out: 'Yes, your brother is grumpy in the morning, but he is also very generous with his things and always lets you have a go on his Xbox.'

Conclusion

One mother told us:

> The greatest hardship for me as a mother has been the arguments between my children. I used to try to sort things out by questioning the children and establish the cause of the row. This was an almost impossible task as fresh tears and shouting would erupt. The younger, less articulate child would not be able to put his or her case forward, especially since the present row would normally be an escalation of things that had happened previously. All the old grievances would be revisited to inflame the situation further.
>
> In acting as judge, not only was I frequently getting it wrong, but I was also left pointing my finger at a perceived 'wrongdoer', which delighted the 'victim' and caused more jealousy to the one blamed. This caused more fighting, and the wrongdoer would return this time in the hope of being vindicated.
>
> I eventually changed tack. I now try to remain dispassionate in disputes. Each child, in turn, may have their say and I will listen, but I won't

blame or sympathise with anyone. I will conclude by saying that I cannot tolerate fighting and that, if it continues, the children must play separately. Real progress. This draws the children together in a united sense of grievance against me, the new unpopular one. A far happier conclusion. For me, this progress was life-saving.

Pause and consider

- What could you do to build the friendship between your children?
- Could you allow them to sort out more of their own disputes?
- Do your children feel that you show favouritism to one of them?
- How could you help your children to appreciate each other's different qualities?
- How could you make sure each of your children know they are a special part of your family?

Section 2

Meeting our children's needs

Chapter 5

The five ways of showing love

I know Mum and Dad love me because they are very nice to me. They do stuff with me – take me to museums and things.

Lena, aged 8

When children feel genuinely loved, their whole world looks brighter. Their inner spirit is more secure and they are far more likely to reach their potential for good in the world.

Dr Gary Chapman
Author

Be nice to your kids. One day they'll choose your nursing home.

Phyllis Dillon
Singer

Scene 1

It had not been a good day so far. Nat, aged five, had refused to get dressed. He had lost a fight with his four-year-old brother over the treptasaurus in the cereal packet. He had known perfectly well that it was Cole's turn to have it. So he had a tantrum. 'I hate school,' he shouted. On arrival there, he made the same point to his teacher by pouring a bucket of sand into the freshly made papier mâché. 'Why is Nat sometimes so easy and sometimes so impossible?' his mother wondered, anticipating the battle at teatime.

Scene 2

It is early evening. Kate is getting ready for a party. 'Have a good time at the party, darling,' her dad calls up to her. 'Remember to be back by eleven o'clock.'

No answer.

Kate appears in a see-through top. Both parents are taken aback. The rules are 'no see-through tops'. Mum bites her lip. She had been too busy to discuss the outfit with her daughter for the special party.

'You know you can't wear that, darling – you need to change.'

No answer. A short mumble. Kate goes to get her coat. 'If you don't change, you can't go to the party.'

'You can't stop me. I am fourteen and I can do what I like now.'

'No, you can't. Now go and change.'

'You are the meanest parents of anyone I know. I hate you.'

Kate runs out and slams the door.

'Why has Kate been so angry lately?' her parents wonder, dreading the next showdown.

Is any of this familiar to you? Of course there are many reasons for bad behaviour in any child. He may be tired or hungry. She may be dealing with a surge of teenage hormones. It may be a one-off incident. They may be worried about school. But if bad behaviour becomes the norm, one of the first questions we should ask is: does this child feel deeply loved?

The need to feel loved

Children long to know that they are loved unconditionally. Whether they are good at sport or not, whether they win academic prizes or not, they need to know that they are accepted and valued. There is an empty space inside our children – an emotional tank, if you like – crying out to be filled with love.

Their behaviour is often a gauge indicating the level at which they *feel* that love to be. When a young child has a tendency to whine, to cry, to snatch, to throw tantrums, or to hurt other children, the chances are that they feel that the level of love in their tank is low. It needs to be filled up. In teenagers the symptoms are more serious when the gauge registers low. Antisocial and rebellious behaviour often stems from an adolescent thinking, 'No-one loves me. No-one accepts me.'

As parents we may be horrified that our children could feel this way. Of course we love them. There is no one who occupies more of our thoughts. We have made extraordinary sacrifices for them. They have cost us thousands already. So, what is the problem? The main issue is that many of us do not know how to meet our children's emotional needs in a way that makes them feel deeply loved. We may think that because we love our children and have said, 'I love you,' they automatically know it. But our children do not only need to be loved, but also to *feel* loved; not only to be accepted, but to *feel* accepted.

Tom Marshall, in his book *Right Relationships*, reflects on years of talking to people about difficulties in forming close relationships: 'I have lost count of the number of those who, looking back on their childhood, have said sadly, "I guess my parents loved me, in their own way, but I never felt it." '[1]

How, then, do we ensure that our children feel loved – in their heads and in their hearts? Sometimes we may not feel very loving towards them – we may be tired, cross, at the end of our tether, in a bad mood or generally critical. Meanwhile they annoy us. They seem to be rude, ungrateful, incredibly self-centered, lazy, or are just pushing our buttons.

Love is an act of the will, regardless of the temperature of the heart. Love involves action. It requires a decision; namely, that we are going to act lovingly, particularly when we feel unloving.

Children who are certain of their parents' love have many advantages – in particular:

- They are deeply secure.
- They are equipped to cope with life's ups and downs.
- They are better able to make friends, having the confidence to reach out to other people and to trust them.
- They have the confidence to make themselves vulnerable by sharing with others what they think and feel.
- They are able to stand out from the crowd and be different when they need to be.

- They are enabled to influence others rather than always be influenced by them.

So how do we go about it?

Discovering love languages

We are indebted to Gary Chapman for the insights in his book *The Five Love Languages*.[2] We have found them enormously helpful in recognising how people come to feel loved. He shows that there are different ways we can express love to another person and that each of us responds better to one or two of these 'love languages' than to the other ones.

Five ways to show love

1. Words

Our words can express love powerfully. Through praise: 'Well done!

I am so proud of you.' Or compliments: 'You look gorgeous,' or, 'That's really thoughtful, darling.' Or affection: 'I have loved you every single day of your life.' Or encouragement, 'I know you can do it.'

2. Time

When we set aside some of our precious time to be with another person, we show them they matter. When we focus our attention exclusively on them, when we do something together with them, listen to what they are saying or watch what they are doing, we communicate that they are special to us.

3. Touch

Physical affection demonstrates that we enjoy being close to that person. Touch can communicate welcome, support, care, consolation and security all at once with a simple gesture.

4. Presents

A present is a tangible, visual symbol of our love. It shows the recipient that we were thinking of them when we chose the present and it will remind them of our love each time they look at it or use it.

5. Actions

When we do something for another person, when we show kindness to them, we demonstrate our love in practice. We can make people feel very loved through meeting their needs with kind actions.

Gary Chapman describes these five ways of showing love as 'love languages'. For each of us there will be one that communicates love in a way that touches us and that fills our 'emotional tank'. We will instinctively understand and respond to that love language just as we immediately understand our native language. Some people, of course, are bilingual. Similarly, with these love languages, we may discover that we feel loved through more than one of them.

Nicky In our marriage it was invaluable to realise that Sila and I feel loved in very different ways. Sila feels most loved when we spend time together – just the two of us – and especially when I have initiated it. Whereas I feel most loved by Sila when she speaks encouraging words to me. After time, Sila would put touch, while for me kind actions come next.

Understanding those differences has helped us avoid inadvertently hurting each other and enabled us to show love to each other in ways that count.

Recognising signs of an empty tank

If we are to fill our child's emotional tank, first we must identify their primary love language.

Sila When one of our sons was four and at nursery school, his behaviour was not dissimilar to that of the little boy at the start of this chapter. He would swing from being helpful and compliant one day, to bolshy and contrary the next. We were at a loss to know why.

Then, on one of his off days his teacher asked me if we'd been giving him much one-to-one time recently. I tried it that same afternoon. I spent thirty minutes focusing my attention on him and playing with him. The effect was electric. Never had I seen a more helpful four-year-old at teatime that day. And even his sister and brothers found him unusually accommodating! His emotional tank had been filled right up.

Learning to use all the languages

Typically each of us shows love in the way we most like to receive it. We may give lots of hugs because physical affection is particularly important for us to feel loved. We may be an excellent present-giver because receiving them means a lot to us. Or we may instinctively find ourselves encouraging others because hearing affirming words is what keeps us going day to day. It is all too easy to become an expert in the one we respond to most ourselves, but our children may well be different from us.

Before focusing in on each language, it is important we recognise the value of *all* these love languages for *every* child. All children need to hear positive, encouraging words from their parents. All children flourish when their parents set aside time to be with them – a large quantity of time given consistently over many years. Children thrive on presents from both their mother and father to mark their birthday, to celebrate achievements and to show support at difficult times. All children require huge amounts of affection – cuddles, kisses and hugs – given frequently when little, and then at appropriate times and places as they grow older. And all children feel loved through knowing that their parents are willing to serve and help them practically – feeding them, washing their clothes, collecting them from school, taking them to parties, expending bags of energy for their wellbeing.

Reading each child

Knowing which of the five expressions of love is the most significant is hard to read in young children, but by the time they are about seven years old we will usually be able to discover this. Not only will each child within the same family respond differently, but the relative importance of each of the five will also vary at the different stages of growing up.

Nicky We asked Kirsty as a teenager which love languages were most important for her. She said 'time' was first and, much to our surprise, 'presents' came second. When we asked her why, she talked about the importance for her of time to be together to talk – at meal times, last thing at night or on holiday.

She also recalled an occasion some months earlier when she was facing exams and was under a lot of pressure at school. She came home one evening to find that Sila had put flowers in her bedroom. She told us that the flowers put the exams in their proper perspective. They communicated to her that our love for her was unconditional and not dependent on what grades she achieved.

Being genuine

Children see through parental attempts to 'buy them off'. We cannot use these love languages as a way of trying to make up for ways we let them down. So, buying them lots of presents because we are never there, or giving them an over-abundance of physical affection because we are always short-tempered, will not work. Love languages need to be a genuine communication of our love, not an attempt to cover up other omissions.

Providing an example for our children

As with everything else in life, children learn most about loving through imitation. So when three-year-old Fergus lost a toy recently, his five-year-old brother said, 'I'll help you find it,' because that's what he had seen his mother do. When Ellie, a thirteen-year-old, was in tears, her sixteen-year-old sister gave her a hug because that is what her parents had always done when she has been upset. Through example, we show love is a two way street.

Some of us will be aware that when we were growing up we never experienced one, or perhaps any, of these ways of being loved, in which case it will probably feel very unnatural to show love in this way ourselves. The good news is we can all learn. Like learning a foreign language, it will take determination, effort and practice before it starts to feel more normal and we become adept at showing love in a particular way.

Many parents feel in need of love themselves, which is why our adult relationships are so significant, particularly for our parenting. The mutual giving and receiving of love between us as parents helps to meet this need, as well as showing an example to our children. As we find out what is important to make our partner feel loved and then show love in this way, we become a positive role model for our children's present and future relationships.

If you are a single parent, you may feel daunted at the prospect of this challenge on your own. A single father, whose wife died when their four children were under ten, said to us, 'The love between husband and wife acts as the powerhouse of the family. Single parents have to find other ways of being nurtured in order to keep giving out love to their children, which may not be reciprocated.' Our suggestion is not to be afraid to get help. If you have a good relationship with your extended family and they are nearby, ask them to help fill the gap. If not, then look to friends, particularly longstanding friends you can trust, or a church community.

Doing this will be important both for you and your children and will enable you to meet your children's emotional needs more effectively.[3]

Putting the languages into practice

The concept of love languages has been revolutionary for us, and has proved an invaluable tool in parenting. Sometimes, while mentally rehearsing the list of five, we have thought of a new way of putting love into action. Occasionally we have become aware that we have been neglecting the very one a child has been craving, and we have suddenly understood why there has been increased squabbling and tension in the home. As we have tried to put them into practice, we have seen the difference in each of our children and in our family as a whole.

Conclusion

Gary Chapman and Ross Campbell, co-authors of *The Five Love Languages of Children*, give an example of the difference it can make when a parent puts into practice the expression of love that is most important for a child:

> Leigh Ann is nine years old. After her mother learned about the five love languages, she made some changes in their daily routine. 'I simply can't believe the difference it made in Leigh Ann's life,' she told us later. 'Mornings at our house were always rather hectic; my husband left home at 7:00, Leigh Ann's bus came at 7:30, and I left about 7:50 for work. We all did our own thing and about the only meaningful contact we had with each other was a good-bye as we left the house.'
>
> Knowing that Leigh Ann valued acts of service, this mother asked Leigh Ann, 'If I could do one thing for you in the morning that would make your life easier and more enjoyable, what would it be?'

'Mum, the greatest thing you could do for me would be to fix my breakfast. It's such a hassle to get the bowl, the spoon, the cereal, the milk, the banana. If you would just put everything on the table and I could sit down and eat, it would be wonderful.' Leigh Ann's mother was surprised at the request but agreed, and the next morning breakfast was waiting.

'Right away I could tell a difference in her morning attitude. She even said thank you most days. And, when she left for school, she seemed to be in a better mood. Three days later, I instituted an act of service in the afternoons when she returned home …

'All of this began four months ago. The biggest difference I notice is that when we talk about school, her comments are much more positive than they were before. It seems to me that she is having a better time and is more motivated than she was. Also, I feel that our relationship is closer.'[4]

For teenagers, the impact of knowing which love language is most important for each of them can be at least as great, as another parent discovered:

For my thirteen-year-old daughter, touch is her number one love language. If I give her a little massage when I am saying goodnight, she loves it. It's rather like a cat that purrs. She has my undivided attention and she just chats away whilst I stroke her back.

For my fifteen-year-old daughter, it has taken me ages to discover and then respond to it. For her, it's making a delicious meal that hits the bull's eye. That's a real stretch for me as I don't enjoy cooking that much. But if I do, Tilly will talk about it afterwards and I know she has appreciated it. Unlike her sister, all she wants at night is a quick kiss and to be on her own in her bedroom.

Pause and consider

- What do you think your children's love languages are? If they are old enough, one way to find out is to ask them for examples of when they have felt most loved. Get them to be specific about when, where and what it was you did that made them feel your love.
- Which love language do you find easiest to use?
- Which one is the hardest?
- Do you know your partner's number one love language? Are you showing them love in the most effective way?
- If you are a single parent, how could you nurture other emotionally fulfilling relationships with friends or family?

Chapter 6
Words

My parents always told me I was special. And I believed them.

Jack, aged 34

Mostly I remember my Dad's critical words and feeling tense around him.

Marisa, aged 43

Most important of all in knowing my parents' love for me was they gave me lots of encouragement. For example, I would be sitting at the bottom of the stairs when Dad came home from work and he would drop everything and say with a massive smile, 'How ARE you?' (Now I work myself I have no idea how he did that after a long day at work.)

Alice, aged 26

As parents we can say things to our children that will affect how they think about themselves for the rest of their lives. A newspaper article about the actress Dawn French included this description of her upbringing:

> When Dawn French was fourteen years old, overweight and about to go to her first disco, her late father sat her down for a talk. She was expecting the usual father/daughter stuff about boys with high testosterone levels and what time she should be home.

> He did spell out what he would do to any over-enthusiastic lad who dared lay a finger on the young Dawn. But it was what he said next that had such a lasting effect on her life.
>
> He told her that she was uncommonly beautiful, the most precious thing in his life, that he prized her above everything and was proud to be her father.
>
> No father could have given his daughter a more valuable start in life. Instead of approaching adolescence as the short, fat girl, who couldn't get a boyfriend, Dawn was secure in the knowledge that she was loved for who she was, not for what she looked like.
>
> That confidence has remained throughout her adult life. And, yes, she is uncommonly beautiful. It is a soft, warm beauty enhanced by a ready, generous smile.
>
> 'How wise of my father to say that,' she reflects. 'It affected my whole life. How could you not come out of it well-equipped to deal with life, when you felt so loved and supported?'[1]

Our words also have the power to crush. A friend of ours played the piano as a child until one day her grandmother said to her, 'What an awful noise! You'll *never* learn to play well.' So she stopped permanently.

The way we talk to our children can become a habit – for good or bad. We can easily become fixated on our children's failures, mediocrity or irritating behaviour. We go on … and on … and on about these, instead of seeing their uniqueness and good points. In fact, such criticism may well spring from our own problems – from what is going on inside us. We are feeling inadequate. We are desperate for others to be impressed by our children. We are feeling stressed. But if we only speak negative, critical words to them, they will grow up feeling insecure.

One mother, with two children under five, said to us, 'The hour before bedtime is the hardest time to remain positive. The house looks like a bomb site, the children are tired and petulant, the chores seem endless, I feel a wreck, and to top it all we have some people arriving for supper at eight o'clock! It's so easy to be sharp and to say: "Why on earth can't you undress more quickly?" or, "I've had enough of your messing around – you're hopeless," and other such comments which I regret later when I look at their little faces all snuggled up and sleeping peacefully. It took me two years to realise that, if I started bedtime routines half an hour earlier, I would be less hassled and would end up being less critical.'

The psychologist Professor John Gottman asserts that, for every one critical comment from their parents, children need at least five positive comments. We will look at four ways we can use words positively to keep filling up our children's emotional tank to ensure they feel loved.

1. Words of affection

Expressing our love

The three words 'I love you' have great power. John, now in his twenties, said, 'I cannot remember ever hearing my parents say that, or any other affectionate words to me throughout my childhood. It left me feeling very alone and insecure.' He is still waiting to hear those three words.

Parents need to speak frequently of their love from the earliest months of their children's lives all the way through the teenage years. The words, 'I love you,' might be part of the bedtime ritual when they are younger or the last words spoken to older children before they leave for school. They might be sent by text or written in a letter for a child to keep and read over again.

Teenagers long to hear their parents speak these three words to them more than their parents usually realise. As they pass through adolescence they are besieged by questions about their identity and value. They are undermined by their own unfavourable comparisons with their friends and siblings. Hearing they are loved can help provide the security and self-worth they need to carry them through.

Phrases like, 'I love being with you,' 'I love playing with you,' 'I really enjoy talking to you,' 'I like watching you draw/seeing you play hockey/watching the way you play with your little brother,' 'You're wonderful,' 'You're so funny,' 'You're great fun,' should become part of our regular vocabulary to express our affection.

Saying what is best for our child

It is important that we say these words of affection for our child's sake, not ours, as otherwise they can be used to manipulate. 'I love you. Do you love me?' is more about meeting a parent's emotional needs than the child's. A friend said to us, 'I know my dad loved me, but he only ever said the words, "I love you," when I was supporting him through a crisis. It felt conditional. The more worthy deeds I did, the more I felt his approval.'

We may have to think about what will be of most comfort to a young child in the moment of being separated from us. To say, 'I love you,' when we are prising her off our shoulder to put her into school could make separation harder. Equally to shout, 'I love you,' to an eight-year-old from the touchline is likely to be counterproductive. A timely wink might mean the same thing and not be embarrassing.

Learning to express affection

Some parents find it difficult to express their love in words, particularly if, during their upbringing they did not hear affectionate words being spoken in their family. The book, *Guess how much I love you* can provide a springboard for parents of little children to start to articulate their thoughts.[2] Breaking the sound barrier is usually the hardest part. Once we become used to hearing ourselves speaking affectionately, we will find it gets easier and easier.

2. Words of comfort

One seventeen-year-old boy was asked how he knew his parents loved him when he was a young child. He said: 'They told me they loved me, allowed me to sleep in their bedroom when I was scared and comforted me. I remember Dad always said, "It's all right," when I cried or had a nightmare.'

There will be moments in our children's lives when they are frightened, worried, confused or do not understand what is happening to them. At such times our words can reassure and comfort them at a deep level. What we say is likely to stick in their memory and be a help to them years later when they are lonely or worried.

3. Words of praise

Looking out for opportunities

Steve Chalke, author of *How to Succeed as a Parent*, writes, 'The golden rule is this: catch your kids red-handed doing something right and praise them for it.'[3] A friend of ours who teaches children aged six to eleven commented, 'As any primary school teacher will tell you, praise is the only sustainable strategy for managing behaviour and encouraging hard work in a class of thirty children.' In a family with more than one child, praising the child who is behaving well, rather than telling off the one who is misbehaving, is a powerful means of encouraging good behaviour, particularly if the misbehaviour might be attention-seeking.

Carefully chosen words of praise do much to build the relationship between parent and child. We have some friends with two sons, both mad keen on football. Having played football himself, the father watches every move of their weekend games with avid interest. If one of them loses a match badly and comes home in the evening discouraged, the father tells him what a brilliant tackle he did five minutes into the second half. The boy's mood begins to change and father and son then spend the next ten minutes to an hour happily analysing the whole game.

It is worth considering whether we are praising our children equally. A friend of ours with an older brother felt that his brother got eighty per cent of his parents' praise. This was very hurtful.

Praising a child's character

To counterbalance our celebrity culture, which defines success in terms of looks, fame or income, it is important to look out for the positive qualities of each child's character. In doing so, we encourage the values we care about most. We might praise them for their generosity in sharing their possessions; for playing nicely with a friend; for looking after a sibling; or for their ability to cope in a difficult situation. One mother noticed how good her six-year-old son was at making friends with lonely children in the playground. She commended him and then asked him why he did it. He replied, 'They need my help.' Her praise reinforced his kindness. Not only will our children thrive on this sort of encouragement, but they will take on the role of being encouragers themselves.

Praising achievements

Our aim should be to commend our children more often than we criticise them. One father told us, 'I take our oldest child to school in the morning on the back of my scooter and every day I try to tell her one thing she is good at.' But what if our children do not seem to excel in any arena? They are not athletic; they struggle with school work; and they have neither musical nor dramatic gifts. In this case our words of praise will be even more important as our child is unlikely to be hearing them elsewhere. That does not mean using false flattery. That will make our children trust our words less. We must be honest in our praise.

We need to look for those achievements that no one else will notice. For younger children this might mean congratulating them for dressing themselves: 'That was really clever putting your shirt on this morning, Tom,' even if some of the other clothes are on back to front.

We can encourage them as we watch them forming the letters of their name: 'You wrote those letters so carefully,' even if they are several months behind their peers. We can congratulate them for brushing their teeth or tidying their bedroom, even if we have just asked them to do it. Or we might be able to say, 'That was really generous of you to share your new toy with John.'

To an older child, we might say: 'Well done! You are really persisting with your maths,' even if the rest of their school work leaves a lot to be desired. 'Thank you for not slamming the door when you left this morning,' particularly if we talked to them about it the day before. 'You were a real help at lunch today.' 'Thank you so much for staying and chatting to Grandpa – he really enjoyed it.' 'Well done for helping to clear up the garden.' Or, as part of a conversation over a meal, 'These muffins are delicious,' if our child baked them.

These attempts at encouragement may at first sound contrived or insincere to our ears; but as we practise praising our children, they will become more and more natural.

4. Words of affirmation

Showing our pride

Our children may be teased, bullied, come bottom of the class, face disappointment and occasionally even wonder if they are worth anything to anybody. As parents we are in the best position to convince them that they are full of potential and have a unique contribution to make.

We can assure them that we believe in them and value them. During the final of the television competition, *Pop Idol*, the mother of Will Young was interviewed. 'You must be so proud of him tonight,' said the reporter. 'Oh! I was proud of him a long time before tonight,' she replied. 'He doesn't have to sing to make me proud of him.'

Some of us are hugely ambitious for our children. We are determined to help them overcome their flaws and improve their performance.

The result is that we focus on their weaknesses more than on their strengths. This is short-sighted. Children who are confident of their parents' love have a secure base upon which to build their future.

Talking in their hearing

Speaking about our children in front of them will affect how they think about themselves. 'She's a complete nightmare.' 'I am finding it so tedious being at home with him.' 'She's so naughty!' 'He drives me up the wall! I'll tell you what he did the other day …' We have all heard parents talking disparagingly in their children's hearing. They forget that their children are absorbing every word. A child may not react outwardly, especially when very young, but will take on board all that is said. Conversely, when a parent tells a grandparent or a godparent in the child's hearing a story about their child's kindness or thoughtfulness (avoid telling friends, as parents who show off are tiresome), it makes her feel valued.

We may hold back from praising our children for fear of spoiling them. But children are not spoilt through praise, but through a lack of discipline and through being allowed to do whatever they like. (We address this in the next section of the book.)

Affirming their looks

Affirming our children's physical appearance from birth helps them to stop comparing themselves unfavourably with others, particularly during their teenage years. One woman told us how her mother would say to her every time she brushed her red hair, 'What beautiful hair you have! What beautiful hair!' Despite always standing out from others, she never doubted as she grew up that the colour of her hair was an asset to her.

In affirming their looks, we are helping them to distinguish between what they can change and what they cannot. So we might well encourage children to wash their hair, or provide a diet that will help them stay in shape, or ensure they are getting enough exercise, whilst recognising that different children have a different build and we are not expecting them to look like a supermodel. Our aim is to help them to look their best while being confident in the natural shape of their own body. (Of course their definition of 'best' may well be different to ours, particularly as teenagers.)

In a culture obsessed with physical looks, focusing too much on their appearance will be unhelpful to them. Our aim is to assure them that we love them for who they are, with their own unique attributes. Rob Parsons writes, 'The other day, my wife Dianne complimented a teenager on her new outfit. The girl smiled, but her mother poked a finger at her tummy and said, "It'll look even better when she does something about that." Of course a parent will want to help a child who is seriously overweight or has a bad attack of acne, but somehow at the same time, we have to let our children know that we love them anyway. That involves us being manifestly proud of them when they are at their gawkiest, and especially if their features don't happen to fit in with what society at present considers "attractive." '[4]

Conclusion

Words of affection, comfort, praise and affirmation make a deep and life-changing impact on our children. They need us to tell them how much we love them, not only when they please us but also when they least expect it.

Speaking like this requires unselfishness on our part. We have to put aside our own agenda, our tiredness, our frustration with the messy bedroom, or our disappointment at the terrible report, in order to take the time to think of something kind and positive to say. We will have to bite our tongue at times; but we will be astonished at the difference that a little encouragement can make to our child. Speaking this language of love will fill up the emotional tank inside.

Pause and consider

- Try counting the number of positive and negative comments you make to your children today. Is the ratio at least 5:1 (positive to negative)?
- What type of loving, encouraging words do you find the hardest to say?
- Are you aware of any pattern of critical words you want to change?
- Think of three characteristics or attributes in each of your children that you would like to affirm this week.

Chapter 7

One-to-one time

The place of the father in the modern suburban family is a very small one, particularly if he plays golf.

Betrand Russell
Philosopher

Dad took each one of us off to Paris for a weekend after we had finished our GCSEs. I remember that weekend so vividly, it was so special and such a huge amount of fun. It was one of the many times when Dad felt much more like a friend than a Dad.

Julia, aged 23

I always felt my dad and mum were in too much of a rush to spend time with me – and it hurt.

Emma, aged 19

I love going on a girls' day out with my mum and going for a walk together. If I had a dad here then I would like to play chess with him.

Elena, aged 13

'Will you come and play with me?' Most parents' hearts sink, especially as the request usually comes at the worst possible moment. 'Later,' we say without stopping to breathe.

A recent TV programme involved two children working with professional designers to change their house while the parents rather bravely went to stay in a hotel. The son wanted the designers to make a chair that would automatically steer Dad away from the television and through the French window into the garden. The chair would then catapult him onto the lawn to play football. The message was clear.

No amount of material abundance can replace a parent's time. Our children may tell us they want a Lego helicopter, a bike, a mobile phone or the latest iPod, but none of these will begin to compare with the love they will feel as we give them the most costly commodity we have – the gift of our time. Try asking a group of adults to recall a happy childhood memory and the majority will probably describe something they did on their own with a parent.

As one parent with three children put it: 'Even with good family time, our children still benefit disproportionately from a dose of one-to-one time. These occasions have helped us to "read" each child, which is difficult to do when they are all together.'

Most of us know the importance of building in individual time with each child but we all need help in working out how we are going to make it happen. Everyone and everything else seems to shout more loudly for our urgent attention. We may think it is impossible but, if we understand the impact of time spent with a child, we can overcome virtually anything.

A couple we know, with two children under ten, recently re-arranged their evening programme so that the children would go to bed one after the other, creating some one-to-one time. They have reaped huge benefits.

Sila With four children to look after, giving them one-to-one time was a real struggle. Looking back I don't think I achieved it very often, but I see now that it meant a lot to them when I did. When they were young, even a short period of time went a long way to maintaining their sense of feeling loved.

I remember a floor puzzle I used to do with one of our sons when he was three. It was a large jigsaw of Noah's Ark with the ark at one end and all the animals going in two by two stretching across the room. When we first started doing this puzzle it took us about twenty minutes and he loved it. After we had done it several times, he could have knocked it off in three minutes, but he used to spin it out for a good quarter of an hour, just for the enjoyment of having me all to himself down on the floor.

Giving focused attention

Our children have an in-built longing to be noticed by us from the moment they are born and throughout their growing up. Psychiatrist Ross Campbell, explains why:

> Focused attention is giving a child full, undivided attention in such a way that they feel without doubt that they are completely loved, that they are valuable enough *in their own right* to warrant their parents' undistracted watchfulness, appreciation and uncompromising regard. In short, focused attention makes a child feel they are the most important person in the world in their parents' eyes.[1]

Individual attention will be especially significant for a young child if a new baby comes along. The child watches the baby receiving endless attention and cuddles and can easily feel insecure.

As our children grow older, the intervals between the times we spend on our own with them can be further apart but the length of it will need to be longer. A friend of ours with four children took one of them – her eleven-year-old daughter, Kate – shopping alone. This, in itself, was a rare occurrence. They were going to buy a new folder for school.

Not having the three other children in tow, our friend found herself uncharacteristically not minding at all as Kate went through every variety and colour before settling on the shiny cover with silver stars. They then engaged in the same lengthy deliberations to choose a pencil case. Not only did the mother enjoy the experience of this time alone with her daughter, she also noticed that Kate's habitual whining and irritating behaviour with her siblings had disappeared when they returned home.

Children know if we are distracted or would rather be elsewhere. The activities that take on special significance will be those in which our children know they have our full attention. It may require planning ahead to make these happen, whether it is an outing or just playing a game at home.

Sila Our sons have each in turn enjoyed playing cricket with Nicky in the narrow alleyway next to our house. There is only enough space for one bowler and one batsman which meant that there were no distractions from other people joining in the game. They knew during these times that they could rely on having Nicky's undivided attention.

Suggestions for one-to-one activities

- Going for a bike ride
- Watching a sports event
- An indoor game of their choice
- Going swimming
- Walking the dog
- Taking them bowling
- Playing an outdoor game
- Visiting a favourite café
- Cooking with them
- Painting a picture
- Fishing
- Going camping
- Praying with them
- Going out for breakfast
- Reading them stories
- Doing play dough or making a model toy
- Practising throwing and catching a ball
- Going shopping to the shops they like
- Sitting on their bed in the evening discussing the day

Creating conversation

One-to-one time with a child creates natural opportunities for communication. One father said, 'My fourteen-year-old son does not say much at all right now. But if I drive him to a football match and watch him play, then we often have our best conversations in the car. To be honest, it's not how I want to spend a Saturday, but it's worth it.'

We should not be put off by the fact that some of the conversation will involve disagreements. A shopping trip may show up our different tastes in clothing, divergent views about hair colours, or the desirability of tattooing or piercing every part of one's anatomy. Grab the opportunity to discuss and discover their opinions. These are invaluable opportunities for talking about peer pressure, school, how they like to dress – as well as showing them that we want to give them as much freedom as we can.

Going out for a meal with a child on their own is a good way of ensuring that we have time to talk.

Nicky I found a local Chinese restaurant where from time to time I have taken our boys, one at a time, to have a meal. The great advantage of this place is that the son in question can eat as much as he likes at a reasonable price. As they all have huge appetites, I am guaranteed at least an hour's talking.

We may be afraid of running out of topics of conversation. If so, it is well worth thinking in advance of questions that require more than a 'yes' or 'no', such as, 'What sort of holiday do you enjoy most?' or, 'If you could be anyone, go anywhere and do anything, what would you choose?'

Some children will be easier to talk to than others. Keeping up-to-date with the topics that interest them enables us to talk more easily and naturally. Watching their favourite programme with them will usually give rise to animated conversations. One father has told us, 'If I'm not in front of the TV for *X Factor*, my son yells for me to come immediately. He likes us to discuss who I think is the best performer and then loves to cross swords with me. I always have other things I ought to be doing, but this is a good opportunity to be together and have a laugh.'

Sometimes a father will share his son's interests and a mother her daughter's. But children also benefit hugely from opposite-gender parental relationships. One mother reported, 'Many of my longest conversations with James involve which of Beckham's or Rooney's midfield passes I thought was best, and whether I think Rio Ferdinand is England's best defender. I have had to climb a steep learning curve.' This same mother will sometimes take her son to play football on a Saturday morning while the father stays at home doing arts and crafts with their daughter.

Using eye contact

One of the great benefits of one-to-one time with our children is that it affords the opportunity for eye contact. Looking directly into someone's eyes signals our interest in them and has the potential to create a profound connection. Eye contact can be a way of pouring love into our children. Our expressions matter as much as our words.

Sila I realised with four young children that more often than not I was using eye contact only negatively. I might say, 'Josh, come here, right now!' I would be standing with my head thrust forward and, if he ignored me, I would repeat, 'Josh, come here and look at me.'

This might have been repeated several times during a day, and therefore the only association that our children would have with eye contact was, 'I'm in trouble.' I had to learn to rescue eye contact from the negative realm and begin to use it to build up our children's self-confidence.

A mother told us that sometimes she would look at her young children in turn and ask them, 'What am I saying?' and they would know from her eyes she was communicating her love for them.

The more we model positive eye contact for our children, the more they will copy us in giving good eye contact to others. Children with the confidence to look people in the eye signal their interest in others. Such a skill is hugely beneficial in making relationships, with people of any age.

Nicky Our children were met at the door of their first school every morning by their head teacher looking them in the eye, shaking their hand and saying, 'Good morning,' and then their name. They were expected to reciprocate. For one of our children this was particularly challenging as he was very shy, but we saw how the requirement to look her in the eye day by day helped to build his self-confidence.

Being a good listener

We can easily spend one-to-one time correcting our children's behaviour. Sometimes we find it hard to resist simply lecturing them. But, unless we make a point of listening to what *they* are saying and try to understand what they are feeling, we will not build up the trust that enables us to guide them. A father's story demonstrates how quick we can be to offer advice rather than to discover what the real issue is:

> Danny is eight years old. He's my high-energy, everybody-wants-to-be-his-friend child. He loves school, loves his teachers, loves his assignments; he has to be the best, do his best. Most of the time he does. Schoolwork comes very easily to him.
>
> I arrived home from work one evening about six-thirty. He was waiting for me … Before I could even turn the car off, he yanked open my door: 'Dad, I hate school. I'm not going back – not ever, no way. I'm not going back to school. I hate my classes … I'm not going to school ever again.'
>
> 'Hi, Danny, you must have had a hard day …?'
>
> 'Yeah, and I'm not going back to school. It's stupid.'
>
> 'Oh, you'll have a good day tomorrow,' I said as I gathered up my briefcase and suit coat. I hadn't

even really looked at him yet. I was giving my totally stock responses to an eight-year-old's ranting. As I turned to get out of the car, I saw his face. He was red to bulging. So I switched into, 'Come on, you know … blah, blah, blah.' That sort of settled him down.

Bedtime rolled around and he started up again: 'I'm not going to school tomorrow. I'm really not going.' I'm clueless. So I asked him why he was so upset. Ten or fifteen minutes later, it turned out he hates Mr Bisset, his art teacher.

Okay. So he doesn't like his teacher. But that doesn't mean he shouldn't go to school tomorrow. So I said, 'Oh you'll survive. It'll be better tomorrow.' 'I'm not going to school tomorrow. I'm never going back to that stupid place as long as I live.'

Obviously, I hadn't quite got to the source of what he was trying to tell me by his tears and shouting. I realised I needed to practise empathetic listening. Don't listen to the words; focus on his feelings. Listen with your eyes and heart. So I tried that:

'You must be really angry, Dan.'

'I'm mad. And Mr Bisset is mean to me.'

'Really. That must feel terrible when he's mean. What does he do that he's so mean?'

'Well he makes kids cry. And he gives us all these stupid assignments. And he doesn't teach us anything. And he made Jessica cry yesterday. You've got to go and see him, Dad, make him stop. You've got to, Dad; otherwise I can't go back to school.'

On and on he went. Most of what he said didn't even make sense. But I just listened and reflected his feelings, until we got to the very heart of the matter about fifteen minutes later. Mr Bisset had given Danny an assignment to be completed in two days. Danny didn't know how to do the assignment …

After probably twenty minutes of me just listening to him, he was a different kid: 'Dad, you probably don't need to go see Mr Bisset. I'll be okay. He's okay, really. He's kind of a fun teacher, anyway.'

You know, I did go and see Mr Bisset, because I promised Danny I would. But the thing I realised is that when my kids are upset, I tend to give them a cheer-leader kind of speech. That's my stock reaction. I probably never recognise eighty per cent of the underlying reasons for their emotions when I do that. Just listening to Danny helped me understand his little heart far more than I ever have. I was able to help him because I took the time to listen.[2]

Sila That story really resonates with me. Looking back I recognise that I was too quick to pre-judge the reason our children were upset. I would try to fix the issue with my good advice, and short-circuit what I knew would be the more lengthy process of looking them in the eye, trying to get inside their mind and heart and really listening to them. I would often respond on 'auto-pilot' (not listening is all too easily my default mode) and I know there were many times when I came up with solutions that didn't address their real problem. I came to realise I had to slow down and practise effective listening, and the response from our children, when I did, was always positive.

A mother with a six-year-old child, Chris, said to us: 'I notice that I have to listen to what may be behind his words. It is not always immediately clear. Chris came back from school the other day and was out of sorts. He said he'd fallen over. Later on, as we talked, he told me he'd got locked in the loo. This was the reason he was upset, not his knee.'

The skills of being a good listener are fundamental in parenting. Some of us are naturally better at it than others, but the good news is we can all learn. Admittedly, effective listening always takes time and effort. But if we want our children to talk about their feelings, we need to be ready to listen, and to listen whenever they want to talk, not just at the moments that are convenient for us.

Nicky My danger has been that I can be too quick to jump in and to try to reassure our children when they have been telling me they are unhappy. In effect, I deny what they are saying in order to make out things aren't really all that bad. This can be confusing for them as well as making them feel resentful.

It might have been as simple as one of them taking off a jumper and saying, 'I'm really hot – it's boiling in here,' and I might stop them with, 'No it's not. It's quite cold – keep your jumper on.' Or, another of them says, 'I had a really boring time at Sam's house – it was no fun at all,' and I'd reply, 'I'm sure it wasn't that bad. Sam's such a good friend of yours.' Or another says, 'I think someone at school stole my new pencil case today. I left it on my desk,' and I'd respond, 'Well that was a silly place to leave it.'

I realise now it would have been more helpful for our children if I had listened and allowed each of them to tell me what they were feeling, perhaps responding with nothing more than, 'Mmm! …' 'I see …' 'Yes …' 'Oh really? …' 'That must have been annoying, or boring, or upsetting,' as appropriate.

Six ways to become more effective listeners

1. Give your full attention

Continuing to look at the computer screen or read the paper when our child is wanting to tell us something will eventually cause them to give up trying.

By contrast, putting down whatever we are doing, even in the middle of a busy day, and giving a child our full attention sends a powerful message. Sometimes we may have to say, 'I'll be finished in ten minutes and then you can tell me.' Then we must be true to our word.

Our body language – turning to face them, looking them in the eye and adopting a sympathetic pose – speaks volumes to them. Equally, of course, their body language will have much to say to us if we are paying attention.

2. Cope with distractions

There will always be distractions and demands that make it hard for us to listen – other people, our work and urgent tasks needing our attention. The telephone may interrupt the conversation. Declining to answer it, or saying we're busy and will ring back later, helps us to stay focused and hear our child out. Or, again, we may be consumed with our own worries and agenda. Effective listening requires us to put aside what is going on in our mind and to focus on what our child is saying to us, paying particular attention to any anxiety being expressed.

3. Show an interest

We are unlikely to share all of our children's interests and some may be totally alien to us – even dull. Listening takes generosity and means concentrating on what appeals to them, whether it is a sport that we know little about, a style of music we dislike or television programmes that leave us cold. As we take an interest in their world, they will open up to us.

4. Listen uncritically

Communication with our children is crushed by criticism, but flourishes when we give recognition to their views. Some children feel that they have never pleased their parents, nor that they could ever please them. They stop communicating their thoughts and feelings. We need to be able to listen without butting in with a lecture.

5. Identify feelings

If we can fathom what our child is feeling, we will be at least halfway to resolving difficult situations. The problem is that children cannot always identify their own feelings. We can help them by giving them a vocabulary. So if they are upset, we might say, 'You look sad,' or, 'It sounds as though you are really angry,' or, 'Did you feel jealous?,' or, 'Were you embarrassed?' They will then start to recognise why they feel as they do, and to tell us.

6. Reflect back your child's words

When our children come to us hinting at a problem, or with a half-voiced concern, they need to know that we have understood. The best way to achieve this is by repeating back to them the feelings they may be struggling to express. So, if they have said,

'I don't want to go to that boring games lesson at school again,' avoid replying, 'Oh, don't be silly! You love games, and anyway everyone has to do games.' It would be better to say, 'It sounds as if you're not enjoying games. Tell me why.' When we do this, our children no longer feel alone in their troubles. We have entered their world to give sympathy and support. They feel understood. And if they feel we are on their side, they are likely to open up more.

A woman in her twenties talked about her parents' approach: 'They would listen to everything I needed to say about arguments at school, friends, work, my latest crisis – however repetitive, serious or seemingly petty – and then remember to ask about those things a few days later, ready to hear the next episode. When I was in difficulties they listened, listened and listened. I felt they cared and that they gave me wise advice. They also helped me realise that everyone else was going through similar trials. So I knew I wasn't weird or stupid.'

Without such open communication children become isolated and turn in on themselves, or they may seek the advice of others who do not have their best interests at heart. Sometimes a child is unable or unwilling to express her worries or fears and we may sit with her in silence. But our presence is saying to her, 'I care. I'm still here for you whether or not you choose to tell me what's troubling you.'

Finding opportunities

Nothing can substitute for the gift of giving a child our focused attention. Some opportunities can be planned well in advance. Of course the more children we have, the more planning will be required and the more determined we have to be. We heard recently about one couple who invited each of their children to choose a weekend away on their own with their mother for their thirteenth birthday, and with their father for their sixteenth birthday. Not surprisingly, each child chose a different type of weekend. The children, now grown up, still talk about these trips as highlights of their lives.

If one parent works away from home or for longer hours than the other, then time with this parent will be even more memorable for the children.

Nicky I was less available than Sila for our children when they were aged ten and under. Yet what amazes me is the way our children, now in their twenties, remember those occasions when I did something special with each one of them on their own.

For example, I took our daughter Kirsty to a restaurant for her eleventh birthday. Sila and the other children were away in Scotland with grandparents. I remember it because I thought I had booked a table at quite a cheap restaurant, only to discover on arrival that it was one of the most expensive for miles around! Kirsty remembers the occasion for quite different reasons. It was time spent alone with her father.

Other opportunities present themselves unexpectedly. A twenty-four-year-old woman recalls a moment during her childhood: 'I remember going to a water park, falling into the swimming pool and crying. Dad came and got me out, and took me to a café to eat pancakes together – just the two of us. It was an adventure. I felt as if I'd had the whole afternoon with him, even though it had only been half an hour.'

Sila When one of our sons was eleven, he sometimes found it difficult to go to sleep at night, and the more he tried, the more he wound himself up. One evening I was sitting on the edge of his bed commiserating with him about it while also thinking of all the things I needed to do downstairs, when he said, 'Draw a picture on my back, Mum, and see if I can guess what it is.' I drew the shape of a sailing boat, which he guessed after two or three attempts. 'Do another,' he said. Next I drew a person holding an umbrella.

And so started a ritual between us on those nights when he couldn't sleep. It was one-to-one time for fifteen minutes or so with our son that I could no more have planned than fly to the moon – but it was a window of opportunity that lasted almost a year, and I could so easily have missed it through allowing the pressure of other things to pull me away.

Conclusion

Whatever our situation, whatever the size of our family and whatever our job, most of us will struggle to make one-to-one time with a child. There are demands on all of us that seem more urgent and it is so easy to say yes to other people and other things, rather than yes to special time with a child.

Rob Parsons, in his book, *The Heart of Success*, writes of the struggle for parents who find the exhilaration of the business world more stimulating than the company of their children:

> Some years ago I was asked to speak to a large financial institution on how to balance home and work. I commended them for their success and pointed out that, to achieve it, somebody somewhere had worked long hours and made many sacrifices.
>
> But then I urged those successful men and women not to forget that, although work is important, when they are older it is in the area of relationships that they will crave success. I warned them that, if they had children, those kids would be grown and gone before they knew it. As I spoke I saw the usual looks of disbelief from the young, and knowing nods from those with a few grey hairs. Then I said, 'The days when your children want you to watch them in school plays, teach them to fly a kite, and listen to that story over and over again are very limited. The time is hurtling towards you when you're going to say to a fourteen-year-old, "Do you fancy going fishing this weekend?" and he'll reply, "Do you mind if we don't, Dad – I said I'd go out with some friends." '
>
> I told them of a little maths I did one day that changed my life. I worked out the number of days

in the first eighteen years of my children's lives – 6,575. No amount of success, money or prestige can buy us one day more. If your child is ten years old, you have 2,922 left. I said, 'I understand as well as anybody the pressures of modern business life, but those days of your children's lives are irreplaceable. So far as is possible, try not to miss one of them.'

When I finished, the chairman, a man of about sixty, stood up to thank me. He was obviously having some difficulty speaking, but somehow he concluded his remarks and took his seat next to me on the podium. Then I saw that his eyes were full of tears. As unobtrusively as I could, bearing in mind that we were in full view of the audience, I asked him if he was all right. He turned towards me and said, 'I'm OK. I just found it all very moving. I've been overseas for five days and when I got back I said to my fourteen-year-old boy, "Well, have you missed me?" He said, "No, Dad – because you're never here." ' He went on, 'You know what really upset me? It was that my son wasn't being sarcastic. He was just articulating what has become for us a *lifestyle*.'

I reached out and touched his arm and said, 'It's never too late.' I was well-intentioned but I wasn't being completely honest. The truth is that, although that man may still build a wonderful

> relationship with his son, nothing could give either of them back the years that were gone. At the time, the chance to stand on the touchline of football matches seemed as though it would be there forever, and when that father said, 'Next week, son – I'll be there then,' he meant it. It was just that there were always business plans to write and accounts to listen to: there were hundreds of people who had demanded a piece of him. But his son hadn't demanded; he had just *asked* – until one day he had just stopped asking.[3]

There are no shortcuts. We have discovered over the years that it requires a conscious decision and careful planning to make the opportunities, to adjust what we do according to each child's age, and to take advantage of weekends and holidays. Make plans with your partner if you are parenting together. Time with a child might mean sacrificing time with each other for an afternoon, a day or even a weekend. Even parents who are at home with their children much of the time still need to give them periods of focused attention.

If you have regrets over lost time with a child, do not allow that to prevent you from starting again. Whatever you have done or not done in the past, initiating one-to-one time with a child can make a profound difference to your relationship today and in the future. Knowing the long-term benefits and remembering that the window of opportunity will soon pass are the greatest incentives.

Pause and consider

- What is the one-to-one activity you find easiest to do with each child? How often have you done that in the past month?
- What is most likely to prevent you giving your child one-to-one time?
- What activity would your child most like you to do? When could you next do that?
- What stops you from listening effectively to your child?

Chapter 8

Touch, presents and actions

I used to long for my father to hug me but he never did – and now I can't make myself hug him.

Simon, aged 38

Children need four hugs a day for survival, eight hugs a day for maintenance and twelve hugs a day for growth.

Virginia Satir
Family therapist

My most abiding fear in my childhood and thereafter was of my mother. To say that she did not love me is questionable. But to say that she never gave any outward sign of loving me is to state no more than a fact. At the age of 69 it may sound ridiculous to record that after babyhood (and for all I know during it) my mother never once showed me by a kiss or a cuddle the slightest vestige of physical affection, but that is how it was.

Ludovic Kennedy
Journalist and author

I am quite a tactile person, so just being held and hugged is really important to me.

Thea, aged 15

Touch

An article written about the golfer Greg Norman commented on his aloofness and cool temperament. He explained that he had inherited these traits from his father: 'I used to see my father, getting off a plane or something, and I'd want to hug him but he would only shake my hand.'

The article described how Norman lost the 1996 US Masters tournament to Nick Faldo, having gone into the final round with a six-shot lead. The journalist wrote:

> As Faldo made one last thrust into Norman's heart with a 15-foot birdie putt on the 72nd [final] hole, the two of them came towards each other, Norman trying to smile, looking for a handshake and finding himself in the warmest embrace instead. As they held that hug, held it even as both of them cried, Norman changed just a little. 'I wasn't crying because I had lost,' Norman said the next day. 'I have lost a lot of golf tournaments before. I will lose a lot more. I cried because I have never had a hug like that in my life.'[1]

Being demonstrative with our children

The medical profession has known for a long time that physical affection is vital for newborn babies. Without touch they fail to thrive. This need for human touch continues throughout our lives. Perhaps the best known figure to demonstrate its power was Mother Teresa. In her life of looking after the orphaned, the destitute and the dying she never stopped touching people to show them she cared.

Showing physical affection to our children does not just mean hugging and kissing them. With young children physical contact happens naturally and easily: at bath-time, while helping them get into pyjamas, during story-time, when they sit on our lap, as we snuggle them into bed. Touch can have a wonderfully calming and soothing effect on our children as we are trying to get them ready for sleep.

One mother said, 'When I say goodnight, I hold my child's hand and give it a double squeeze. He knows that means, "You're great!" '

One of our children's godmothers had a wonderful way of calming our children down at bedtime when they were little. Once they had got into bed, she would run her fingers through their hair, giving them a gentle head massage with her finger tips, and ask them about their day. This had an amazingly soporific effect on them and they all adored her.

Touch for some people conveys love more powerfully than words. A thirty-four-year-old man told us he never doubted his parents' love for him because of all the hugs, cuddles and kisses they gave him as a child. Even now he still greets his father with a bear hug.

Sila Touch is very important for me to feel loved. This has a lot to do with how much physical affection both my parents gave me during my childhood. I particularly remember bath time in winter. (The bathroom was the only warm room upstairs in our house.) When I got out of the bath my mother would wrap me up in a big white bath towel, hug me close and then dry me to rhymes such as, 'Rub a dub dub, three men in a tub.' In the summer she would roll down a grassy bank in our garden with us and we'd finish up in a laughing heap at the bottom.

My father was tall and as a little girl I remember him getting down on all fours so my brother, my sister and I could climb on his back and pretend he was a horse. And after Sunday lunch, when we had walked to the top of a hill, there was often a cold wind blowing so my father would open his coat or lift up his big jumper and shelter my sister and me underneath.

I don't suppose my parents thought of it in these terms, but those occasions were filling up that emotional tank inside me.

Opportunities for physical closeness occur naturally when we sit side by side with our children in a comfortable chair while reading a story, or we put a hand on their shoulder when they are busy drawing or doing a puzzle. Equally valuable, especially for boys, can be playful wrestling.

Sila One of our sons, when he was five, made a Father's Day card for Nicky. Inside he put his own words, written with the help of his teacher: 'I love you Daddy because you love me and you play rough and tumble with me.' Nicky had always enjoyed play-fighting with him, but he had far underestimated the effect it was having on that child's emotional well-being until he read that card.

We know some single mothers with sons who have struggled to provide this sort of rough and tumble. For some of them a grandparent or godparent has been a helpful source. Others have built friendships with carefully chosen and trustworthy male role models to give opportunities for healthy physical contact.

Choosing our moments

As with words of affection, it is best to choose our moments and be sensitive so as not to embarrass our children in front of their friends. While once they expected a hug when dropped off at school, they get to the age when they would rather be hugged in the privacy of our home.

With the arrival of puberty, teenagers (and some pre-teens) typically become self-conscious about all contact. A daughter may withdraw from physical contact with her father as she becomes more aware of her own femininity. Fathers need not feel hurt by this and it is important to respond with sensitivity, while finding appropriate times to continue to hug and kiss her. This will help to affirm her sexual identity and build her confidence. Boys and girls may crave parental attention and simultaneously be embarrassed by any demonstrative show of it. We find one moment they fight us off and the next they relax and enjoy hugs.

During those periods when they really do not want contact, particularly with the opposite sex parent, we can look for alternative ways of maintaining physical contact in as natural a way as possible – perhaps a hand on their shoulder while helping with homework, throwing a playful punch, giving them a quick hug or a kiss on the cheek when saying hello or goodbye. Before too long they will be open again to normal physical affection.

Overcoming our own awkwardness

For some parents showing physical affection does not come naturally, especially if they have not come from a physically demonstrative family.

A friend of ours remembers, aged seven, going to his father to hug him and being told, 'Now you're seven we only shake hands.' He was never hugged again by his father and commented, 'Something in me died towards him when he said those words.' This has made him determined to react very differently with his own sons and to keep giving them lots of physical affection.

Nicky Years ago I remember being with some great friends outside their house when their son arrived back from his first term away at university. They are quite a traditional family and I wondered how they would greet him. The father walked towards his son. I watched to see if they would shake hands and whether the father might put a hand on his son's shoulder. Without a moment's hesitation they hugged affectionately and walked into the house together with their arms around each other's shoulders.

At that moment I decided this unembarrassed show of affection was what I wanted with our children as they grew up.

For some children touch will make them feel good about themselves in a way that nothing else does. Physical contact can build strong, affectionate bonds and has the potential to reinforce memories of special times spent with a parent. Eloise, now married with three young children, spoke to us about her relationship with her father: 'If we were upset as children, Dad would sit us on his knee and without fail he would pull out his spotted handkerchief and wipe the tears from our faces. This proffering of his handkerchief continued as we grew up. He even pulled it out at my wedding (although they weren't tears of sadness on that day, I hasten to add!).'

Maintaining appropriate boundaries

What is good, healthy physical affection at one age with one child can change to them feeling invaded at a later stage. A child may signal that nakedness with the opposite sex parent has become inappropriate. We need to respect their privacy, and certainly we should be knocking on their bedroom door before entering by the time they become teenagers.

Part of our duty to protect our children involves teaching them from a young age that they do not have to be touched or kissed by anyone with whom they feel uncomfortable. Talking about 'good touch, bad touch' can help children distinguish between appropriate and inappropriate physical affection, whether this is from a stranger, someone at school, a friend or a family member. Tragically, sexual abuse is often perpetrated by those whom parents (as well as the child) trust and least suspect. Often, only the child knows what is happening and the best protection is to arm our children with words to say, such as, 'No, I don't want you to touch me,' and the confidence to tell a parent what has occurred straight away.

Any kind of sexually motivated touch by an adult will be highly destructive to a child's future. Parents who struggle to control sexual feelings towards their children should seek professional help immediately. This will take courage, but it is nothing compared to the awful damage caused by sexual abuse. Equally important is taking action if we suspect that an older sibling is taking advantage of a brother or sister sexually, or that another adult is misleading our child. Children who have felt ignored when in need of help can struggle with anger against their parents' failure to protect or rescue them, as much as against the abuser. This is a huge and delicate subject with longlasting consequences that can be perpetuated from one generation to another. We would urge anyone whom has been abused themselves to get professional advice from their doctor. The advice of a doctor should also be sought by those who suspect that abuse may be happening to their child or another child they know.

Helping teenagers

Inappropriate touch should not defer us from giving appropriate physical affection. A youth organisation, commenting on the high number of pregnancies among teenagers in the UK, stated, 'Young people, who feel the need for love to be expressed to them in touch due to a lack of it in their parental home, are much more likely to seek sexual encounters as teenagers.'[2]

A twelve-year-old bridesmaid was given this piece of advice by the bride after the wedding: 'Don't stop cuddling your dad when you become a teenager. He's still your dad. It's the other boys you need to think twice about cuddling.' The girl, now twenty-three, had never forgotten those words and spoke of the confidence that physical contact with her father had given her to relate appropriately to boys of her own age.

Showing our love for our children through healthy, affectionate touch builds self-esteem and confidence in an easy and pleasant way.

Presents

I love presents. Why can't it be my birthday everyday?

Andrew, aged 4

All I ever wanted was for them to say, 'I love you,' and not to get a big present.

Carrie, aged 34

Receiving a present – even a tiny one like a bar of chocolate – makes me feel really warm and happy inside. I know I've been thought of.

Emma, aged 17

Presents are the fourth way of showing love. They signal our interest in our children and can show our understanding of what each child enjoys.

Nicky I sat down at my desk one day to find a note: 'Buy Benj a VERY expensive surprise present for being such a great son!' It made me laugh, but it also made me think, 'When had I last given any of our children a surprise present?'

Showing love through presents

Some people never stop buying things for their children, which arguably makes each present less meaningful or memorable. Others dismiss present-giving as a shallow substitute for showing love in other ways. But a well-timed and well-chosen present is a powerful symbol of our love. A present tells our children that we have been thinking of them and that we care about them. It may be something very small, such as a notepad for drawings or a muffin after school.

One mother remarked, 'From time to time I tell my children I have specifically bought their favourite ice-cream for them because I know they like it. It is not just the ice-cream, but hearing why I got it, that makes them feel loved.'

Giving presents at special moments

A present is a powerful way to show our appreciation when a child has made a special effort, needs to be consoled, or is celebrating an achievement. If we have more than one child, we do not always need to buy everyone a present to keep it fair.

The attitude we have tried to adopt within our own family is that a present given to one child at such times is an expression of the love and support of the whole family.

Making birthdays special

Marking our children's birthdays with presents is a way of honouring their unique place in our family. Our care in choosing and wrapping their presents and our home-grown birthday traditions can create memories of our love that they will remember throughout their lives. When asked what reminded her most eloquently of her parents' love, Maddy replied, 'Birthday mornings in my parents' bed, with all my presents brought in on a tray.'

If a child is desperate to acquire a particular toy or gadget, he could save up his pocket money or we may decide to give it to him for his birthday. Waiting for a present teaches children the value of delayed gratification. This is particularly important in our instant, 'have-it-all' culture.

Combining presents with another love language

Busy parents can easily use presents to buy affection. For those who are separated or divorced, present-giving must never become a competition with the other parent. All of us must resist being manipulated by a child who demands a present as proof of our affection. It is unhelpful to give presents because we are fed up with hearing, 'I want it,' or as a bribe, 'If you eat your supper, I'll buy you a lolly,' to make them do something they should do anyway.

Present-giving is never a substitute for love expressed through words, actions, time or touch. If we give a child an indoor game, he is likely to say, 'Come and play it with me,' or if we give him a bike, 'Come out for a ride with me.' We know of someone who was given a sports car for his seventeenth birthday by his father. But the present provoked more anger than gratitude. The son was a talented sportsman and played in the first team for his school in three sports. Yet his father had never come to watch him play a single match. The sports car could not possibly make up for the lack of loving interest.

By contrast, a friend told us about the squash racquet she received from her parents on her ninth birthday. She said, 'It was one of the best presents I ever had.' She was very good at sport but had never had the opportunity to play squash. When giving her the racquet, her father said he would teach her to play. She went on, 'The present demonstrated to me my parents' understanding of my love of sport, and I had some of my most memorable times with my father on the squash court.'

Nicky For Sila and me, presents are less important than the other ways of being shown love. As a result we have tended to underestimate this language of love in our children's lives. However, we began to realise that for two of our children, receiving a present means a lot more to each of them than to us. Since then we have tried to be more thoughtful and creative in using this love language.

Teaching our children to give presents

We may find our children starting to imitate this way of showing love at a young age. Little children will sometimes go around the house selecting objects, wrapping them up in a scrumpled piece of paper and giving them to us as presents.

The parents of one young boy, David, were trying to teach him and his siblings to be kind to lonely people at Christmas. He took their message to heart. He went round his home wrapping up favourite trinkets, such as his mother's jewellery and a rather nice silver bowl, and gave them to friends and neighbours for Christmas. It took his parents weeks to track the items down.

Some they never found!

Children love to help if we are planning surprises. Getting them involved in preparing for family birthdays, choosing presents, making cakes and drawing cards will help them discover the fun of giving, as well as receiving. As they grow older, using their own limited funds is a good way of learning that it is the thought behind the present, rather than the size of it, that counts.

Actions

> *She broke the bread into two fragments and gave them to the children, who ate with avidity. 'She hath kept none for herself,' grumbled the sergeant. 'Because she is not hungry,' said a soldier. 'Because she is a mother,' said the sergeant.*
>
> **Victor Hugo**
> **Author**

The fifth way of expressing love to our children is through acts of service. These may range from cooking endless meals to washing piles of clothes, from tidying up toys to helping with the homework. The list will be a mile long when our children are little. Sometimes we will wish we could bill someone for the time involved.

When they become teenagers, the requirements will be no less demanding as we find ourselves providing a free twenty-four-hour taxi service with unlimited mileage for them and their friends. Parenthood involves sacrifice. Gary Chapman writes:

> Parenting is a service-orientated vocation. The day you found out that you would have a child, you enrolled for full-time service. Your contract called for a minimum of eighteen years of service with

> an understanding that you would be on 'active reserve' for several years after that.[3]

Finding the right approach

Parents respond to the physical demands of bringing up a child in different ways. Some engage in non-stop hard work to provide a full-on five star service with an immaculate home, neatly ironed clothes and delicious meals on time like clockwork. But then there is no time for fun or play. Other parents are very laid back, and on Sunday night there is no food in the fridge and every item of the school uniform is dirty. But children find too much chaos stressful. Our task is to strike a happy medium.

Teaching children to show gratitude

Of course, young children take the things we do for them for granted. They assume that this is what their parents are there for – to provide for their needs. A busy mother, looking back on her own childhood, said, 'I could never understand how Mum could be even five minutes late to pick me up from school because, as far as I could see, she had absolutely nothing to do all day. It's only now that I have two young children of my own that I see, through the haze of my own exhaustion, the hundreds of things she did for me without being thanked. Twenty-five years later I'm really grateful.'

Certainly it is never too early to teach our children to be appreciative. They will eventually get into the habit of saying 'Thank you' if we remind them often enough. An important part of their education is learning to express gratitude for meals, clean clothes, being taken to a friend's house or collected after a party. Teenagers will probably still need to be reminded to write thank you letters promptly, but hopefully they will be starting to follow our lead by now and to imitate the way we show gratitude (or not, as the case may be).

Encouraging our children to help

As well as showing our children love through our actions, family life is the place where they first learn to be helpful themselves. The headteacher of a primary school observed, 'My experience at school shows me that many children see their parents as slaves who answer to their every need.' Giving each of them a daily chore or two, appropriate to their age and ability, teaches them to do their bit. They may groan and take ages doing it, but whether it is taking out the rubbish, laying the table, clearing the plates or washing and drying up after meals, they begin to learn patterns of responsibility. Sometimes their help might make our tasks longer, but they are learning to play their part.

Virginie, a single mother, told us, 'I used to have a night a week where we all cooked and prepared the meal together; this was generally messy but great fun. I am a great one for doing chores as a team.' There are all sorts of ways we can help to make it more fun. Paula, another single parent with six children, has a bucket in which she puts little bits of paper, which list all the jobs that need doing. Each child dips in a hand and pulls out the tasks for the day.

Part of helping our children to grow in responsibility is to gradually increase the household chores that we expect them to do, so that, by the time they leave home, they are competent to look after themselves. They are able to cook, buy food, do their own laundry, use an iron, do basic DIY, clean the kitchen, clean their room (including changing bed linen), maintain personal cleanliness (by buying their own soap and shampoo, etc) and do their fair share of the housework. Our children will generally only learn to do these things by actually doing them, first under our supervision and then on their own. If we do everything for them until they leave home, we are not equipping them for life, and they may not pull their weight when they share a flat or home with others.

Of course generally children want to help when they are too young to be of much assistance, and are less keen to help when they are old enough!

Nicky I remember setting aside a Saturday morning when our children were little to plant out the pots and window boxes on our balcony. The children were very keen to get involved. I knew that not many plants would survive their enthusiasm. I decided it would be quicker and more successful if I did it on my own. Perhaps the balcony was the prettier for it, but I later regretted that I had missed an opportunity to let them help and have the fun, not only of doing it together, but also of being able to review our gardening efforts during the following months.

Having the right attitude

The attitude with which we undertake the acts of service that parenting demands will have an impact on our children. If we are resentful, they will notice our grudging attitude and may end up feeling guilty or worried. They will also probably be less likely to put themselves out for others. However, if we are aware that serving our children is a way of demonstrating our love, what we do will help them realise that they are special to us.

Sila One of my least favourite jobs as a parent was making a packed lunch at seven fifteen each morning, and I used to look forward to the day when our children could all make their own. However, I somehow found myself still doing it when our children were teenagers and perfectly capable of making the sandwiches themselves.

We once asked Benj, who was fifteen at the time, which of the five ways of expressing love was most important for him. After several moments of deep thought as he munched his way through his third bowl of cereal, he chose 'actions' as number one. He went on to say, 'I know Mum loves me because she makes my sandwiches for me every day.'

My attitude towards the packed lunches changed overnight! After that, when I made them, I was aware that I was doing far more than filling their stomachs with food.

Conclusion

Words, time, touch, presents and actions – any one of these five expressions of love may be important for us to feel loved, while another may be quite irrelevant. What matters, however, is not how much a particular love language means to us, but how much it means to our child. We should judge the degree of significance not by our own response but by theirs. And when we show love in the ways that mean most to them, we will see their emotional tanks being filled up. They will be loved, and *feel* loved. As Rob Parsons observes:

> We send our children into a world that will continually judge them. They will be forced to ask themselves, 'Am I clever/determined/successful/sociable *enough*?' And, of course, 'Am I attractive *enough*?' Matching up to the demands of others is a wearisome business. But we do our children a wonderful service if we send them into the world with an unshakeable belief that there is at least one person who, irrespective of their grades, weight or athletic genius, loves and accepts them unconditionally. It really is the greatest gift.[4]

Pause and consider

- When did you last hug your children?
- What sort of presents does each child most enjoy?
- What actions could you carry out today to show love to your children?
- Do you show love to your children regularly in all five ways?
- What new ways could you use to demonstrate your love?
- Do you know yet which is most important for each child? If not, ask them. You may be surprised by what you hear.

Section 3

Building character through setting boundaries

Chapter 9

The foundation of discipline

Young children are supposed to be defiant. It's in the job description. They are learning the rules of the game. Let them have a tantrum. Eventually they will learn that when you say 'no' it means 'no.'[1]

Dr Tanya Byron
Clinical psychologist

If you always give in, they don't learn that somebody can stay firm, so when they become young teenagers and adults they don't have the capability to say no to themselves when they are under peer pressure in terms of drugs, delinquency or sex.[2]

Jane Cassidy
Child psychotherapist

I wish I had put down firmer boundaries with my elder children when they were teenagers. I just let them find their way and actually they needed my help.

Anthony, aged 57

No discipline seems pleasant at the time, but painful. Later on, however, it produces a harvest of righteousness and peace for those who have been trained by it.[3]

The New Testament

Most parents have vivid memories of their first baby: the innocent face, the dimple, the tiny hands, the smiles and gurgles. How could such a sweet child ever need any sort of firm handling? A year later they are shocked by the strength of his will and his ability to defy them!

"No"
CHOX
DELUX

CHOX
delux

CHOX
delux

CHOX
delux

It is never too early and it is never too late to think about boundaries and discipline.

Discipline involves teaching, guiding and training, as well as correcting – with unpleasant consequences, if necessary. Putting appropriate boundaries around our child's behaviour lays a good foundation on which character, self-discipline and maturity can be built.

Sila Sometimes I wondered whose character was being built the most – theirs or mine. Teaching, guiding and training all sound like good ideas until our children blatantly ignore what we say, particularly at a friend's house or in front of their grandparents.

A week-long visit to my parents in Scotland with four children under the age of twelve was just about to end and I was happily thinking to myself that things had gone relatively smoothly. We were all packed up and I had given them strict instructions not to go anywhere as we had to drive to catch the train to London. But Barny, aged eight, was nowhere to be seen.

Having searched and shouted at the top of my voice for him for several minutes, I heard a rather muffled cry coming from upstairs. I eventually tracked it to the linen cupboard, a walk-in cupboard with hot pipes and no window. I put my hand on the handle to fling open the door and say very firmly, 'Barny, what do you think you're doing? This is no time to play games,' but the door wouldn't open.

> It turned out he'd been unable to resist seeing whether the key, which normally lived on the outside of the door, also locked the cupboard from the inside. Well, it most definitely did. However, it had got jammed and he was well and truly stuck and we were meant to be leaving immediately.
>
> Nicky, who is the practical one, had already returned to London several days earlier. My mother and I struggled with a very old lock, a motley array of screwdrivers, and a seriously hot child who wasn't sure whether it was more frightening to be stuck in a hot, airless cupboard or to face his just-about-to-lose-some-cheap-train-tickets mother! Somehow we got him out after twenty minutes, and with red faces, cross words and a mad dash for the station, we just caught the train.

You do not need to be a parent for long to discover that children do not always do what we ask of them. Nor are they born thinking about the needs of others. If in doubt, try putting a new toy in front of a group of two-year-olds and ask them to 'share nicely'! Within seconds, there will be yelling, grabbing and tears. Children have to learn how to behave in a civilised and sociable way, and it is our responsibility as parents to be their principal teachers. If all we do is to excuse bad behaviour, we will fail in our task.

Many parents want to be their child's best friend, but our children need us to be in charge. They need to know that we are placed in a position of authority over them. In today's society the word 'authority' often carries negative associations. But authority, exercised fairly and kindly, provides a structure within which children feel secure. When we show them love and set appropriate boundaries, our children will grow up to see authority as helpful and be willing to respect it at school and in society. Hard as it is for them, they need to discover that they are not the centre of the universe. And family life will be a lot happier for this understanding.

What puts us off setting boundaries?

Our job is first to decide where the boundaries should lie and then to impose them firmly. Easier said than done, of course. We may be reluctant to discipline our children for one or more of the following reasons:

1. Discipline is exhausting whatever the age of our child
We prefer to opt for short-term peace at the expense of the long-term benefits. We think we will start tomorrow, or next month, or when the exams are over, or when we are feeling stronger, or when they can understand the reasons for a boundary. But the more we put it off, the more trouble we store up for ourselves and our children. The tantrums of a two-year-old and the sulking and shouting of a thirteen-year-old often occur because they cannot get their own way. It is in their best interests to learn that this type of behaviour will not make us change our minds or move the boundary.

One mother with three young children was trying to settle them down one evening. They kept leaping out of their beds and charging around yelling their heads off. At the end of her tether, she said crossly, 'Fine – I'm going to bed – you can do what you like,' and promptly went to her own room and got into bed fully clothed. Lying there, listening to the pandemonium, she realised this would not work. Tempting as it was to pull the duvet over her head, she dragged herself out of bed and imposed some order.

2. We think discipline is the opposite of love

In reality, children, even when they know where the boundaries lie, will often push against them to see if they are firmly in place. This is part of the security they need as they grow up. An Old Testament proverb says, 'Those who love their children are careful to discipline them.'[4] Our children need to know that we love them enough to say, 'No,' even when they do not understand the reasons. Discipline is part of love. As parents we have to make important decisions for our children before they are old enough to do so themselves. This poem shows how hard it can be:

> I loved you enough to ask you where you were going,
> with whom, and what time you would get home.
>
> I loved you enough to insist that you saved up
> your pocket money
> to buy a bike for yourself
> that we could have afforded to buy for you.
>
> I loved you enough to make you return a Milky Way
> with a bite out of it, and to confess, 'I stole this.'
>
> I loved you enough to let you see hurt,
> disappointment and tears in my eyes.

I loved you enough to let you stumble, fall and hurt.

But, most of all, I loved you enough to say, 'No,'
when you hated me for it.
Those were the most difficult battles of all.
I'm glad I won them, because in the end you
won, too.[5]

3. We are worried that our children will not like us if we discipline them

In the short-term they probably will not. Bart, a five-year-old, said to his mother after she had told him off, 'I want another mummy!' Our concern that our children will reject us if we discipline them will be magnified if the relationship between us as mother and father is not working well. Insecurity can make us vie for our child's affection. This will always affect children badly and may cause them to reject us altogether when they are older.

4. We are frightened of our children's reactions

Tantrums, crying and shouting in protest at the boundaries we have set are nothing to be frightened of. The reactions may be loud, embarrassing and disturb the household. Do not be put off! We have to teach our children how to behave. It is no good tiptoeing round them worrying that we might upset them.

5. We do not want home to feel like school

This is more about *how* we impose boundaries rather than whether we have them at all. We gradually learnt from experience what works and what does not.

Nicky When our children were all under eleven, I bought a new computer. I decided I would do an A4 page of rules for our home.

I was so pleased with my handiwork that I not only included well-recognised boundaries for the children's behaviour, but I found myself adding a number of new ones that I knew would make the household work like clockwork from then on. Mealtimes would be transformed with punctual and well-dressed children; arguments about bedtimes would be a thing of the past; bedrooms would be ready for inspection by any unexpected visitor.

I presented this impressive list at the next family meal and carefully took them through the various points. I was, I confess, a little disappointed by their cool response. I had expected to be congratulated for the presentation and for the clarification of the house rules. I put the silence down to thoughtfulness. I announced that the list would be pinned inside the cupboard at the top of the stairs for easy reference (I did not want to embarrass anyone by displaying it publicly) and I put it up that evening.

A week later I had some reason to go to the cupboard. Not a sign of my list remained. I do not know to this day whether it was one child or all four working together who quietly removed it. I also came to see that children do not respond well to lists of rules, however well presented.

6. We ourselves had bad experiences of inappropriate or unjust discipline in our own upbringing
We may be worried about being unkind or too controlling, and thereby causing our children to become angry and resentful. However, the remedy to inappropriate discipline is not an absence of discipline but appropriate discipline. Resentment usually springs, not from the imposing of boundaries but from an absence of love.

Authoritative parenting

The key to effective discipline lies in the combination of showing love and being firm.

Psychologist Sue Palmer writes: 'There are four broad styles of parenting, based on the balance mothers and fathers strike between two elements: warmth and firmness. Warmth is the measure of how much love and support they give their children; firmness relates to the level of control they exercise over their children's lives.'[6] The following diagram describes these styles:

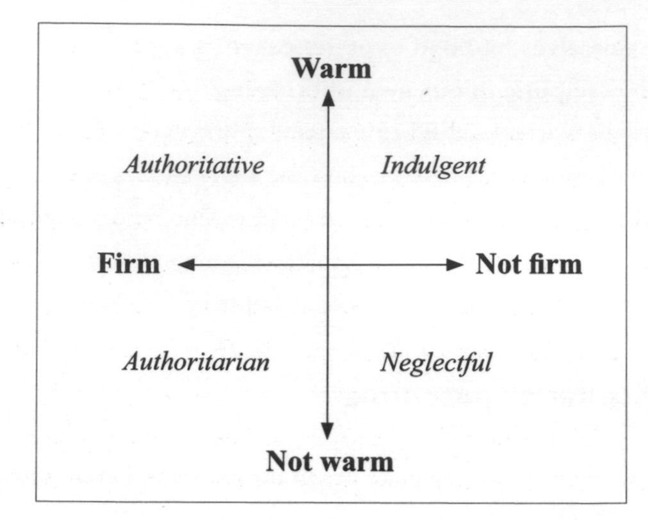

Four styles of parenting

1. Authoritarian

Parents who adopt this style tend to be rigid, domineering and lay down the law; they do so without listening to their child's point of view and without offering opportunities for discussion, choice or negotiation. They could be repeating the parenting style they experienced themselves. Or they may be too unsure of themselves to feel able to handle an argument.

Providing that punishments are not cruel or harsh, this style can give stability and security. The result is generally a well-behaved and obedient child. But the failure of parents to consider their children's feelings can result in a lot of repressed anger. This may eventually lead to destructive or anti-social behaviour once the children are out of their parents' immediate control. This style can also produce children who are fearful and anxious to please.

2. Indulgent

Indulgent parents are high in warmth but low on firmness. These parents make a habit of giving-in to requests, putting their children's interests above other people's and automatically springing to their children's defence if they get into trouble. Some are over-reacting to their own authoritarian upbringing. Some want to be their children's 'friends' rather than their parents. Others have allowed their children to do what they like from an early age and then found themselves unable to take back parental control.

These children usually feel loved and are generally self-confident, but they often have problems conforming at school and getting along with other children or adults. As one teacher put it: 'Their sense of entitlement is breathtaking.' They may also go off the rails later. As adolescents, they are more likely to be involved in drug or alcohol abuse and may find it difficult to accept that the world does not owe them a living.

3. Neglectful

This style is neither warm nor firm and involves giving a child neither attention nor boundaries. It may be the result of the parents' own neglectful upbringing. Sometimes deprived circumstances cause the parents to be too preoccupied with the dramas of their own lives to expend much effort on their children. It can also occur in more economically successful families, when parents are simply too wrapped up in their work to spare the time for child-rearing or cannot be bothered to take on the responsibility of discipline. Children brought up in neglectful homes grow up with poor self-esteem and a far higher than average chance of behavioural problems leading to self-destructive and antisocial behaviour.[7]

4. Authoritative

This style, involving warmth and firmness, was recognised by developmental psychologists such as Diana Baumrind in the 1960s. It produces the qualities most of us would ultimately want to see in our children, including independence, maturity, self-respect, self-control, curiosity, friendliness, initiative and optimism. Sue Palmer writes:

> The advice of every expert I spoke to while writing *Toxic Childhood* pointed towards an authoritative parenting approach … Authoritative parents treat their children warmly, which in practical terms translates into giving them plenty of time and loving attention, listening to them and responding to their concerns and allowing some (safe) choices. But they're also firm, ensuring rules and routines to provide stability, security and safety – for instance, regular family meals, bedtime schedules and rituals, monitoring of TV viewing (and no television in the bedroom).[8]

Examples of the four different parenting styles[9]

Scene 1

Annie, aged four, has snatched a ball from Sarah, another child the same age, in the playground.

- The authoritarian parent: 'Come back here this minute and give the ball back to Sarah.'
- The indulgent parent, believing that Annie should be allowed to give full expression to her desires, looks on benignly and

does not comment.

- The neglectful parent does not even notice what is happening as he is speaking on a mobile phone at the other end of the playground.
- The authoritative parent: 'The ball belongs to Sarah. I know you'd like to play with it, but come and ask her nicely if you could have a turn after her.'

Scene 2

Richard, aged twelve, wants to rent a Certificate 15 DVD that his friends have been talking about.

- The authoritarian parent gets cross and does not allow him to rent any more DVDs.
- The indulgent parent lets him rent it after a lot of pleading.
- The neglectful parent lets him watch whatever he likes in his bedroom on his own.
- The authoritative parent says, 'No,' explains why, and then helps him choose a more appropriate DVD.

Our natural style

Of course no two parents will have exactly the same 'parenting styles'. None of us will be a neat, clear-cut authoritative parent! In fact, each of us will probably have elements of more than one style in our own natural way of parenting, which is why couples have to agree on their approach when setting boundaries.

Sila I recognise my natural style is to tend towards being too firm and not as sympathetic and warm as I would like to be.

Nicky Meanwhile I tend to be high on warmth and to err on the side of over-sympathising with our children and letting them get away with too much.

As a result we have often had to discuss our joint approach, ideally before laying down a boundary, but sometimes it has been after the event!

Teaching consequences

An important part of setting boundaries for children is teaching them that their actions have consequences for good or for harm. If they throw stones, they may hurt someone or break a window. If they repeatedly pour milk on the carpet, the house will smell. If they hit other children, they will be unpopular and may be hit back.

Logical consequences

Sometimes we can make sure our children reap the unpleasant consequences of their actions. So, if they are old enough to know they should not throw their food on the floor, we can insist they clean it up themselves. If they have broken a toy in a fit of rage, we do not replace it. If they break a window because they were throwing stones when we told them not to, they contribute to the repair out of their own pocket money. If they do not complete their homework in time, they get in trouble with their teacher. Allowing children to suffer unpleasant consequences is often the best way to encourage good behaviour.

Imposed consequences

Sometimes there is no logical unpleasant consequence for a child's misbehaviour. In this situation a parent must impose an unpleasant outcome not naturally connected with the event. For example, a child who has been rude to Granny might not be allowed to watch TV that evening, or a child who has hit a sibling may be sent to bed earlier than usual. This is the basis of *punishment*. Some people immediately identify punishing with corporal punishment – smacking with the hand or using an instrument like a wooden spoon – but that is a totally separate issue.

Punishments can take many different forms: from sitting on the 'bottom stair' to the withdrawing of privileges. We use the terms 'punishing' and 'punishment' in this sense of imposing some kind of negative consequence. You will need to decide what words you use in your own home so that your child takes you seriously.

Where to begin

The prospect of setting boundaries can easily make us feel overwhelmed. Where to begin? You may feel inadequate, lack confidence or feel out of control. If that is your situation, you are not alone. Begin where you are.

Six principles for setting boundaries

1. Do not try to solve everything all at once! Begin with one or two suggestions from the chapters in this section or from friends.
2. Do not feel that your family has to be like any other family. There's no blueprint and what works with one child may not be appropriate for another.
3. Do not compare your child with other children, or yourself with other parents. As one mother constantly reminds herself, 'Comparisons are odious.' Some children are more compliant while others are much more strong-willed. We know a number of parents who thought parenting was quite straightforward (and looked somewhat disparagingly at those who were struggling) until they had their second child!
4. Talk about your situation with your partner (but not in front of your children), or with another adult if you are parenting on your own, and decide what to tackle first. A few changes can make a big difference.
5. Do not expect immediate results. Children thrive on consistency and routine but they may take a while to see if you are serious. You may think they are taking no notice of your 'new' boundaries – but that is probably a deliberate ploy to test you out.
6. Praise good behaviour. This is a powerful incentive for children to make good choices. Children will feel their efforts are recognised and appreciated, and parents will see that reinforcing boundaries is not just about saying, 'No.' Take every opportunity to encourage positive behaviour.

How do we do it?

1. Stopping to think

A child's bad behaviour is not always due to a defiance of authority. When our children are being fractious and obnoxious, sometimes it is simply because their blood sugar levels are low or their emotional tank is empty (see Chapter 5). They may be having a tough time at school. They may be exhausted or upset.

HALT

Pausing to think about why children are 'acting up' helps us determine whether to meet their behaviour head-on or to cut them some slack. The acronym HALT provides a useful checklist.

- *'H' is for hungry.* Do they need feeding? If so, it would be better to discuss a contentious issue after they have had something to eat.
- *'A' is for anxious.* Are they worried about something at school that they may not have told us about? Could they be anxious about something they have overheard us say, perhaps about our money, or our marriage? They may not know fully why they are upset and bedtime may be the best moment to draw from them what they are feeling. (See Chapter 7 for tips on becoming a good listener.)
- *'L' is for lonely.* A mother told us that her eight-year-old son had come home from school in a terrible mood. On enquiring about the cause she was met with a determined, 'Nothing.' So she sat on the stairs with him in silence for five minutes and hugged him. That was all he needed. Later he told her he was unhappy because he had been left out of a game in the school playground that afternoon.
- *'T' is for tired.* Children who have been in a busy school environment may benefit from some 'down time' on their bed away from the rest of the family, or in front of the TV with no requirement to talk. Children or teenagers who have had a sleep-over at a friend's house usually come back exhausted – physically and emotionally – and a quiet day and an early night may be all that is required to correct poor behaviour.

It is also well worth thinking, 'Does HALT apply to *me*?' It is all too easy to overact if our own blood sugar levels are low, or we are feeling stressed, in need of a hug, or exhausted. Does the situation need dealing with immediately or can it wait until we have had some sleep or a cup of coffee?

A five-year-old recently started at his 'big' school. He came home each afternoon grumpy and overdone. At first his mother was cross with him. But then she realised that he was not being naughty. It was just that he was worn out, feeling that he had had to be well-behaved and grown-up all day. What he really needed was not discipline, but her love and care. Similarly, a teenager, who had just broken up with his girlfriend, was monosyllabic with his parents for a few days. They told him off for his rudeness. But what he needed was their understanding and extra hugs.

2. Setting an example

As in all areas of parenting, our children learn more from what they observe in our behaviour than from what we tell them. Our discipline of our children is built on the discipline we exercise in our own lives. So, if we become aware that our eating, our anger or whatever are out of control, and that we are not maintaining healthy boundaries in our own lives, it is important to look for help.

3. Working together

A mother said to us recently:

> As parents you need to agree on the boundaries you are setting. I remember one time when our sixteen-year-old told me she was off to the cinema miles away in Brighton with her boyfriend, who had just passed his driving test. And worse still, my husband had agreed to lend them our car. I was horrified. 'No, you are not,' I said. 'Dad says it's fine and we are going anyway,' she told me.
>
> So then we had a situation where everyone was cross. I was mad at my daughter, her boyfriend, my husband and myself. It took us ages to realise we needed to decide together on a unified approach.

All children try to play one parent off against the other in order to get their own way. They mysteriously acquire an instinctive mastery of the 'divide and rule' tactic and they can tell which parent will be the 'softer touch'. Every parent knows how irritating it is to hear, 'Dad says I can,' or, 'Mum thinks it's fine,' just when they have set a boundary. It is even worse to undermine the other parent by saying to our child, 'Let's do this, but don't tell Mummy,' or, 'You can do that as long as Dad doesn't find out.'

Parenting goes much better if we support and encourage each other when one of us has said, 'No.' Even when parents are separated or divorced, the more they are able to lay aside animosities and act together to provide clear, mutually agreed boundaries for their child's behaviour, the more secure their child will be.

Sila Nicky and my different parenting styles caused problems when we did not have a common line. I was definitely stricter over food in bed when our children were little. I gave them as much to eat for tea as they wanted with the clear understanding that this was the last meal of the day.

But then, if Nicky was around to say goodnight, one child might complain that he was too hungry to go to sleep. Nicky would proceed to offer him sandwiches, fruit, biscuits – in fact, a five course meal, if desired, with full room service. Lights-out was delayed by thirty minutes and I felt totally undermined.

We realised a discussion was needed and a compromise found. We decided that Nicky would check with me first before giving them more food

> to see if they had had an opportunity at teatime to eat as much as they wanted. If so, he agreed to steel himself against their pleas of starvation! However, we also agreed that occasionally he could break all the rules – as a treat – and I would let it go.

Tips for working together and resolving differences

- Do not argue in the heat of the moment. Choose a time when the children are not present and when neither of you is overtired.
- Identify the main issue that is causing the conflict. Visualise taking the issue from between you and putting it out in front of you. This will help you to face the issue together instead of attacking each other.
- Take it in turns to listen to each other's points of view. Accept that you may have different perspectives and try not to blame. Digging in on your side and not budging will not solve anything. It will only mean more conflict. Discussion opens the way for finding a solution.
- Brainstorm possible solutions. Write out a list.
- Find a solution that is acceptable to both of you and try it out.
- Agree that, if the solution does not work, you will go back to your list and try another.
- If you cannot agree, seek help together from someone with an outside perspective.

Within our agreed boundaries, each of us needs freedom to parent in a way that is natural to our personality. One mother, who spent more time than her husband with their children, reacted bossily to the way he was getting them ready for bed, saying, '*This* is what we do.' To which he replied, 'No, that is what *you* do. I do it differently.'

Some couples come from families with very different parenting styles and each may feel strongly that theirs is the 'right' way. Difficulties arise when we try to compensate for our partner's approach by being much stricter or more lenient ourselves. Ultimately, unless our partner is being abusive or cruel, deciding together on a common approach is more important than exactly which way we go. Working together like this will usually mean both parents making compromises for the sake of their children's wellbeing.

Step-parenting makes the task of agreeing the boundaries more complex but also more urgent. One new step-mother was horrified when her step-son told her that he was allowed to play computer games all night in his mother's home. A phone call by the father to his ex-wife revealed that this was not so, and they were quickly able to establish a common rule for both households. The step-mother then felt empowered to set up some other important boundaries.

In a family where there are children and step-children, a big challenge for each parent will be not to favour their own child or children. Of course this is not easy, but everyone needs to be treated equally to avoid jealousy and resentment. A friend of ours, with three children from a previous marriage, married a man with three children of his own. 'When I remarried,' she told us, 'my husband and I did a parenting course together to work out how we were going to parent from the same platform. It took a lot of discussion, but we needed to agree on the boundaries we would establish as a new family. I also found that giving time to each of my step-children has been a vital key to success. By giving them time, I won their love, and then I could set the boundaries.'

4. Maintaining a sense of humour

Children's behaviour can test our patience to the limit and a sense of humour helps us to keep things in perspective. One mother wrote about the moments that she finds most challenging:

> I have two children with an extraordinary propensity to spill drinks. For some reason this really annoys me: a sticky table, wasps, wet clothes, unnecessary expense, and, worst of all, a happy moment ruined. However, I know perfectly well that they don't do it on purpose and that these are just childish mistakes, but I find it easy to over-react, get grumpy and shout. Happily, my husband, John, has a good sense of humour, and this enables me to recover my sense of proportion. He is always threatening to publish a book entitled *Places I have spilt my drink around the world.* His response each time is, 'Excellent! We have a new entry. I don't think we've had Pisa Airport before!' He and the children laugh, and even I manage to produce a wry smile.

Disciplining with humour goes a long way towards making the setting of boundaries more pleasant, both for us and for our children. Saying to a five-year-old, 'I hope I haven't seen you wiping your Marmite hands on the chair,' or to an eight-year-old, 'The clothes on your bedroom floor look as if they are not wanted. Let's give them away,' lightens the whole tone as we teach them how to behave.

Humour with teenagers is also helpful but requires careful

handling. They are generally more sensitive to being patronised or laughed at and are likely to find our humour annoying at times.

5. Creating the balance

In our own experience, knowing where and how to set boundaries for our children has been the hardest area of parenting and has often caused us much self-questioning. In aiming to avoid the two extremes of harshness and permissiveness, sometimes we feel we have erred in one direction, and sometimes in the other. We have come to realise we are not alone. As one father put it, 'Parenting is an inexact science. My wife and I tend to stumble along together, making it up as we go.'

Parents must set the boundaries somewhere between the two extremes. We are not walking a tightrope along which every step is critical to our children's well-being. A better image is a broad track on which there is freedom for us to work out our own path, and then to be confident and consistent with our decisions. No two families will take exactly the same route. Some will be closer to one edge, some closer to the other.

Of course children are acutely sensitive to being treated unfairly and are quite likely to complain: 'Segun doesn't have to …,' or, 'Gemma is allowed to …' But we must refuse to be manipulated by the decisions other parents have made. What is of primary importance to some parents will be secondary to others. Choose your own battles. One couple with young children told us, 'It matters a great deal to us that our children learn to tell the truth and are kind to others. We are really tough on that. However, on tidiness and snacks between meals we are more lenient than other parents. Those are not so important to us.'

6. Adapting our approach

Adjusting the boundaries according to the ages and personalities of our children can be difficult. Our children may have moved on to a new phase and we are stuck in the past. Discussing this with parents who have children the same age can help us move on. A mother of teenagers commented, 'Talking with other parents and agreeing a consensus on sleep-overs or weekend activities can be empowering and helps us not to feel like ogres.'

We also found that what worked for one child at one age was ineffective for another child or for the same child a few years later.

Nicky Our oldest child, Kirsty, needed very little encouragement to do her homework. She was conscientious and not particularly interested in TV. Sometimes, in her teenage years, we had to encourage her to take proper breaks. But with our sons, it was a different story. We had to have clear rules about how much TV they could watch and when they should do their homework in the hope that it would get done at a reasonable time.

As they got older, we tried to adjust when we ate together to be helpful to them. We also gave them increased responsibility in deciding when and for how long to do their work. I'm not sure we got it entirely right. With the older ones, we were probably too strict and with our younger ones, too lenient.

7. See it as a process

The process of a child learning self-regulated boundaries for their own behaviour is a gradual one. Sam, a mother with four children under eight, said, 'A young child cannot see the big picture – all they can see is the chocolate biscuit they want now, or the game they want to start playing at bedtime. Whereas, as a parent, we can see the big picture and it's our job to make decisions for them until we have trained them to make good choices for themselves.'

Parents initially exercise total control for their child's welfare and protection. As children grow older, they need to be allowed to make more and more of their own decisions until eventually (around the age of eighteen) they are choosing their own way. By then, the benefits of looking at the long-term consequences of their actions and of exercising restraint when appropriate should be deeply embedded in their thinking. They have learnt to show respect for people and property, and have developed proper self-control.

Conclusion

Damian Whitworth, a journalist reporting on the lack of confidence among parents in disciplining their children, observed:

> NO. One of the shortest, easiest, most used words in the English language. It can also be one of the hardest to utter in any meaningful way – particularly if you are a modern parent. Those who work with children believe that a generation of parents have forgotten how to say no, with the result that as their children grow up

> they lack the self-esteem needed to negotiate adult life successfully.[10]

A senior school teacher, Fiona Hammans, who sees the effect on pupils when there is a lack of discipline at home, observed: 'You've got a generation of parenting that does not believe in punishing their kids. They say, "You're grounded for a year." And the kid cries, and then they say, "Oh all right, then!" A whole lot of parents don't know how to control their kids. The kids are in charge.'[11]

All of us will feel like giving up at times. The arguments are endless and the days are too long. 'Let their school, or their youth leaders, or the police, or Granny instil some discipline,' we think. But we cannot devolve the responsibility to others. If we do not teach our children how to behave, they will be at a disadvantage wherever they go. And in the long run, family life will be more fun, and considerably more peaceful, when good boundaries have been set.

We will never get it entirely right. We will never be perfect parents. Sometimes we feel our attempts at improving our children's behaviour are getting nowhere. And what is really irritating is that other people see the effects more than we do. 'Your children are so polite,' they say. And we wonder if they have the right parents as we think of the children's behaviour at breakfast.

Pause and consider

- Do your children know where the boundaries lie?
- Do you know where the boundaries lie? Are you happy with them?
- When did you last say, 'No,' to your children and stick to it?
- Do you and your spouse/partner have different views on discipline? Are you prepared to discuss the most difficult issues together – or do you need help to find a joint approach?

Chapter 10

Setting boundaries with pre-school children (aged 0 to 5)

You know that the beginning is the most important part of any work, especially in the case of a young and tender thing, for that is the time at which the character is being formed.

Plato
Philosopher

It's easier to say, 'No,' to a one-year-old than to a five-year-old. So, if you start young, you'll reap the benefits later.

Sam
Mother

When my kids become wild and unruly, I use a nice, safe playpen. When they've finished, I climb out.

Erma Bombeck
Columnist

Train up children in the way they should go and when they are old they will not depart from it.[1]

King Solomon

Setting and enforcing boundaries with young children is tiring and inconvenient. We may be shocked when our child first challenges us and deliberately throws their lunch at the wall. We need to work out how we will respond. Tessa Livingstone, who was part of the BBC's parenting series, *Child of Our Time*, writes about this critical moment:

At some stage between one and a half and two, your child is likely to recognise the distinction between accidental and deliberate wrongdoing. Causing trouble can be very appealing, partly because parents or carers react so strongly, and partly because it generates an intoxicating sense of power. Whatever the reason, most children feel a combination of enjoyment, aggression and personal distress, and it is within this turbulent context that conscience will start to develop at the age of two. It is then that issues of discipline become more important.[2]

Starting young

1. Understanding the need to set boundaries

Some parents are reluctant to discipline their children when they are young for various reasons. Some because they do not know how to, some because they do not think they need to, and some because of what other people might think. A mother described to us what changed her attitude:

> I suffered real heartache in dealing with my eldest child Alex as a toddler, because I did not discipline him early enough. My mistake was that I did not want to discipline him in front of others. I felt that this was a demeaning, humiliating loss of face for both of us. So, when he became rough, I was embarrassed but reluctant to tell him off.
>
> I was one of those mothers who vainly hoped that no one was noticing! Then, a near disaster happened. One suppertime Alex threw a fork at the head of his godmother's child in an entirely unprovoked attack. It nearly hit her eye. There was no excuse to be made.
>
> At last, and really for the first time, I disciplined Alex in front of someone else. I had been doing him a great disservice in not doing this before. The other mother's reaction moved from horror to respect. Far from losing face, I had finally done what a parent ought to do.

2. Teaching right and wrong choices

The concept of 'right and wrong choices' was invaluable to us. Tessa Hardingham, the founder of our children's nursery school, explains how toddlers who join the school aged two and a half can understand right and wrong choices very quickly:

> To use right and wrong choices effectively with children, they must be told three things. First of all, they must understand what is and what is not acceptable behaviour. They need to know that there are certain boundaries in place. So, for example, a two-year-old is quite old enough to understand that it is not acceptable to throw food around, to pull hair, or to throw hard toys. They must know clearly what we expect of them.
>
> Secondly, they are told the different consequences of keeping within or crossing those boundaries. They quickly discover that the consequence for one is pleasant and for the other is unpleasant.
>
> Thirdly, they learn that they are responsible for their own behaviour – the choice is theirs. So, if they continue to throw a hard toy across the room when we have told them to stop, we say to them, 'It is your choice: if you do not stop throwing the toy, you will go and sit on the stairs.' If they choose to stop, we encourage them by saying something like, 'Well done! You made a right choice.' Otherwise they experience the disagreeable consequence of their own wrong choice.

This simple technique teaches young children vital lessons for life. In particular:

- They cannot always do what they feel like.
- Good behaviour is rewarded.
- Bad behaviour will result in an unpleasant consequence.
- They must take responsibility for their own actions.

One of the best ways of reinforcing *good choices* is through praise. We should make it clear what we are praising them for. Here are some examples: 'That's really kind letting Aidan play with your car,' or, 'Well done for putting your clothes on the chair,' or, 'Thank you for leaving your muddy shoes at the door.' Reinforcing a right choice with praise will generally motivate them to want to do it again.

Meanwhile the consequence for a *wrong choice* must be something they do not enjoy and therefore acts as a disincentive – sitting at the bottom of the stairs on their own, not being allowed to watch TV or a DVD, going without sweets, not being able to play a game or having a favourite toy confiscated for a time.

3. Distinguishing between natural childishness and naughtiness

When our children do things we are unhappy about, the question to ask ourselves is: 'Should we engage in a battle over this?' We found making a distinction between normal childishness and naughtiness very helpful in trying to work out where and how to set boundaries.

Naughtiness is when children are being deliberately disobedient and are challenging our authority. They are looking to see if the boundaries we have set are going to be enforced. They will often test us to see what they can get away with, such as not getting out of the bath when we have asked them for the third and final time, running away from us when we have explicitly told them not to, or deliberately hurting a sibling when we have just warned them to stop fighting.

Natural childishness, on the other hand, is simply children being children. Annoying as it may be children are bound to make mistakes and have accidents. Some children are particularly accident-prone: a three-year-old knocks over a mug of milk; toys get left out in the rain because children do not think about rust; they come back from swimming and a wet swimming towel is left on a dry bed and soaks the duvet; or they are outside playing in their best T-shirt, which they catch on a branch and tear.

Unless we have just told them not to, these actions are all the results of their age and immaturity, and should not be punished.

Sila I found that the key to disciplining our children when they were young hinged around my seeing the difference between them acting childishly and behaving defiantly. Having the distinction clearly in my mind halved the battles I had to fight and helped me to stand my ground when an important boundary was being breached.

Nicky Equally important was trying to restrain ourselves from getting cross with and punishing our children when they damaged property unintentionally as a result of their age.

We used to have some downstairs neighbours who had a valuable collection of old books. Once a year the husband would put the books on their dining room table and carefully oil the leather covers. Our bathroom was directly above their dining room.

One year, leaving the freshly oiled books on the table, our neighbours went out for the afternoon. Barny, aged four, was having his bath. He discovered for the first time a small hole in the silicone seal between the bath and the wall. Taking his small plastic bucket, he proceeded to pour water down this hole. Our neighbours returned home to discover water dripping onto the books – rapidly reducing their value.

On receiving an alarmed call from downstairs, we rushed into the bathroom to witness Barny concentrating hard on his next bucketful in his attempt to empty the bath. Our instincts were to be furious with him, but actually he needed to be stopped (with an explanation that the bathwater had to stay in the bath) and not punished.

In situations like this, we must ask ourselves whether we have told our children what we expect of them. Friends of ours were apoplectic when their four-year-old son decided to climb up their best curtains and swing on them, and in so doing pulled the curtain rail off the wall. They were about to explode with fury, but then they both realised they had never actually explained that curtain-climbing is out of bounds. It would therefore have been unfair to discipline him. Now, however, he knows. Should he try it again, he will be in trouble.

Natural childishness also means young children have a lack of awareness of time and little appreciation of deadlines. We may be expiring with stress as we try to hurry them into the car while they dawdle, oblivious of our timetable. It is unfair if we take out our frustration at being late on them, or if we get annoyed at their indifference to our busy schedule. This is part of being a child. One solution for us is to build in extra time for all the unexpected delays we encounter. It is amazing the difference these small adjustments can make. Leaving five minutes extra to get to nursery can make the whole experience more fun for everyone.

For high-achievers, who are used to driving themselves with deadlines, this is likely to be a hard aspect of parenting. We may have to alter our expectations radically as to how much we can achieve in a day. Otherwise everyone ends up frazzled as we drag our young child around at high speed, ticking off all the things on our to-do list. Reducing our expectations helps us all to be more relaxed and even to enjoy activities at a child's pace. One parent commented, 'As we dawdle along, picking up sticks or other random objects, watching caterpillars cross our path, or a crane unload a lorry, I tell myself through gritted teeth, "One day I will cherish this memory." '

4. Giving age-appropriate instructions

As we set boundaries for our children, there are questions we need to ask. First of all, are they old enough to understand what we are telling them? If we are on the beach, there is a difference between saying to a two-year-old, 'You mustn't go out of my sight,' and saying the same to a six-year-old. The six-year-old is able to remember our instructions and understand something of the dangers involved. If the two-year-old wanders off, that is our responsibility as a parent and we have no right to be cross with the child.

What can be frustrating is that young children forget so quickly. If we say once, 'Don't take your pillow outside,' and they do it three days later, they are not being naughty. This is still part of their natural childishness. Young children do not hold the same values as adults and they will often fail to remember our instructions from one day or week to the next, and they need reminding.

5. Using our voice strategically

One of the main lessons we are teaching our children is to respond to what we say. Our children pick up whether or not we expect a positive response. The tone of our voice will have as much of an impact as the words we use. If we say, 'No', consistently, in the same serious tone of voice, to put a boundary in place, it will be one of the first words our children understand.

The first 'no' will probably apply to their physical safety.

If newly mobile children start crawling towards a point of danger, such as the stairs or a hot cooker, they need to be told 'no' in a firm voice and lifted away. They understand amazingly quickly what we mean, provided we use a strong tone of voice and back it up by lifting them away from the source of danger. A rather weak 'no' said in the same tone as our 'yes' will be ineffective or even counterproductive.

Making requests in a calm, firm voice will be much more effective than constantly shouting and always sounding cross. This is part of planning for success and our children will tend to live up to our expectations. If we approach each situation anticipating disobedience, then that is what we will get. When we say calmly, 'Emily, you know you don't help yourself to a juice carton without asking Mum or Dad first. Put it back in the cupboard please,' she will pick up from our tone whether or not we expect her to comply. Sometimes, of course, Emily will choose not to, and we will need to use a firmer tone and impose a consequence if she still refuses, but that should not be the norm.

Increasingly, the boundaries we put in place will be for their emotional safety. The principle is exactly the same. They learn our 'no' means 'no' because we love them and are concerned about their well-being.

Pre-empting bad behaviour

It is worth being aware of the typical situations when a child is most likely to be disobedient or to throw a tantrum. These will probably include most of the following: mealtimes, leaving the playground, going shopping, having to share toys, leaving someone else's house, clearing up at the end of the day, dressing and undressing, getting out of the bath, going to bed. This, of course, covers most of the day, which is why parenting never ends!

The following tactics can help us to be one step ahead.

1. Being aware of triggers for bad behaviour

Remember HALT (Hungry, Anxious, Lonely or Tired) in the previous chapter to check on other reasons for children playing up. One mother discovered her eighteen-month-old was impossible to handle if he did not have a sleep in the afternoon. So she now organises her day around his rest. If we are aware of the triggers, we will avoid many unnecessary confrontations.

2. Using distraction

This brilliant tool is underused and undervalued by many parents. It is highly effective, particularly with pre-school children. In the playground, when Owen is about to climb up the slide that is too big for him, we can say, 'Owen, look! There's Luke. Luke is having a great time on that big swing. Let's go on the one next to him.' Using distraction means thinking of something interesting enough, quickly enough.

Sila My mother was an expert at distraction with our children when they were young. If they were crying as we left them with her, she insisted on a proper goodbye and then, holding them by the hand or in her arms, she would say something like, 'Now, let's go and feed the birds.' And off she'd go, weathering the crying, which usually stopped the moment we were out of sight, as suddenly getting the nuts for the birds became more interesting.

3. Giving options

Options defuse head-to-head conflict. So, rather than saying, 'No, Ruth, you can't take all those toys to Sally's house,' a better approach might be: 'Ruth would you like to take your ball or your book to Sally's house? You choose. Which one would you like to show Sally?'

Thinking ahead and giving our children alternatives can also avoid recurring struggles. If we know that the sweet aisle at the supermarket may cause trouble, we could decide to have a 'sweet tin' at home. Before going to do the weekly shop, we can check to see if we need to refill it. On the way we tell each child they can choose a packet of sweets to go into the tin.

Choices are also often the vehicle by which we give our children a way out if we are locked in a contest of wills and they stubbornly refuse to give in. If a child is determined not to eat anything out of protest at an earlier incident, we could give them the choice of either staying at the table until they have eaten at least five mouthfuls or going without TV later on. We are not giving in to their sulks and tears but we are making it easier for them to back down when they know they are not going to win.

As with distractions, this technique is helpful when they are young, but we should be weaning them off it as they approach school age. Otherwise they will not learn to be obedient, to us or their teachers.

4. Providing rewards

With pre-school children, rewarding good behaviour as much as punishing bad behaviour needs to be immediate. One parent said, 'I sometimes tell my children aged four and two that if they behave nicely at teatime we can play "hunt the Smartie" afterwards. This is a tiny incentive but it seems to work.'

This strategy should be distinguished from offering a screaming child a Smartie in the middle of a tantrum to try and shut him up. This would be to reward bad behaviour. Nor should we get into the position of having to bribe our children every time we ask them to do something.

As children get older the gap between the behaviour and the reward can be extended. A father commented, 'We found a system of simple cumulative rewards, such as for five good mealtimes or ten good bed-times, worked really well for our children aged three and five. They then chose a small prize.'

Handling temper tantrums

There is hardly a parent of a toddler who does not live in dread of the next tantrum. The scene is familiar: we are doing the shopping with our child in the trolley. Everything looks fine on the outside but on the inside we are on edge, bracing ourselves for the inevitable. We go around the corner into the next aisle and *it happens*. Our toddler spots the biscuits and demands to have some *now*. We say, 'No', in as calm a voice as we can muster and then she explodes – screaming, writhing, kicking, arms flailing – and everybody turns round to see who is responsible for the disturbance.

A friend of ours with two children, Sam aged six and Amy aged four, describes how she and her husband, Colin, cope with such scenes in public:

Our first rule is: 'Ignore all comments from passers-by.' In fact, pretend you are foreign and don't understand. When Amy had a total, all-out, writhing tantrum in the desk section of Ikea, Colin grabbed Sam and joined the gathering crowd of spectators, claiming to be entirely unrelated to this screaming child. (Colin has refused to go to Ikea ever since.) I sat next to Amy and pretended to be reading a magazine, without taking any notice of her Oscar-winning performance.

Another time I gave each of my children a £2 budget to spend in a book fair. Amy would not believe me that Sam's two books cost the same as her one book. She was incensed: he had two books and she only had one. So she lay in the confined space of the school library between the shelves, tripping up parents and other children, and screamed. I did try and shift her to the edge where she was less of an obstacle, but a child mid-tantrum is hard to move. Eventually, I had to sit down and wait until the whole event was over to get her out. People kept saying, 'You're very calm,' but actually there was no option. Finally, she stopped crying; we bought the books and went home. Funnily enough, there were very few people left by then. I imagine the school book fair reported huge losses that year.

Dr. Dorothy Einon, a child psychologist, explains the value of staying calm:

> Tantrums affect 80% of children between twenty months and four years and these displays of fury are reserved mainly for the mother. When you face the prospect of a tantrum at any time, it helps to understand what is going on in your toddler's mind, especially as your reaction to a tantrum can greatly influence how long it lasts and whether it is repeated. If you get angry, you are playing into the toddler's hands. Children of tantrum age want their mother's attention and, if they can't get your smiles, they will take your anger in preference to being ignored.[3]

All this requires self-control, and the ability to press the 'pause button' on our reactions when necessary. (We will describe this idea further in Chapter 14.) Having been through tantrums four times ourselves we found the following advice helpful. And take courage! The tantrum years do not last forever.

Surviving tantrums

- Tantrums are normal toddler behaviour.
- We are not bad parents and our child does not hate us.
- It helps to think ahead as to how we can be prepared for the most obvious times when our child might have a tantrum.
- The best thing to do when a child is having a tantrum is not to make a big deal of it. Assume an impassive face, refuse eye contact and say nothing (or very little). If we pay too much attention they are likely to repeat the behaviour.
- We can either pick the child up and remove him from the situation, or go into another room leaving the child alone if it is safe to do so.
- If possible, particularly when in a public place, hold her in a strong bear hug until the anger subsides and tell onlookers, 'It is just a tantrum.'
- Once the tantrum is over, do not show relief or give extra attention. This will encourage more tantrums in order to gain more attention.
- Laugh about it later with your partner or friend (but out of earshot of your child).

Dealing decisively with bad behaviour

There is no escaping the fact that setting boundaries requires not only the right tools, but also a great deal of effort. Many parents give up on discipline because they simply do not have the energy to persevere. Here are seven ways to make the job more manageable.

1. Take decisive action

Children learn at a (surprisingly) young age what they can get away with. Imagine the scene: we take our child to the playground and they are running around with a friend, when our mobile rings. We answer it and start talking; we are half-concentrating on what our child is doing as he goes to explore a large muddy puddle. We glance over our shoulder from the bench we are sitting on and say, 'No, Samir, don't go in the puddle. You haven't got your boots on.' We turn back to resume our conversation. Meanwhile Samir is standing on the edge of the puddle about to walk right in. We turn round again and say much louder this time, 'Samir, I said NOT to go in the puddle! Samir! I said, "DON'T GO IN THE PUDDLE!" ' We are still sitting on our bench, still on the phone. Samir looks up and without a moment's hesitation walks straight into the puddle knowing he can probably get through to the other side and run off to the slide before we, the startled parent, can even leave our bench. Anyhow, we have not finished our conversation.

Such a scene usually arises out of our desire for an uninterrupted adult conversation and, frankly, feeling too tired to want to bother. We have all been there! If only we could have our child on one of those retractable dog leads – we could press the button and carry on chatting to our friend.

The alternative, and better, scenario is that we take action. As soon as we see Samir near a puddle, if we do not want him to get wet, we stop our conversation, get up, go to him, bend down and say, 'Samir, please do as I have asked. You are not to go in the puddle as you do not have your boots on.' And then we take him away to play on the slide or climbing frame. Usually the new activity will distract him from the appeal of puddle-stomping.

If Samir returns to the puddle and, despite our repeated instructions, he deliberately disobeys, there needs to be a consequence. Hard as it is, we have to demonstrate to Samir he cannot get away with it. Perhaps we leave the playground. Perhaps we take him to sit on a bench for five minutes and do not allow him to play. Whatever we do, we need to take action. It will feel far easier to let it go and carry on chatting to our friend, but making the effort now will be an investment that bears valuable returns in the years to come.

2. Remove the problem from the child or the child from the problem

We have asked our three-year-old not to hit the chair with the plastic cricket bat, as he is systematically destroying our last decent piece of furniture. If he continues the demolition work, we ask him, 'Euan, was that a right choice or a wrong choice?' Euan may see it for himself (admittedly, the less likely option), or we may have to help him: 'That was a wrong choice. I've already told you bats are for hitting balls, not furniture. I'm going to take the bat away.' Then, ignoring the screams, the tears and other protests, we take the bat away quickly, without being drawn into negotiations. We put it out of reach, and ideally out of sight. We then say, 'Let's go and find something else to play with.'

In other situations we may need to remove the child from the problem by sending him or her to a 'cooling off' place. One minute for each year of their age is a useful rule of thumb – longer is generally impossible to enforce and shorter is usually ineffective.

Sila We used various parts of the house as a cooling off area, depending on the offending child's age. The area had to be safe and of course less enjoyable than staying where they were. The punishment would have been meaningless if they were able to sit playing with their toys elsewhere. We never locked a child into a room as that could have frightened them.

I can remember one of us frequently taking a child who had been throwing food on the floor to the bottom of the stairs and saying for the umpteenth time, 'You are to stay here for three minutes. Then you can come back and sit with the rest of us.' Often we had to put the child back there four or five times until the three minutes were up, and we wondered if this was really going to make a difference. In the long run the children got the message and realised we were serious about manners at mealtimes.

3. Give advance notice

Giving an advance warning can help everybody. For example: 'We have to leave soon, so this is the last go with the bike.' Or, 'It is nearly time to go home – one more turn on the swing.' But children have got to know we mean it. They see through weak, half-hearted instructions and are adept at delaying tactics. When the time comes, we need to get up, pack up our stuff and go.

Our warnings need to be appropriate. It is not fair to young children of pre-school age to shout from another room, 'Time to tidy up the toys because it's bathtime in ten minutes,' and then to come through five minutes later and be angry with them because nothing has happened.

Sila When our children were little, I was getting more and more frustrated with their failure to take my instructions seriously. So I started to use a timer.

> I would tell them they had ten minutes more to play and that, when the timer went, I would come through to help them put away the toys and then it would be straight upstairs for a bath. Once the children knew that I would implement the timing and had not added on twenty minutes leeway, they started to be more co-operative.

4. Make warnings realistic

A mother described to us how she and her four-year-old daughter, Anna, went with Anna's friend, Sarah, and Sarah's mother to a special children's fair as a Christmas treat. On the journey there Sarah punched Anna. Sarah's mother warned her that, if she did it again, she would not be allowed to go on the merry-go-round or to buy any toys or sweets at the fair. But that was the whole purpose of the outing. So, if she carried out her threat, the whole day would be ruined for everyone. Sarah did do it again. Of course, when they arrived at the fair, the mother could not carry out her threat. As Sarah enjoyed her third turn on the merry-go-round, she muttered something about Sarah missing her favourite TV programme the next day.

It is all too easy to fall into the trap of issuing idle threats. If we fail to back up our words with consequences, we create real problems for ourselves and for our children. They are learning that they can get away with wrong choices. We are not being kind to them. It would have been far better if Sarah's mother had said something like, 'If you hit Anna again, you will miss your first turn on the merry-go-round,' and then had sat in the car with Sarah for ten minutes when they arrived.

5. Follow through with consequences

Following through with a punishment is often inconvenient. The younger the child, the more important it is that we act immediately. The child is then able to link the punishment with the offence. If we are in the park and have said, 'If you go on pushing Sean, we will have to go home,' we must be true to our word. This is the last thing we want to do having only just arrived, particularly if we have other children who are enjoying themselves. But they too will take in whether we issue idle threats or back up what we say. So it is worth deciding what punishment is most appropriate (and workable) in any given situation. We can usually find somewhere in the park for an offending child to sit while not being allowed to play for five minutes.

Children are acutely aware of parental injustice and favouritism. Of course, continuing to be fair is much harder if we have one child who is more compliant and another who is very strong-willed.

Sila That was certainly true for us, not least over bedtimes. The rule in our home was that after storytime the children each got into their own bed and, after praying with them, we turned the lights out. Of our four children, one was particularly strong-willed at a young age. This child, aged two and a half, decided that bedtime didn't need to be adhered to. He kept getting up and disturbing the others or coming downstairs whilst the other children stayed in bed. Fairness meant we had to continue to impose an unpleasant consequence on this particular child every night over a two week period so that both he and the others knew that this boundary was non-negotiable. We were close to giving up, but the message eventually got through.

Finding the right punishments

These should be selected according to the seriousness of the misbehaviour and the age of the child.

- Put the child in another room for one minute for each year of the child's age.
- Make the child sit at the bottom of the stairs, or on 'the naughty step', for the same length of time as above.
- Confiscate a favourite toy.
- No *Bob the Builder* (or their current favourite) DVD that day.
- Shorter bath time if they enjoy playing in the bath.
- Missing out on a game that they would normally play or missing a trip to the playground.
- Going to bed without story time (as long as only used rarely).

6. Avoid arguments

Many parents wear themselves out arguing with their children – seeking to persuade, explaining, cajoling, desperately trying to make their children co-operate with their instructions – but without success, as the children know there will be no punishment for misbehaviour. Thomas Phelan, best-selling American author and clinical psychologist, recommends that, instead of arguing, parents give their children two chances to stop misbehaving before imposing a consequence. He describes his system as '1-2-3 magic' (although he says there is no 'magic' involved). He explains:

> Suppose your six-year-old son wants a biscuit while you are making his tea. You say, 'No,' as tea will be in fifteen minutes. He starts complaining, whining or kicking the kitchen cupboards and screaming in protest.
>
> Without arguing (in fact, showing absolutely no emotion) you simply hold up one finger and say calmly, 'That's one.' If he continues to plead for a biscuit, or accuses you of cruelty to children, or throws himself on the floor and yells loud enough to be heard next door, you let five seconds go by and then hold up two fingers and say, 'That's two.' If the behaviour continues for a further five seconds, you hold up three fingers and say, 'That's three. Go to your room for six minutes,' (based on one minute per year of the child's age), or give some other punishment such as no TV, or an earlier bedtime.[4]

Some behaviour, such as hitting a parent, earns an instant, 'That's three.' The child is not allowed another two swipes before being disciplined. The author then describes what happens after the 'time out' is served: 'Nothing. No talking, no emotion, no apologies, no lectures, no discussions. Nothing is said unless it is absolutely necessary.'

A British parent we know uses a similar approach by giving her children three chances if they are behaving badly, and will say to them, 'You've lost a chance,' or, 'You've lost two chances.' Because they know she is serious about the consequences, simply warning them, 'You're about to lose a chance,' is usually enough now for them to start behaving properly.

Whatever words we use, a clear system like this has a number of benefits:

- Children learn there are consequences for poor behaviour and parents are not constantly arguing with or shouting at their children.
- Whining, shouting, tantrums or other types of manipulation by children are not rewarded.
- Children start to take responsibility for their own behaviour by being given clear warnings.
- The parent is in charge.
- Parents are not required to give endless reasons for every boundary, vainly hoping to persuade their children and wearing themselves out in the process.

7. Be consistent

Children do better when they know where the boundaries lie. Consistency in what they are allowed to do makes life easier for them and us. That means when we leave our children in the care of other people, it is important we outline to them our approach to discipline. If grandparents or other child minders are more lenient or much stricter than we are, it can cause friction.

One mother said to us, 'I explain to my child minder what I expect and she follows *our* principles. There is no point in us having worked out our approach if, for two days a week, she takes a different line and, for instance, buys them sweets when they ask her to or allows them to watch TV all day.'

Conclusion

Setting boundaries early on will make our parenting much easier as they grow older. A mother, who understood the role of discipline in training, and sometimes punishing, her children when they were toddlers, spoke of the long term effect in their family life:

> I don't believe that 'reasoning' – that stalwart of the over-educated, over-anxious middle-class parent – works at all. Parents who politely ask their two and three-year-olds, 'Would you like to go to bed now?' or, 'Do you think you have watched enough television yet?' are asking for a blunt, 'No,' and a whole lot of trouble later on.
>
> I have found now they are older, they don't need punishing all that much. Sanctions, yes. Incentives, yes. But they know that 'no' means 'no'. The threat of losing pocket money is usually enough. Maybe it is because they learnt about boundaries as toddlers. Discipline makes happy children – children who know how far they can go and even have the fun of pushing a little bit further now and then.[5]

Pause and consider

- Identify examples of behaviour in your children that are natural childishness rather than naughtiness.
- Do your children know what you expect of them?
- Are they old enough to understand and carry out your instructions?
- What negative consequences or punishments are most effective for each child? Have you discussed these with your partner?
- Do you give realistic warnings and do you carry them out when the misbehaviour continues?
- If you have more than one child, are you being fair in your discipline?
- Could your child's poor behaviour have a medical cause? If you suspect this might be so, talk to your doctor about it.[6]

Chapter 11

Setting boundaries with 6 to 10-year-olds

My job involves negotiating but it's a cinch compared to negotiating with my kids, who use every trick in the book.

Father of three
City trader

I wish I had been shouted at less and talked to more. And I'm trying to do it differently with my own children.

Jim, aged 36

My parents pretty well let me do what I liked and now I struggle to say 'no' to other people when I know I should.

Sara, aged 27

Training includes sanctions which are designed to refine behaviour. Refined behaviour leads to growth of character.

Jo Glen
Head teacher

My daughter has a problem picking things up in her room. So, if she leaves her clothes on the floor, we put them in a bin bag. She has to earn them back by being tidy.

Madonna
Musician

By the age of six our children are moving on. And so must we. They are becoming more independent. Their focus is now turning outwards to school and to building friendships. They are becoming more aware of the feelings of other people, showing pleasure when people are happy, and sympathy if someone is sad. Life has become more demanding.

They are expected to behave well in the classroom, to co-operate with their teachers and to do their homework. They need opportunities to talk about what is going on at school, who their friends are and their feelings about life – whether positive or negative. And they need us to listen. They still want a lot of love and reassurance, as well as clear boundaries to distinguish between the kind of behaviour that helps relationships to flourish and the kind that spoils them. These boundaries we set are the foundations of their self-control, ensuring that our children are good company for others.

At this age we can give them more responsibilities at home so that they learn to contribute to family life: laying and clearing the table; tidying their toys and clothes; stacking the dishwasher; making their bed. All these are helping them to grow in independence and in their awareness of others.

As our children interact with more people, it is important to teach them good manners. This will include how to address adults politely – to say hello and goodbye, please and thank you – how to show respect, how and when to show their emotions, how to recognise what others are feeling and how to respond appropriately. A tall order. But we are neither expecting nor aiming to achieve it overnight.

Nicky Sometimes, during these years, we felt as if we were taking one step forward and then two back. We seemed to be addressing the same issues and reminding our children about the same manners

> again and again. We were tempted to think that nothing we were doing was working.

Our encouragement to you is keep your nerve! More is being taken on board from these day by day lessons than we realise at the time.

You will need to think carefully about how you can enforce the key boundaries. The aim is to be firm, not harsh; to guide, not to crush; to teach obedience, not to squash individuality; to enjoy a relationship of love and respect and to avoid long-term anger and resentment.

In this chapter we will look at some principles for setting boundaries with six to ten-year-olds. We are building on the last chapter, but with subtle differences. Our children are now more open to reason and logic, and the length of time between misbehaviour and punishment can be longer.

Remember that HALT (see page 189) still applies whatever age they – or we – are!

Take some time to think about each child

Have a cup of coffee, or go for a walk, and reflect on these questions:

- What are the regular issues you have with this child?
- Which battles do you need to win? Which are unimportant?
- What in the past has helped this child to take responsibility for his behaviour?
- How could you help her to grow in responsibility?

Set the rules clearly

We owe it to our children to be clear about what we expect of them and what the consequences are if they do not do what we say.

Sila I do not pretend to have managed to do this in every area of disciplining our children, but some rules I was very clear about, particularly those that had to do with their safety.

When our children were eight, six, three and one, I would walk to the park with the two youngest in the double buggy and the other two walking. I had already trained the older two sufficiently about road safety and I was confident they wouldn't run out into the road or try to cross it on their own. So I allowed them to run ahead on the understanding that they were not allowed to go out of sight or around a corner without me. If they did, they knew very clearly that they would have to come back and hold onto either side of the pushchair. That was

> the consequence of going against the rules, which
> I had to remind them of regularly.

We need to be reinforcing instructions like this to young children again and again, not assuming that they have remembered them from last time.

Some rules are not so important, but still need to be worked out for the sake of peace in our home. Rob and Jean's strong-willed six-year-old refused to wear the blue pyjamas that were under her pillow. She wanted the pink pyjamas. But if she was wearing the pink ones, she would want the blue.

Her mother would say, 'No – blue pyjamas tonight, but you can wear pink tomorrow.' When her father put her to bed, it was, 'Blue! And that's it! Tomorrow we will discuss tomorrow.' Yells and screams of protest followed both. Eventually they had to institute a three-night rule – blue for three nights and then pink for three. And the conflict largely came to an end.

Nicky For us, battles over the length of story time before bed almost made us give up reading stories at all. Eventually we made a rule about the number of stories and stuck to it. After a while, cries for yet one more story died away.

In setting the rules, we must ask ourselves if we are making unreasonable demands of them. Parents who expect immaculate tidiness at all times, or who require their children always to be quiet, need to recognise this is their own problem, not their children's.

Use incentives

Effective discipline includes not only punishing wrong choices but also rewarding right choices. For many families 'star charts' are a useful incentive to good behaviour. (A star chart involves a child earning stick-on stars for good behaviour. When the line, the column or the whole chart is full, the child is given a reward.)

In one household we know with three sons, when one of them fills up his chart, the whole family goes on an outing at the weekend, chosen by the child in question. Rewards might range from a small toy to going out for a pizza, or to a film.

Star charts will only work if they suit our own personality and parenting style. A friend of ours said they never worked for her as she could not cope with the administration involved. She kept forgetting to put the stars up and no-one could remember who had earned what.

Sila Our own experience was that star charts tended to work well for limited periods and for specified activities, such as tidying clothes, getting dressed, good table manners, getting out of the bath without a fuss or behaving well in the car. Each child needed a roughly equal chance of success so the stars were given out for age-appropriate achievements.

We found that earning stars provided a big incentive to behave well initially, but then, after a few weeks, it would be ignored. Some of the improvements in behaviour did remain, however, until we saw the need for a fresh scheme.

One mother told us she used a negative star chart – black marks for misbehaviour. Unsurprisingly her children were often angry and resentful. When she stopped and began focusing on good behaviour, they were much more co-operative.

Another simple reward system for the younger end of this age range is the 'marble jar'. Put a number of marbles (say twenty) in a jar, well out of reach of your children! Add a marble each time they do what you are asking. Take one away each time they repeat the behaviour you are trying to change. If by the end of a decreed period (say one week), there are more than twenty marbles in the jar, they can be converted into a reward.

Some parents make their children's pocket money dependent on their behaviour. We did not do this because we felt that an important purpose of pocket money was for our children to learn to save, to give and to spend, and to work out their own balance between these three choices. Even a small, steady source of income makes this possible. Occasionally, if one of our children was saving up for something special, we would find a way in which she or he could earn more through doing extra chores; equally, a week's pocket money was sometimes forfeited for bad behaviour.

Rewarding good behaviour does not mean using bribery to get children to do anything we ask of them! 'If you behave nicely, I'll buy you an ice-cream,' or, 'If you are kind to your brother, you can stay up later,' are tempting strategies, but our expectation should be that they will behave well and be kind to others without bribes. If bribery is extended to every area of life, our children are not really learning obedience. They will start to see the reward as their right and end up bargaining over everything we tell them to do.

Keep your word

Our children will only learn that our 'no' means no and our 'yes' means yes if we are consistent. If a child asks, 'Can I have a biscuit?' or, 'Will you buy me a new T-shirt?' or, 'Can I go to the cinema?' and we say, 'No,' we must hold firm (unless we have good reasons for changing our mind). If we eventually give in as a result of their whining and complaining, then quite clearly our 'no' does not mean no. In fact we are telling them that they can get whatever they want if they keep wearing us down for long enough. At the same time, if our children feel that every request is met with a straight 'no', they can become frustrated. It helps if we can sometimes suggest a positive alternative. So, 'Can I have a biscuit?' might elicit, 'Not now, but I'll make you a banana milkshake if you like.' Or our answer to, 'Will you buy me a new T-shirt?' could be, 'Would you like one for your birthday?'

We must be equally consistent with a 'yes'. We may have said, 'Yes,' to our six-year-old that we will come and help him make his model, or to our eight-year-old that we will go swimming, or to our ten-year-old that we will take her shopping. Before we know it, the telephone has rung. We have sat down for a twenty minute conversation and the opportunity has passed. That tells our child, 'When Mum or Dad says "yes", they don't mean yes.' By being consistent and sticking to our word, we are helping them to know the importance of keeping to their own promises.

Act decisively

Sila For ten years I did a twenty minute school run with at least five children in the car. To make the experience as pleasant as possible, I had some clearly explained rules. Being rude to, shouting at, or fighting with each other were not acceptable, not least because I would be distracted as the

> driver. The consequence for such behaviour was missing their turn in the much coveted front seat. This was a forfeit I could use with them all equally and they quickly discovered that I would impose it when necessary without discussion.

Taking decisive action with our children when they are pushing the boundaries is much more effective than nagging and shouting. As someone has said, 'Trying to control a child by nagging is like trying to drive a car by sounding the horn.'

The action has to be something our child minds about if it is to be effective. One parent told us, 'When my son was six, he repeatedly behaved badly as he came out of school, being demanding, rude and difficult. I tried everything to solve this, but finally warned him that one more bout would mean no friends to play that week. I carried it through, cancelling the friend who came round to play each Thursday. His behaviour changed overnight, which was a great relief both to him and me. I remember feeling it would have been so much easier not to follow through, especially as his friend's mother seemed very disappointed and perplexed about the cancellation, which made me feel bad.'

So much of our energy as parents can go into arguing with our children about what they can or cannot do. But this is usually ineffective because generally they are not persuaded by what we say. We may be creating great lawyers, but we are not producing well-behaved children. That is not to say we should never listen to our children. Far from it. But when we have established rules and codes of behaviour that are non-negotiable, such as what time they need to be in bed, no hitting or name calling and sitting down at mealtimes, it is far better to use our energy enforcing them calmly and consistently than being caught up in cajoling, arguing and shouting.

Label the action not the child

We want our child to understand that a particular *behaviour* is wrong, rather than have him believe that *he* is innately wrong. Children who are frequently told they are naughty will tend either to fulfil the prophecy or to feel wretched inside. We need to help them to understand: 'That was a naughty, or unkind, or thoughtless thing to do,' rather than say: 'You're a very unkind girl,' or, 'You're a silly boy.' Sometimes, talking about the incident later when everyone has calmed down is more productive than laying into them in the heat of the moment. As Rob Parsons writes:

> Remember how fragile the self-esteem of a child can be. When we discipline we must never attack the *person* of a child – only their behaviour. If we hold to that principle we may still have a lot to say about what they've done, but it won't include – 'You are *so* stupid.'[1]

Do not be manipulated

Children will naturally try to avoid unpleasant consequences by manipulating their parents. This is a normal developmental process and does not mean that anything is wrong with our children. They are trying to lure us into an emotional discussion where, eventually, they hope to wear us down to get what they want: 'You're so mean! That's why you didn't buy me that computer game.' 'You love Michael more than you love me.' 'That's not fair – my friends stay up much later.' 'If you take my phone, I'll run away.' 'It's your fault I broke the mirror. You made me cross.' 'Banning TV is silly! It won't make any difference.'

Do not be drawn into defending yourself. Do not feel the need to endlessly explain every rule. This will only encourage a child to keep up the fight. Explanations can be helpful as long as they are aimed at training and educating the child, rather than justifying every action of the parent. So, in response to bedtime being unfair, we could reply, 'I know, but bedtime here is 7.30 pm.' Or, in reply to the accusation of meanness, 'I've told you why I'm not happy for you to have that particular game.' And we move on.

Sometimes we have to hold to what we believe is right even if other parents disagree with our discipline or boundary. At the same time we may find it helpful to discuss with other parents what boundaries they have set.

Avoid idle threats

We can all make wild threats in the heat of the moment that are wholly unrealistic such as, 'If you don't behave, next time we go on holiday we'll leave you at home,' or, 'You won't have any Christmas presents next year.' Some parents say that sort of thing all the time, and children are not stupid – they know we will never follow through on them. We need to have a few realistic threats up our sleeve, especially for those times when we are at the end of our tether and have dispensed with rational thought. A father told us this story:

I remember being on holiday with some friends. One of their children had done something wrong that morning and had been told, 'No ice cream today.' We didn't know this. Later that day I spotted an ice cream van and offered to buy everyone an ice cream. Our friends explained the situation to us. The poor child recalled the punishment and started to cry.

The next bit really impressed me – they kept to the punishment, gently and quietly reminding the child why he was not having an ice cream. Then one parent took him, crying, for a walk down to the river to see the swans whilst the others ate their ice creams. He was fine when he came back. That's called effective parenting – not vengeful, but fair, firm and consistent. And I bet the child remembered it too.

Find the right consequence

Discipline is a journey. Some techniques that worked well when our children were younger may have lost their usefulness. It is important to review our practices from time to time. What was right at five will not be appropriate at nine – and may even be humiliating. Disciplining in front of others, for example, becomes less and less advisable as they grow older. It is best to take them aside to protect their dignity. Sometimes we can talk about it later and not in front of their siblings.

Finding the right balance of consequences that are effective but not too harsh requires constant juggling. If we know we have a tendency to be too lenient, we must make sure that the action we take makes an impression on our child. Meanwhile, if we know we have a tendency to be harsh, we must be careful not to over-react and create resentment.

The punishments we give must fit our child's offence. This way, our children learn that there are degrees of wrong behaviour and they will also learn which are most serious in our eyes. The consequences for stealing or lying would obviously be more severe than those for failing to get into bed, or a child helping himself to a banana just before a meal.

Finding the right consequence also involves 'reading' each child. What will be effective with one child will be water off a duck's back with another. Look at the list below and ask yourself which punishments you have found to be most effective. Which should be kept for serious misbehaviour? Are there other appropriate consequences that you could add to the list?

Possible disagreeable consequences for 6 to 10-year-olds

- Confined to a bedroom
- Earlier bedtime
- No TV for one day
- No pocket money that week
- Playstation or favourite toy or game confiscated
- Less time on the computer or no computer games that day, weekend or week
- Not allowed to play or stay with a friend or have a friend to stay.
- No sweets, crisps, ice cream
- Extra chores (eg, washing the car, sweeping up leaves)
- Not allowed to go swimming/play football/go shopping with a parent

Keep shouting to a minimum

It will help us considerably if we can keep a loud and urgent voice for what is dangerous or urgent and a quiet but serious voice for disobedience. If we are constantly screaming at our children, they will not respond in an emergency.

A friend of ours, called John, with four children under twelve is softly spoken. He told us that recently he was walking all four to the park. At the first junction the nine-year-old waited for the traffic lights to turn to red and then stepped out into the road. John, a few paces behind her, realised a speeding car was not going to stop and shouted her name at full volume. Unused to hearing him raise his voice, she instantly froze. The car missed her by inches.

Moving on

We have all disciplined in ways we have regretted later. We need to forgive our children when they have made mistakes and let us down, and to forgive ourselves when we get it wrong (as well as apologising to them). They, like us, must be able to move on. It is unhelpful to refer back repeatedly to when a child was naughty. A friend told us, 'As a child I liked to know that I was forgiven and the discipline had finished.'

Conclusion

Disciplining our children is exhausting. Most of us would do anything for peace – now! Doing nothing is often infinitely preferable to doing something. Good discipline requires effort and energy. *Mañana* is the much easier option. But the reward is great for both us and our children when we decide to act rather than ignore the misbehaviour, to nip it in the bud rather than let it escalate. A seven-year-old can feel great when he finds he can cope with not being at the front of the line at school or when the teacher says 'no' to him. It is rewarding as a parent when we hear that our ten-year-old, whom we have disciplined for selfishness, has been kind to another child.

As we hold our nerve and persevere with enforcing the behavioural boundaries – alongside providing affirmation, encouragement and humour – the family becomes an enjoyable and secure place in which our children can grow up. They are more likely to mature into the sort of children who naturally and easily respect others, while feeling confident in their ability to take responsibility for their own behaviour.

Pause and consider

- Are there aspects of your children's behaviour you need to address?
- What manners are most important to teach your children now?
- Are there some positive incentives you could use to encourage good behaviour?
- What unpleasant consequences are enforceable for bad behaviour? Do your children mind about them?
- Are you clear which degree of naughtiness deserves which consequence?
- Do you and your partner agree on your methods of discipline?
- Do you carry through your threats? Are they fair and realistic?

Chapter 12

Letting go gradually with 11 to 13-year-olds

There are two things we should give our children: one is roots and the other is wings.

Hodding Carter
Journalist

Youth is wholly experimental.

Robert Louis Stevenson
Author

Some of us as parents have a characteristic that is almost certain to make the process of letting go agony for us and almost unbearable to our teenager: it is the need to control.

Rob Parsons
Author

At that age, if we didn't agree with a rule, we could talk it through.

Leanne, aged 28

'You wouldn't understand if I told you.' 'You treat me like a seven-year-old.' 'I am easily old enough to go out on my own to that party.' 'You are so strict.' 'Everybody else's parents let them.' 'Huh!' (Or some other, even less communicative, monosyllabic grunt.)

Do any of those sound familiar? If so, you probably have an eleven to thirteen-year-old at home. Some of the moodiness is due to hormones. Some of the conflict is the result of children angling for more freedom than they have the maturity to handle. But much of the stroppy behaviour is down to the natural processes of a child becoming increasingly independent and getting ready to leave home.

This is a transition stage. A father with two children in this age bracket explained, 'At this age you are veering between disciplining and steering your children – and sometimes it all goes completely wrong. But that's okay. You can start again the next day. Neither parent nor child can be the controller and so I find setting boundaries requires lots of patience and a regular dose of humour.'

Of course this process of becoming more independent has been going on for some time. We may have felt the impact of the separation and loss of control when they went to nursery school for the first time or when they went to stay at a friend's house on their own. However hard it is, we must gradually let go of our children. This lies at the heart of our role as parents.

Letting go becomes especially important as they approach adolescence and through the teenage years. These are the crucial years for learning about independence. Teenagers need space – to explore, to handle increasing freedom, to discover themselves and to build relationships outside their family. Our role through these years is gradually to extend the boundaries that govern this space until the independence is complete and we relate to our children as adults. It begins typically when they are eleven to thirteen-years-old. The rate at which we let go will depend on their maturity, and every child is different. The following principles helped us as we began the complex process of letting go at the right speed for each child.

Recognise what is normal

The onset of adolescence brings a change in our children's emotions and behaviour that can be sudden and startling to parent and child alike – and this may begin sooner than we expect. It is helpful to be reminded that what might seem thoughtless and irritating is often typical pre-teen and teenage behaviour.

Normal pre-teen and teenage behaviour

- Shutting the door and shutting parents out
- Being monosyllabic
- Being slow to react and being oblivious to others' feelings
- Needing to sleep a lot
- Feeling embarrassed to be seen with a parent in public
- Rejecting guidance and doing the opposite
- Oblivious of time and deadlines
- Winding up parents and siblings – sometimes deliberately
- Being angry and sarcastic
- Being forgetful
- Hogging the computer or TV, oblivious to anyone else wanting them

Feelings pre-teens and teenagers typically experience (and sometimes express)[1]

- 'Nobody likes me.'
- 'I feel ugly.'
- 'Nobody understands me or cares about me.'
- 'Any place would be better than here.'
- 'I feel like running away from home.'
- 'I just wish everyone would leave me alone.'
- 'My parents treat me like such a baby.'
- 'I feel like crying all the time.'
- 'Sometimes I feel like I am going crazy.'
- 'Everyone is looking at me.'

Remember we are on the same side

As our children push for more independence, sometimes all we seem to do is to nag, criticise, complain and say 'no'. We feel embattled, and so too can our children. But really we are on the same side, working with them, not against them, to equip them for life. Both parents and children need to adjust to the new status quo.

Helping our children become responsible, independent adults involves more than worrying about the boundaries. The pre-teen and early teenage years produce conflicting desires: one moment wanting to be grown up, the next wanting to be protected and comforted and to be a child again. It is important to keep 'reading' each child in order to sense when to 'hold on' and when to 'let go'.

Even while acting older than they really are, they still need frequent assurances of our love. They want to know whether we are interested in them and, as they face all the normal self-questioning of the teenage years, they still require masses of our encouragement and affirmation. They need to know we are there for them, that we believe in them. Finding an activity that both you and your pre-teen child enjoy may well provide a good opportunity for talking together. For one mother that involved taking her eleven-year-old son to watch football matches at their local club. A father we know took up kite-surfing in order to go out with his twelve-year-old daughter. The talking took place on the hour-long car journeys to and from the coast.

Extend their freedom

When our children were little, we organised their whole lives. We knew what they were doing every moment. We organised their friends, their time, the food they ate and the clothes they wore. Then suddenly, all of that changes. It can be hard. As one parent reflected, 'It can happen overnight. It's a big shock.' We can feel rejected and misunderstand their intentions. Why do they want to pull away from us and spend more and more time away from home? It feels as if they would rather be with anyone but us.

Nicky I was horrified the first time our eldest child asked if she could stay away for the weekend. (This wasn't with a granny or close friends of ours but with a school friend whose parents we did not know very well.) From my reaction you would have thought she had asked to go backpacking round Europe aged ten. I struggled with a cocktail of emotions – possessiveness, anxiety, suddenly feeling dispensable – at the thought of our daughter being out of our sight, out of our control and under the influence of other adults for a whole weekend.

Sila I was the one who found it hard later on when our boys wanted to be with their friends on a Friday evening and to stay overnight. I think I felt hurt that they didn't want to be with us any more. Saturday morning breakfast had always been a special family time for us ever since they were small. And suddenly they didn't want to be there; they didn't want the breakfast I made for them. Or, at least, that's how it seemed to me from a mother's perspective.

We will struggle with different things. They may suddenly want to keep things secret from us, to have a world independent of ours. One mother said her son had told her he was thinking over something, and for the first time did not want to tell her what it was. She felt like bursting into tears. For single parents, this can be exacerbated – obviously providing the opportunity for more time to themselves, but potentially causing them to feel very lonely.

Our children's push for freedom is a right and natural part of their development. Like young birds, they have to leave the nest to learn to fly. We must allow them to spread and strengthen their wings, ready for the time when they will fly without our supervision.

Give them time with their friends

Today, this age group typically spends a huge amount of time making their own arrangements with each other by phone, texting, via MSN or through messages on social networking sites like *Facebook*. Much of the excitement is quite simply the fact that they are making their own plans apart from us. There can be a lot of secrecy and shrugging of shoulders when we make enquiries. This is normal behaviour and part of learning to make their own decisions. A parent with a son aged twelve told us a typical scenario:

> At half-term my son and his school friend started to mutter that they had a few plans for the Easter holidays, and my son asked me not to over-book his three-week break. Long phone calls ensued behind shut doors with several volleys of texts each day for the next month as the mystery event was organised for the Saturday before Easter. These were backed up by elaborate emails and intensive MSN-ing.

As the great day drew nearer we enquired who was coming and where they were going. 'We can't say,' they replied. We gently reminded the boys of the non-negotiable golden rules: we need to know where you're going, with whom and when. A few girls' names were provided plus 'lunchtime' and a rather unpromising venue – a shopping street with the odd cheap café. 'And how are you getting there?' we asked. Ah! This obstacle clearly had not been anticipated. Neither my husband nor I were available to drive so they considered the train briefly – and then went back to their Xbox.

When I arrived home on the day in question around 3.30 pm, I was surprised to find the boys still languishing in their pyjamas. Thinking back to the six weeks of fevered planning, I casually enquired about their schedule. 'Could you drive us?' they asked – and I duly dropped them at their planned destination a little concerned that it was now about three hours after 'lunchtime'. 'Will you pick us up?' they asked. 'No,' I said. 'I think you should get the train and please be back by seven.' I abandoned them and returned home. They scraped back in by 6.59 pm, somewhat unsettled by some 'weirdos' on the train, but still looking reasonably pleased with themselves. I felt sure the meeting had been a success. An hour or so later I enquired, 'So, did you meet the girls?' 'No,' they said, 'We played football in the end.'

Give them more responsibility

While this age group can typically be very self-absorbed, we should not be afraid of extending what we expect them to do at home. They are, after all, bigger and capable of giving more help. Through increasing their responsibilities in such things as washing-up after meals, tidying the house or helping with outdoor chores, we are teaching them to look beyond their own needs. They are learning to take care of others and to play their part, first in the home and ultimately in society.

Help them become responsible

In setting limits for their behaviour, our aim is to move from externally imposed boundaries to helping them develop internal, self-imposed boundaries. This means moving from us saying, 'It's time for a bath,' 'It's time for bed,' or, 'You can only watch two programmes on television,' and then making sure they do it, to their deciding of their own initiative to turn off the television, to do their homework, to wash, or to go to bed. They are becoming self-regulating. This process involves our trusting them, which in turn breeds trustworthiness. Self-confidence grows as we give our children greater responsibility. Penelope Leach, author of *Parenting*, comments:

> It is our refusal to welcome them as apprentices into the adult world which drives many [teenagers] to reject adults altogether and rely exclusively on each other's company. It is our difficulty in

> trusting them to be kind, sensible or responsible which makes them doubt their own goodness as people so that they sometimes act out the anti-social roles that we seem to expect of them. And it is our inability to take them seriously, and to do to them as we would like them to do to others, that makes it so difficult for them to trust us.[2]

A watershed for many parents and children is the transition from primary to secondary school. Moving schools is a big adjustment for most children. Anticipation and eagerness are mixed with anxiety and a fear of the unknown. They are moving into the bigger, more scary world of adolescence and they suddenly become a small fish in a much larger pond. We may well be worried for them, but trusting them with greater responsibility will help them to adapt quickly into this new phase. The process of letting go involves us taking calculated risks.

Sila I remember so well each of our children setting off for their first day at secondary school. They looked as if their heart was in their mouth, and mine most definitely was. How would they cope? Did they have the right things? Would they know where to go for the first lesson? And a hundred other concerns. But most worrying of all for me was whether they would manage the travelling to and from school.

One of our sons, aged eleven, started off cycling to school with Nicky. First he went behind

> Nicky, then in front, and when Nicky saw he had sufficient experience, he was allowed to go on his own. I remember feeling seriously worried for the next week and I realised, if I'd been the only one making the decision, I probably wouldn't have allowed him to do it. However, he managed the journeys well and seemed to grow up visibly as he settled into this new responsibility.

For some families, and in some places, eleven would be too young for our children, particularly girls, to travel to and from school on their own. A female friend of ours said to us recently, 'I remember feeling it was unfair that my brothers could travel in the dark and I couldn't. It was for my protection, but I still felt it to be unfair. Now
I am grateful that my parents did not give in to my complaints.'

There is no fixed timetable for this movement from parent-control to parent-trust. Each family will manage it differently, and the children within a family will differ in character and personality. Some are much more self-contained and confident, others less so. The process is gradual and will depend upon their maturity.

Allow them to make more decisions

Allowing this age group to make their own choices in as many areas as possible helps them grow up. These may include their hairstyle, their clothes, how they spend their pocket money (or 'allowance') and how they decorate their room. Journalist Judith

Wilson describes teenagers' bedrooms as 'a reflection of their personalities: creative, rebellious, fun-loving and, above all, a "work-in-progress".' She goes on to give parents this advice:

> What is it about teenage bedrooms that makes parents blanch and adolescents sigh? The former say their older children's rooms are no-go zones full of junk; the latter moan that they have zero privacy or creative freedom. The problem is, when children hit puberty their bedrooms take on a new significance. Once charming spaces, themed with jolly patterns and lovingly tidied, they become a powerful symbol of teenage independence and a statement of a rapidly developing personality. Suddenly, parents don't get a look-in. Literally – because the door is shut.

Don't take it personally. What children long for is the freedom to create a space that projects their personality. Teenagers are experimental and have the potential to create rooms that are hip, bold, thoughtful – even extremely organised.

The secret is to grit your teeth and hand over the design reigns. Certainly, they may need help – so give advice, if asked – and a modest budget. But don't be chippy about them painting walls or sticking up posters. These are easily rectifiable. Let them get on with it – you never know, you might be pleasantly surprised.[3]

Our children need opportunities to make choices where, if they make mistakes, it is okay, it is safe. So, if they spend most of their money on one inappropriate and expensive item of clothing, they learn to budget. Next time round, they may look out for a better deal. Living with the consequences of their own decisions teaches them to be responsible for the choices they make.

Sometimes it helps to laugh together about bad choices and tell them about some of ours, to let them know it is not the end of the world.

This is also the age when many children start to explore relationships with the opposite sex. One mother described to us how she has helped her daughter with some decisions she would soon be facing: 'Keira is thirteen. I know any day now there's going to be a boyfriend. Whilst I might like her to wait, I can see it's what all her friends are beginning to explore. So I've just said, "Your first kiss is really special – you'll never forget it. Make sure you kiss someone you really want to." I know she's heard me.'

Start stricter

While allowing them more freedom, we should not be afraid of maintaining appropriate boundaries. They will probably complain that they do not need these restrictions any longer and that we are far stricter than any of their friends' parents. But eleven to thirteen-year-olds are not yet sufficiently mature to be allowed to roam free, and, if they cross a boundary, there must still be a sanction.

Starting stricter and then increasing their privileges, as they show they are trustworthy, allows us to be as positive as possible. When they behave well, we can say, 'Well done!' and then increase their freedom. This is a positive move forwards.

So, when our own children first went on a shopping trip without us by public transport, we required the following: they would go with a friend; we knew the route they were taking; they rang us when they reached their destination and they returned by a specific time. As they kept to our requirements for two or three trips, we allowed them to go for longer and they only needed to ring if they encountered a problem. Similar restrictions applied to visits to the cinema, staying away with friends, going to parties and so on. If we allow too much too soon, we find ourselves having to become more restrictive again. This is a step backwards and is hard for everyone.

Talking to other parents about what they allow or disallow when our children are in each other's houses, such as the type of computer games we allow them to play, can give us confidence to hold firm to our rules. Occasionally we may feel that we are under pressure from everybody – from friends, from other parents and from our own children.

It is especially hard when other parents have very different approaches. For example, a group of eleven-year-olds are having a sleep-over at one of their homes and the parents decide to go out for a couple of hours, leaving them in the care of an older brother or sister. Or other parents tell us there are three boys and three girls staying on the same night, or they are going to allow a group of twelve-year-olds to watch a Certificate 15 DVD. The parents may ask us, 'Are you happy?' To say, 'No, we're not happy,' can be very hard. It requires us to have thought through what we feel is, and is not, appropriate and have the confidence to stick to it – even when our child tells us, 'That's *so* embarrassing. No-one else's parents mind.' At such times, we need to remember that ultimately we are responsible, and only we can decide where to draw the line.

Monitor parties

As children approach the teenage years, the kind of parties they want to have, or that they are invited to, can raise all sorts of new questions. What if the party gets out of control? Should we let them go, regardless of what is likely to happen? What is safe and what is irresponsible? How can they say, 'No,' to an invitation without losing all their friends? Such questions can cause us to be constantly worried, or make us hold our breath and hope for the best.

Sometimes, merely discussing such questions will draw out of our children that they would rather not go, but are afraid of being thought 'uncool' by their friends. Saying with a moan, 'My parents won't let me,' can be a helpful way of declining an invitation while keeping their 'street cred' intact.

Party checklist

The following checklist contains questions parents might want to ask their child to assess whether they should let them go to a particular party. (Some of the questions will only apply for older teenagers.)

- Whose party is it and where is it being held?
- Is it a private or a public party? Are you on the guest list? Who else is going to be there?
- Will the parents or other responsible adults be present?
- Can I talk to the adults hosting the party? (This will often be met with huge resistance from the child being questioned. 'It's so embarrassing.' 'You're the only one who wants to,' etc. Do not be put off!)
- What time does the party start and finish?
- How will you get there? Who is bringing you home?
- Will there be alcohol available? What will you do if your age group are all drinking alcohol/getting drunk?
- Are there likely to be people taking drugs at the party? (Help them work out what they will do if they are offered drugs. See Chapter 17 for some advice on this.)

Encourage adventure

The opportunity for pre-teens and young teenagers to face challenges, without their parents hovering over them, is an important step in growing up. Adventure, whether in the countryside, at the seaside or in the city, helps children to grow in confidence and maturity through having to work out boundaries for themselves.

Some children enjoy sports or other outdoor activities with an element of physical danger. These can teach them to work in a team and to discover what they need for survival. Being stretched physically, mentally, emotionally and socially, in ways they are not at home, causes them to grow. As columnist Libby Purves writes, 'They learn that clothes are for warmth and protection – not just for good looks; food is for fuel; cold and heat can kill you and above all, you seriously depend on your companions and they depend on you."[4]

Facing physical challenges outdoors in a group also provides a healthy way of channelling many of the strong emotions that the onset of puberty can bring. There are many opportunities today to go on adventure holidays centred round pursuits such as water sports, biking, fishing, horse riding, trekking or assault courses.

Nicky Each of our own children has thrived on weeks away at different outdoor centres as well as activity weekends with the church youth group.

Other opportunities for adventure have been during our summer holidays. As a family we have gone to the same place by the sea since our first child was born. Part of the attraction for our children has been that they have enjoyed more freedom each year as they have grown older. One of their favourite activities as young teenagers was taking a boat with friends of their own age, catching mackerel, landing on a small island and cooking their fish over a fire. It became something of a rite of passage in our family, and contributed to their growth and sense of responsibility as well as being fun.

Each one in turn has known that a level of trust (to take care of the boat, not to go out into the open sea and to be back before dark) is required for us to allow them this privilege. And they learnt fast that, if the trust was broken, their freedom would be reduced.

Stay flexible

Some of the decisions about boundaries are extremely hard to make with this age group. How do we know what is right? How much freedom should we allow? What is a healthy balance of time with family and time with others? No one has all the answers, but a sense of humour will help us stay somewhere between being a push-over and being rigidly inflexible.

Recently we were staying with a family who have a daughter aged thirteen and three sons aged eleven, nine and seven. The two older boys had two friends over for the day. They made their plans for the evening. They wanted to have supper and then all pile into the sitting room with duvets and pillows to watch a film. There was much debate amongst the children as to which film they would watch. The boys were pushing for a Certificate 12, which was not suitable for the seven-year-old. The film the parents were suggesting was seen as boring by the older ones. The option of telling the seven-year-old he could not watch anything and had to go to bed would have started World War III. Equally inflammatory would have been suggesting to the older ones they had to watch something suitable for the seven-year-old.

As we watched these normally confident and capable parents struggling with the barrage of irreconcilable requests, we sympathised hugely. We were so glad we were not having to make the decision! After much discussion a compromise was agreed. Everybody would start by watching the film appropriate for the seven-year-old. Then at his bed time it would be changed for the one that the others wanted to watch. The seven-year-old was told he could watch the remainder of his film the next day. Peace was restored and they all settled down together.

We have faced many similar situations ourselves. Sometimes we stood firm and bore the fury. At other times, we found ourselves re-evaluating our decision.

Sila Generally at half-term I tried to go to Scotland with the children to see both Nicky's and my families. On one occasion I had already made our plans when one of our sons, aged eleven, announced that he wanted to go surfing in Cornwall with another family instead. We were adamant that it was much more important for him to spend time seeing his grandparents, uncles, aunts and cousins.

With a month to go he would bring the subject up at least every other day. For us there was nothing to discuss and we simply got cross with him for failing to appreciate how important these family relationships are.

Eight days before we were due to set off, we were leading an evening parenting course and our talk stressed the importance of listening to our children. We returned home to find a note on my pillow. On one side was written in big letters: 'Mum – talk to Dad about surfing,' with smaller writing in the corner surrounded by hearts saying, 'Mum, do you want breakfast in bed? Or any washing done? Or ironing or shopping?'

On the other side was written: 'Some parenting

points to go to sleep on: does your son feel deprived? Can he fulfil his dreams? Will he never feel the power of the ocean? Will his hobby only be on his wall [his bedroom walls were then covered with surfing posters]? Will his board fade away physically and mentally?' And underneath that: 'Mum and Dad, on a completely different subject, you don't by any chance like Cornish clotted cream do you? Nice and smooth, cold and creamy, and great as a present from your son.'

His new approach worked. The next day, realising how much the opportunity to surf meant to him, we had another discussion and this time we decided we should let him go.

Conclusion

Most parents have the instinct to protect. Most children have the instinct to explore. For many of us, our over-protectiveness is tied up with not wanting our children to move on. It is a subconscious resistance to the separation process. As one parent put it, 'There's a sort of grieving for the child who was our faithful companion for many years and who is now no more a child.'

At times we can be too strict, at others too lenient. Letting go is not easy, but it is absolutely essential that we do it. It prepares the way for a strong and close relationship with our children as they become young adults.

Pause and consider

- Are you allowing your children to grow in responsibility? Are you trusting them more than when they were ten or under?
- Are there areas where you need to be more strict? Or others where you can be less strict?
- Are you expecting too little/too much of your children?
- Have you discussed your boundaries with them?
- Have they had the opportunity to go on outdoor adventures?

Chapter 13

Teenagers – guiding without alienating

Parents of teenagers face a difficult dilemma; how to help when help is resented, how to guide when guidance is rejected, how to communicate when attention is taken as attack.[1]

Haim Ginott
Psychologist

If you think it's difficult to live with teenagers, spare a thought for those of us who live with our parents.

Joshua, aged 18

When I was a boy of fourteen, my father was so ignorant I could hardly stand to have him around. But when I got to be twenty-one, I was astonished at how much the old man had learned in seven years.

Mark Twain
Author

Parents are relentless – give them an inch and they take a mile.

Henry, aged 14

I was glad there were some boundaries, but not too many. You want to feel your parents are out for your safety and you want them to say 'no' to some things.

Kirsty, aged 28

Our teenagers need us. Often, to their surprise, they *really* need us! Whether or not they admit it, the vast majority of teenagers crave the interest, encouragement and support of their parents. And they still need appropriate boundaries as they are not yet sufficiently mature to make all of their own decisions.

The stock response, 'Whatever,' or, 'Take a chill pill, Mum,' mask the fact they need and want us around to take an active, but changing, role as parents.

In this chapter we look at how we can guide our teenagers in such a way that we enjoy having them around us and they enjoy having us around them – for some of the time at least. The relationship will be strained from time to time. Do not believe parents who tell you otherwise.

However, having lived with four children through the teenage years, we experienced the great pleasure, as well as the difficulties, of continuing to build a relationship of mutual love, trust and respect with each of them. The following points helped us enormously.

Think of their needs

Our own experience is that the same basic principles that we used in parenting younger children still apply, but there is a dramatic gear shift in the way we go about it and the change of speed can be fun.

Nicky We asked a group of parents of teenagers doing one of our parenting courses, 'What is the main parenting issue you are facing?' Most of them replied, 'Knowing where and how to set boundaries.'

Instead of addressing the theme directly, we spent some time talking about the five love languages and the importance of discovering how our teenagers feel loved. The parents went away and made changes in their approach. A month later, on the last session of the course, we asked whether these changes had made

> any difference. Spontaneously, all the parents said that their children were much happier and that the setting of boundaries had become a lot easier as a result.

Libby Purves observes:

> One central truth ... makes the contemplation of all teenage problems a lot simpler. This is it: everything goes better if teenagers are happy. Obvious? Yes. But how often do you hear parents talking of wanting their big sons or daughters to be happier? So, rather than thinking only about remedies to teenage problems as if they were nothing but a crowd control problem, think instead about what contributes to their happiness. Not a spoilt, overindulged happiness – just a plain bread-and-butter satisfaction with life that everybody needs.[2]

Recognise the end goal

Part of our long-term aim as parents is that, by the time our children have gained their independence, they will still want to spend time with us and will seek our advice when they need it. By then we will no longer be in control, but we still have much to offer from our longer perspective on life. Daniel Hahn, a youth worker, writes about the change in our role:

> Parents face two options. We can keep using the same patterns we used when they were young (and frustrate

> ourselves to death) or we can realise that our methods must change as our children develop … As hard as it is, our role must move from controller to consultant.
>
> What do consultants do? They ask questions, offer opinions, share experiences, present options and forecast outcomes. Ultimately, however, they step back and allow the client to make decisions. Consultants understand what they can and cannot do for their client; as a result the client owns the process as well as the results.[3]

This shift in the relationship – from us taking all the decisions to helping them make the best decisions for themselves – is a gradual one through the teenage years.

Maintain communication

Of course, maintaining communication can be one of the hardest things to do. Teenagers typically want more time on their own, often become monosyllabic and usually prefer the company of their friends to that of their parents. One fourteen-year-old said, 'I get mad at my parents when they ask, "How was your day?" and I say, "Fine." And then they keep asking more questions and get cross if I don't tell them anything. But it's the same day at school as the day before and there's nothing to say.'

Being aware of the changes that are taking place within our teenagers will help us not to take this lack of response as personal rejection. The onslaught of new hormones and growth spurts can drain them of energy. In addition, recent discoveries about the development of the brain have shown that the prefrontal cortex, the part known as the CEO of the brain, is not fully mature in teenagers. This is the centre of the so-called executive functions – planning, setting priorities, organising thoughts, suppressing impulses and weighing up the consequences of actions.

While going through this period of growth, teenagers typically find it harder to take the feelings of others into account. The *New*

Scientist reported a survey carried out at San Diego University amongst 300 people, aged between ten and twenty-two years old, measuring the speed at which the respondents could identify emotions in other people. The results revealed a drop of up to twenty per cent at the age of ten or eleven, only returning to a normal speed at the age of eighteen.[4]

Not surprisingly, many children who were articulate and enthusiastic before puberty suddenly become sullen and resentful, and communicate with grunts and sighs when we attempt to draw them out. There is an illusion that, as they grow more independent, we are less necessary. One parent of teenagers commented that it is easy to reach the point where every conversation revolves around, 'Can I do this?' or, 'Why can't I do that?'. However, our parental input beyond saying 'yes' or 'no' is vital. They are facing new situations and conflicting emotions that they want to talk through with us.

Teenagers will open up when they feel ready and safe, when we have been hanging around together, after watching sport, on the way home from a shopping trip, in the car on a long journey and late in the evening, usually when we are longing for sleep.

It is worth trying to recognise when our teenagers are most likely to talk, and to catch those moments.

The key is to give them time so that they do not feel pressured. They will then feel comfortable to broach sensitive subjects, knowing that we will not jump down their throats. This is when listening and asking questions that draw them out are most critical. Saying to a teenager, 'Tell me about …' is more likely to elicit a response than an interrogatory style of, 'Where did you go?' or, 'What were you doing?'

Make as few rules as possible

If there are too many rules, teenagers are likely to ignore them. Why? Because rules and regulations about every aspect of their lives give the message, 'We don't trust you to make good judgments for yourselves.' They will almost certainly go straight out and do exactly what we told them not to do. In doing so, they are saying to us, 'You try to make all the decisions for me. You try to control my every move. I'll show you whose life it is.' Pretty soon our teenagers will ignore whatever we say.

A good maxim is to say 'no' to the things that really matter and 'yes' to everything else. Remind them that the few boundaries we lay down are there to protect them. Remind yourself of the same. A friend, reflecting on her own teenage years, expressed her appreciation for having parents who kept the rules to a minimum:

> When I was a teenager, there were very few rules, but the few were expected to be upheld. My parents allowed us to dress as we wished,

including a phase when I discovered a taste for smelly old male overcoats, which Mum felt old men had probably died in. We were free to experiment with hair styles, room decoration, music and so on.

There were, however, a few things Mum and Dad felt strongly about. One of these was that we were not allowed either to own a motorbike or to ride on the back of one. I remember adhering to this rule even when I was fairly confident they wouldn't find out. It became very complicated when my boyfriend at the time bought himself a motorbike and we wanted to travel home from parties together. I can still remember my father parked in his car – strictly round the corner – coming to pick me up at 1 am as the said boyfriend zoomed past us waving!

When my brother and I reached seventeen, they did all that they could to help us get through our driving tests and to buy a cheap car. This enabled us to keep to the rule they'd set.

Decide what really matters

Imagine your teenage son or daughter is going travelling and will be apart from you for six months. What would you say? They will not remember much. Our own advice would include the following:

- Always tell the truth – that will often be hard but eventually you will be known as someone who can be trusted.

- Be courteous to friends and strangers – 'loving your neighbour as yourself' is the best way to live.
- Do not take drugs or get drunk – that will weaken your self-control and you can easily end up doing things you later regret.
- Keep sex for marriage – otherwise you will hurt yourself and others, and it may cause complications later on, if and when you get married.
- Avoid getting into long-term debt. Only buy what you can pay for, or what you know you can repay.

Nicky I wrote a letter, including all of this advice, to each of our children for them to read as they set off on their gap year after leaving school. I started by telling them the characteristics and achievements Sila and I have admired in their lives, and recalling some of the most special moments in their growing up. I then wrote the five guidelines above, not least for Sila's and my peace of mind.

I did, however, add a sixth which went: 'Try to read the Bible and pray every day – faith grows as you recognise your dependence on God, in the good as well as the challenging times.'

It was several months (and with one child two years) before we knew what they had made of their letter. But we were touched and encouraged to discover that, with each of them, the letters had been treasured and re-read many times, on their gap year and since.

Be ready to explain rules

We must be able to explain to a teenager why our boundaries are important. When our children are young, the answer to the endlessly repeated question, 'Why should I?' sometimes has to be, 'Because I say so.'

For teenagers, rules need an explanation. Of course they may not agree with our reasoning, but we give these rules because we know the longer-term consequences. So, if we forbid our teenagers to smoke, we must be prepared to explain why.

Nicky As one of the chaplains at the Brompton Hospital (one of the leading thoracic hospitals in the UK), I've met any number of people in their forties and fifties whose lives have been threatened by lung cancer. Patients have often said to me, 'If only someone had warned me as a teenager when I first started smoking.' As a result I have felt a duty, not only to warn our teenagers of the dangers, but also to make it as difficult as possible for them to get addicted.

Our explanation of why we did not want them to smoke included the following. First, and above all, there was the long-term danger to their health. Next, the cost. If they were to smoke ten cigarettes a day for sixty years, they would be paying out £30,000 at today's prices. Could they think of some better ways of spending their money? Next, especially as they all loved sport, smoking affected their fitness. Then there was the

> smell – off-putting for most people. Finally, once addicted, giving up is extremely difficult.
>
> We told our own teenagers that, while we were still supporting them financially, they were not to smoke at home or in our sight. If we saw or heard of them smoking, they would lose a month's allowance. This has not stopped all of them all the time, but it has certainly acted as a disincentive. And it has left them with a lasting understanding of the long-term consequences of addiction.

We will look at the explanations we might give for our boundaries concerning alcohol, drugs and the appropriate use of sex in Section 4.

Be prepared to negotiate

Negotiation is important for teenagers. They need us to listen to their point of view, and they need to know that we value their opinion. Tim Smith in his book, *Almost Cool*, writes:

> When we spend time debating with our teenagers, we demonstrate respect by taking the time and focus to spar intellectually with them. This is helpful to the development of their logic and reasoning abilities. It also helps them feel that their viewpoint is valid enough to discuss. A teenager reasons, 'If they value my opinion enough to debate it, they must value me enough to try to understand me.'[5]

We so often get entrenched in an argument and it looks as though there are only two options – ours and theirs. And of course we think we are right! But, as we negotiate with our teenagers and encourage them to communicate to us their ideas, we may find there are other solutions.

Sila When Kirsty was fifteen, many of her school friends were going to pubs and bars. We were unhappy about this and told her she couldn't join them. On a number of occasions she tried to persuade us to change our minds, but we were adamant.

Then one evening, when the subject came up again, she explained that she wanted to go to the pub (where she was legally entitled to be), not in order to drink alcohol, but to meet up with her friends. Knowing that she was telling us the truth, we felt that, considering her motives, it would be better for her if we let her go.

At times, the discussion reveals there really *is* only one sensible solution and we have to be firm. We may have to say, 'You can't go to that party because I can't get hold of the parents to find out any more details.' Or, 'I'm not allowing you to stay out that late as your school work will be badly affected,' adding that we understand they are unhappy with our decision, but we are insisting for their own benefit. If we have a teenager who is irresponsible with money, we will not be helping him if we keep giving in to his demands for more pocket money or a bigger allowance.

It is unlikely that parents and teenagers leave all such discussions with a smile on their face. This is an unrealistic goal.

Nicky A few years ago one of our children, aged sixteen and a half, was desperate to go to a big music gig. A number of his friends, several of whom were eighteen, were planning to go. Sila and I listened. We said we would think about it and discuss it with him the next day.

We decided we were unhappy about him going. He was under age and it was a large event, starting late and finishing in the early hours of the morning. We did not want him to be put into a situation where, if there was an incident, he might be confronted by the police. When we spoke to him about it the next evening, he was very angry and told us for a good twenty minutes how totally unreasonable we were being. We tried to listen with an open mind, but nothing he said persuaded us to change our decision. He kept trying until eventually he realised it was fruitless. He left the room furious with us.

Several days later he brought the subject up again. We were both in the room and proceeded to have another lengthy and heated debate rehearsing all our same reasons for not allowing him to go. We brought it to a close and said our 'no' was final.

At this point he left the room, grabbed the football in the hall, went outside and vented his frustration by kicking the ball hard against a wall for about half an hour. Sila and I were glad that he had chosen to take his anger out on a football rather than us.

Sila On a different occasion, another of our sons, aged sixteen, had been invited to go to a friend's eighteenth birthday party that was taking place in a club. Our son desperately tried to convince us that he wouldn't need to provide any proof of his age. We were quite sure he would need to show some ID to prove that he was eighteen or over. We didn't want him to go.

We had no way of contacting the host of the party and so could not find out one way or the other. So we negotiated what seemed the best solution. He would go to the party but he would not try to get in with a false ID or pretend that he was eighteen.

He accepted this as fair. As it turned out, he was asked his age and ended up coming home.

If our children see us as basically reasonable, they will be inclined to keep within the boundaries we have set. Whereas no discussion and no negotiation will build up resentment in all but the most compliant of teenagers. They must be given opportunities to assert their own ideas and opinions. Otherwise they may well rebel later on.

Welcome their friends

When our children are little, we play a major role in influencing who their friends are and who comes to our home. Once they become teenagers they will be making their own choices. Showing that we accept their choice of friends will make a big impact on them. That does not mean we have to like all their friends, but it does mean welcoming them into our home. A woman we know expressed her gratitude for her parents' attitude:

> Our friends were welcomed with open arms regardless of their appearance. Mum and Dad remember a Spanish guy we invited to stay who appeared from the airport with studded dog collars round his neck and wrists, and a Mohican which brushed the kitchen doorframe as he made his first appearance for lunch.
>
> He became a regular visitor. As did (for a period) leather-clad bikers whose tassels dangled memorably in my mother's creamed leeks. As all were welcome, my parents knew, and generally came to love, our friends. They spent time talking to us and mainly enjoyed the motley crew assembled in the kitchen during our teenage years.

The impact on our teenagers of making our home a place where they feel safe to bring their friends is huge. We may have to adjust our behaviour so as not to embarrass our children. Using the nicknames we gave them as a five-year-old, or acting as if they still need the boundaries of an eight-year-old will probably mean they will not bring their friends home again.

Be prepared for inconvenience and noise. If we have a big enough house, having a space they can make their own is a big draw. Similarly, a darts board or a pool table can provide hours of fun, as well as making socialising easier for a self-conscious teenager. Have some food they like in the fridge. Mealtimes may need to be more flexible. If we insist that they eat breakfast at 8.30 am every day in the holidays, it will be a disincentive for them to ask a friend to stay. A woman said to us recently that, as a teenager, she never invited anyone to her home as they were strictly not allowed to eat breakfast in their pyjamas – and she could not face explaining this.

If the décor is too precious, we may need to relax a bit. One man told us that, in spite of growing up in a freezing and scruffy house, his friends loved to congregate there. His home became their favourite place to 'hang out', mainly because his parents put a higher value on creating a relaxed and welcoming atmosphere than on having an immaculate and smart house.

Sila For me, having lots of teenagers coming and going was one of the best bits of parenting. As they got older we'd often wake up in the morning to discover a number of our children's friends dotted about the house on mattresses in various rooms.

I learnt to have extra supplies of milk, bread, pasta and cereal for these sudden gatherings. At a time in their lives when it was sometimes hard to know if I was making any positive difference, feeding them gave me a great sense of achievement.

We may think some of our children's friends are having a negative influence on them. But it is worth being aware that sometimes we will have prejudices or preconceived ideas that turn out to be altogether wrong. One father of three teenagers commented, 'We have tried to get to know the parents of our teenagers' friends. It has helped us to worry less.'

However, while being open-minded and hospitable, if we recognise that our teenagers are being adversely affected by a friend, or group of friends, we will need to discuss with them how they can stand against peer pressure. Young teenagers need to know that we are not happy for them to spend time with people who use drugs or are involved in dishonest or criminal behaviour. Older teenagers should know by now what we think, and trying to interfere with their choice of friends is more likely to alienate them from us than to separate them from their friends.

In the end teenagers, like the rest of us, will form their closest friendships with people with whom they share common interests and values.

The benefits of choosing their own friends

- Teenagers can learn a lot from even the most ill-advised friendships. Sometimes the only way to learn how to choose good friends is to have a few bad ones along the way.
- When parents try to micro-manage their teenagers' lives, the teenagers cannot learn for themselves. Picking your children's friends is micro-managing at its worst.
- It is virtually impossible to force a teenager to have the friends you want them to have. Try! The result is almost always rebellion.
- The only time you should interfere with your teenagers' choice of friends is when there is a need to protect them from serious and imminent harm.[6]

Avoid over-reacting

Often the contentious topics are the messy bedroom, how long they sleep in at the weekend, inappropriate clothing, the nose ring, the eyebrow stud, the tattoo, hair colour and the like. Do we really want to wage war over such matters? Or do we think that dishonesty, rudeness and unkindness deserve our attention more? It is easy to over-react because we are concerned about what everyone else will think. But whether our teens' behaviour shocks or impresses other parents is not really what matters. One teenage girl said this:

> The main reason I would get a piercing would be to see my parents' reaction. I asked my parents if I could get my tongue pierced – expecting them to say no – and then to get it done anyway. When their reply was, 'Yes, but you have to pay for it,' the idea of having my tongue clamped and a metal bar being shoved through it kind of lost its appeal.[7]

Laughing about such things will usually be the best response. Negotiation – perhaps suggesting that they wait till they are sixteen, or eighteen, or when they have left school – is usually more productive than a straight 'no'.

Manage their concerns

Our teenagers may well be more worried about being out of our sphere of protection than they let on to us. Telling them that we always want to give them a helping hand should they find themselves in a tricky or frightening situation will be reassuring. One woman remembered: 'My dad gave us a twenty pound note when we went out, strictly to be kept for "just in case" emergencies and *not* for anything else. And we knew we could always phone at any time of the day or night, if we were in trouble or were stuck somewhere, and he would come and pick us up. We made sure he didn't need to come out too often and he usually got his twenty pounds back.'

Sometimes teenagers push to be allowed to go to events or parties that secretly they are anxious about attending. It can be a relief to be able to blame their parents for not being allowed to go. Asking them pertinent questions may draw out their concern: 'So you arrive, you don't know anyone and you can't find any of your friends. How will you feel?' Or, 'It's 1 am; you're over the other side of the city; there's no way of getting home and everyone else has drunk too much. What will you do?' Or, 'You get to the party. The drugs are being passed round. No one else has declined. How would you feel?'

Questions like these help them make a realistic assessment of a likely scenario, and they may decide of their own accord they do not really want to go. Or they can rehearse with you how they will respond in different situations. By helping them work out what to say, you will show them you are on their side and that you understand the strength of peer pressure.

Talk through your concerns

This is the time when we worry most about our children. We worry about where they are, who they are with, what time they will be back, how they will turn out, and so on. We may also be concerned about our parenting, particularly whether we are giving them too much or too little freedom. Worrying causes nagging. But nagging will stop them listening to us altogether. Tony Campolo writes about its effect:

> You might not consider it nagging, but it is nagging when you keep on making the same point over and over again, continually trying to drive home the same message. It doesn't take long for children who are under a steady bombardment of repetitious directives to *turn off*. In some cases, nagging even drives children to do the opposite of what their parents want.[8]

Sila One of our children described how my nagging him to work harder for his 'A' levels made him, perversely, do less work. But when his older brother came in and said, 'Oh, don't worry! There's nothing much you can do now,' rather irritatingly it had the opposite effect. He proceeded to learn fifty quotes that were just what he needed for the following day's exam.

Rather than nagging, it is much better to talk through our anxieties, first with another adult, and after that, if necessary, with our children. We can then work out a plan of action together: how they are going to get their homework done; how they are going to say 'no' if they are offered drugs at a party; how their bedroom carpet is ever going to be cleaned again; how they are going to get to school on time.

How to facilitate discussion

The following steps have helped us to discuss the issue at hand rather than nag our teenagers:

- Make an appointment. Teenagers feel they are being treated as adults.
- Set aside sufficient, uninterrupted time. The offer of going out for a meal, a cup of coffee or a smoothie is usually appealing and means that both teenager and parent are less likely to get heated and raise their voices.
- Identify the main concern. Be upfront and tell your teenager what you want to discuss. Plan carefully what you will say. Do not go on the attack or threaten.
- Take it in turns with your teenager to talk. Be sure to listen when they are speaking rather than mentally preparing your next point.
- Brainstorm possible solutions.
- Work out the solution that is in your teenager's best long-term interest. Be firm where necessary, and compromise where you can.
- Agree to review the situation after they (or you) have had long enough to make changes.

Carefully worded advice, even over subjects that are emotive or have caused friction in the past, will usually draw us closer to our teenagers and will help to persuade them that we are trying to support them. Using humour also helps a lot. In one family, a daughter recalls, 'Dad teased us a great deal. I remember him saying things like: "I think I can see the ceiling moving – please could you turn the music down?" and being grudgingly admired by the rest of us!'

Take advice from other parents

Obviously, we must always be loyal to our children and not pass on stories that will embarrass them. Nevertheless, talking about our concerns with other parents, who have similar aged children and who are facing the same issues, is very helpful.

Over-reaction to teenage behaviour is moderated and we are less likely to say things in the heat of the moment that we later regret. We can also share solutions and pass on what we've learned.

Sila We are very grateful to the parents who told us about the 'alarm clock outside the bedroom door' tactic. This was the perfect answer when our teenagers had reached the age of being allowed to return home after the time we wanted to be in bed. We would set an alarm clock for the time they had to be home and put it just outside the open door of our bedroom. The challenge to them was to turn the alarm off before it woke us up. In this way we could sleep soundly through the night knowing that, if we were *not* woken up, there was no need to worry. Equally, if we were woken by the alarm, we would go into action straightaway.

Our children were all keen not to have to face the consequences of us being woken up unnecessarily. On occasions that necessitated racing home, dashing up the stairs and diving for the clock with seconds to spare.

Work out the appropriate punishments when they cross a boundary

For teenagers, knowing there will be consequences if they break the rules or abuse our trust teaches them to take responsibility for their actions. Finding the level of punishment that is in proportion to the offence is important. If we are too lenient, we are teaching our teenagers they can break rules with impunity. If we are too harsh, we may cause long lasting resentment.

Possible punishments

- Reducing their freedom:
  - by stopping them from going out the next Friday or Saturday evening.
  - by making them come in earlier the next time they go out. One parent doubled the number of minutes his teenage daughter was late home, and made her come back that much earlier on the next occasion.
  - by grounding them at home for a weekend (ie, not allowed to go out or to meet up with friends).
- Earlier bedtime.
- Stopping their allowance.
- Refusing the next invitation to a party or not allowing their favourite activity.
- Not allowing friends to stay or not allowing them to stay with friends.
- Banning TV or use of the computer for a night or a week.
- Setting them a task like cleaning the car, sweeping up leaves or doing the ironing.

It is worth having some alternatives and taking time to consider what is appropriate for this teenager and for this offence. That may require discussion between you as parents. Single parents, too, often benefit from talking over the situation with somebody who has a child of a similar age. If the punishment is to be effective, the teenager must mind about it, so that it acts as a deterrent for the future. Sometimes, however, a punishment is not necessary if they have already leant from their mistake. A friend told us this story from her teenage years:

> I remember having a party that went out of control. I had assured my parents wholeheartedly that I was in charge and all would go well; I did not need their help. On the night, various uninvited guests came through an open window to join in and arrived drunk and behaved badly. It all turned into a nightmare for me.
>
> Later on my parents helped me clear up the mess. I was expecting their wrath, but I remember they said very little except, 'Next time you'll know to do it differently.' And they were right. Their understanding at that point was really important in our relationship. I knew I had failed and needed their support, not a big telling off or a punishment.

Encourage independence

Over-protection of our children for fear of their physical and moral safety can be as detrimental to their development as abandoning them to any and every predatory influence. We will not and should not know every detail of our teenagers' lives.

This journey through adolescence must be built on trust. Trust builds trustworthiness. Our respect for their growing independence builds self-respect in them.

Allowing them to travel without us, possibly abroad, teaches them to organise themselves and make sensible choices.

Nicky At the age of sixteen, each of our children went inter-railing for a month of the summer holidays around Europe with a friend. We required them to earn money for the trip through babysitting or some other part-time job, and to put together an itinerary so we knew where they were staying each night they were away. Usually it involved a mixture of camping, staying with contacts or booking themselves into youth hostels.

These trips away always caused us a degree of anxiety. One or both of us would lie awake at night fretting if we had not heard from them for several days. We prayed daily for their safety and their homecoming brought much excitement and relief. But we noticed the way that each child matured through the experience, and they returned to the family more relaxed, more confident, more co-operative and more considerate of others.

Get help if the relationship breaks down

If the relationship between you and your teenager has totally broken down, our suggestion is to seek advice. Blaming ourselves, our teenager, or anybody else, for that matter, will benefit no one. Parenting is a formidable task. Parenting teenagers will often bring us to our wits' end, and we need all the help we can get. A more objective view is often necessary. If you are concerned that your teenager is becoming isolated from you, a trained family therapist can help work through the underlying problems. Similarly, if you perceive self-destructive patterns of behaviour, such as self-harming, anorexia or drug-taking, consult your doctor.

Conclusion

Living in a big city like London did not always make life easy when our children were teenagers. Many times we questioned whether we were being too lenient or were expecting too much of them. Sometimes they broke our trust or failed to adhere to a boundary we had set, and as a result their freedom was restricted.

However, whilst being typical teenagers, we watched them becoming increasingly responsible and more grown up. We certainly had anxious moments and sleepless nights, but usually they came home when we asked them to, phoned if they got into difficulties or were delayed, and generally adhered to the safety measures we had drilled into them. And we all learnt together as we went along.

When we try to see life from our teenagers' viewpoint, negotiate the boundaries with them, appear reasonable, remain flexible, have conversations rather than give lectures and keep a sense of humour, they will increasingly see us as advisers who are on their side. And, when they feel listened to rather than criticised and disapproved of, they may even begin to ask our advice.

We cannot control them now as we did when they were younger. But we can and *must* tell them of the longer-term consequences of their choices. Soon they will be on their own.

Pause and consider

- Think back to when you were a teenager. Reading old diaries can help if you have them. What were some of the things you struggled with, and what did you promise yourself you would never do as parents?
- What causes most tension between you and your teenager? Decide on a scale of 1 – 10 (10 being the worst) how important the issue is and work out what kind of behaviour is worth doing battle over.
- Have you booked in a date with your teenagers recently to have fun together and to do something that they would really enjoy?
- How many of your teenager's friends do you know well? Is there anything you could do to get to know them better?
- How do you deal with conflict with your teenager? Does your method work well? Can you think of improvements?

Section 4

Helping our children make good choices

Chapter 14

Handling anger (ours and theirs)

Anger is a signal, and one worth listening to.

Harriet Dancer
Author

I have been shocked at how angry my kids have made me.

Father of two daughters

I get mad when Dad or Mum won't listen to my side of the story.

Steve, aged 14

I developed this habit of punching the wall and it really hurt my hands. Maybe it's important to let it all out, rather than take it out on your friends or on the streets.

Barny, aged 23

Holding onto anger, resentment and hurt only gives you tense muscles, a headache and a sore jaw from clenching your teeth. Forgiveness gives you back the laughter and the lightness in your life.

Joan Lunden
Broadcaster

Home is a safe place to get mad at each other because you know they'll forgive you.

Ed, aged 18

A young father was pushing his two-year-old son in a supermarket trolley as he did the weekly shop. The child was having a full-on tantrum – screaming, yelling and kicking – but the man was speaking softly in measured tones: 'Don't get upset, George! Don't cry, George! Don't scream, George!'

An old lady felt that she must comment on this shining example of fatherhood. 'Sir,' she said, 'may I commend you on the way you are dealing with young George?' 'Madam,' he replied wearily, '*I'm* George.'[1]

Anger and stress are a part of life, as much for our children as for us. Life is not perfect! We cannot protect our children from experiencing these negative emotions, nor should we. Either the family is the place where children learn to process them in a healthy way, or, if unresolved, the family can be destroyed by them.

In recent years, the rise of eating disorders, depression and destructive behaviour among children shows the urgency of helping our children to be emotionally healthy. That requires us to find ways to guard our own emotional health, because children learn most through what they see modelled in their home. In this chapter we will focus on handling anger, and in the next on managing stress, although they are, of course, closely related and one often triggers the other.

Learning to manage our own anger

We have no doubt that, as a parent, you will have experienced many different shades of anger, from mild irritation and annoyance to stammering exasperation and red-hot fury. It may have been caused by a baby who refused to be put down, a toddler who fought getting dressed down to the last shoe, by sibling rivalry that ended with the older one reducing the younger one to tears yet again, or by the teenager who comes home two hours late with no recognition of the anxiety he has caused.

Acknowledging anger

Anger itself is not wrong – it is a common human experience, a part of our God-given design, our instinctive response to an event that has upset, frustrated, irritated or hurt us. It indicates that something is amiss and needs to be sorted out. We are right to be angry if a child is abused, a teenager is offered drugs or a sibling is hit on the head by her sister wanting to get her own way. Similarly, our children are not wrong to feel angry if a friend deliberately breaks their toy, they get pushed over in the playground or a teacher at school acts unfairly.

The adrenaline rush that accompanies anger is designed to spur us into constructive action – to correct injustice or address the offence. Anger functions rather like the temperature warning light in a car which tells us that the engine is overheating. At such moments we need to pay heed or risk more disastrous consequences (and a large bill) later on. We simply cannot afford to ignore the symptoms of anger, hoping that everything will sort itself out for the best somehow or other.

Acknowledging anger – our own and our children's – is healthy. However, the way we respond when we are angry can be constructive or destructive. When anger is out of control in a home, it becomes a frightening place to live and the other members of the family will become tense, on edge and pessimistic. Parents can dump anger on a child that has nothing to do with that child's behaviour.

If you know that uncontrolled anger could cause you to harm another person, adult or child, or you suspect that you are carrying in yourself buried anger – perhaps the result of a bad relationship in the past – we would urge you to seek professional help.

Rhinos and hedgehogs

The behaviour of two animals when hurt or threatened illustrates two unhealthy human reactions to anger. The first, a rhino, acts aggressively when provoked. It is likely to put down its head and charge at the source of irritation. The other animal, a hedgehog, does the opposite. It throws up a protective shield by curling up into a tight ball and raising its prickles to keep the attacker at bay.

Some of us, when we are angry, act like the rhino – we let others know just how we feel. Our behaviour is loud and may be unpredictable. If we are, by temperament, more volatile, a flash of anger may flare up suddenly and then blow over equally quickly. But, if uncontrolled, rhino behaviour can make our children feel that they are living in a war zone.

Others of us are like the hedgehog. Instead of going on the attack, we try to keep whoever is threatening us at a distance. We become quieter and may withdraw physically or emotionally. It is not that we do not get angry. Rather we express it in less obvious ways and will probably try to bury our feelings. However, buried anger does not go away. Anger that is buried is buried alive. It can then lurk dangerously in our subconscious, threatening to reappear weeks, months or even years later.

Sila I am definitely like the rhino! I wear my heart on my sleeve and my tendency, when I am angry, is to make it very obvious to everyone around. I have had to learn not to react too quickly, as I can easily jump to the wrong conclusion, and not to go into a sulk if I feel hard-done-by. Nicky and the children have discovered over the years that it is better not to take my outbursts to heart and to delay their response until I have calmed down a bit.

Nicky I am much more like the hedgehog. I want to keep the peace at all costs, so I am inclined to keep any hurt to myself. As a result, Sila and the children

> have often been unaware of what they have done or said to upset me. I have to remember to talk about my feelings rather than burying them, and to allow others in the family to bring hurt and anger into the open. Then it can be sorted out rather than left to fester.

Neither aggression (like the rhino) nor suppression (like the hedgehog) are good ways of dealing with anger. Take a moment to look at the following lists. Are you more like the rhino or more like the hedgehog? Or perhaps you alternate between the two.

Responses when angry

Rhino

- Shout and scream.
- Say things you later regret.
- Lose control.
- Lash out and accuse.
- Blame everyone.
- Become explosive or irritable.
- Become controlling and bossy.

Hedgehog

- Try to ignore your feelings.
- Become sarcastic.
- Withdraw behind an impenetrable wall.
- Become cold and clinical.
- Feel nervous.
- Want to run away and hide.
- Get depressed.

Neither rhino nor hedgehog behaviour is good for our own or our family's emotional health. Once we are aware of our tendencies, we can look for ways to control them and try to modify how we behave. Whatever our normal reactions, we have found the following three principles helpful in dealing with our anger.

1. Press the pause button

For most of us, it is what we say or do in the first thirty seconds that we are most likely to regret. Our anger may be justified but, in that critical half-minute, we over-react and the results will usually be detrimental to family life.

Some of us get angry when everything is in a mess or we feel out of control or exhausted. For others it will be when our teenager is unhelpful or seems unmotivated. Once we recognise our vulnerable moments, we can say to ourselves, 'You are about to lose it – watch out!' This is like pushing the pause button on the DVD player.

Simon Carr, a journalist, is a single father with two boys. The mother of his elder child left him and his second wife died. In an article called *A Boys' World – Tears and All*, written when his children were aged fifteen and nine, he wrote about the effect of his temper and how he had to learn to control it in order to protect his relationship with his sons:

> I had half a dozen such serious moods, each lasting a week, sometimes more. And the last was so bad that I sent Hugo [the 15-year-old] back to live with his mother for a while. His absence made me realise how essential he was to our emotional

economy. He stayed away for ten days, until I finally got it straight in my head that he had to be treated a whole lot better, and be protected from these hurricanes. How I controlled the moods I don't quite know. But I learnt to recognise their approach and avoid them – first by agreeing with Hugo's objections (which were, more often than not, sensible enough) and second, by ruthlessly squashing any irritation I felt before it had a chance to develop into something larger.[2]

Nicky I always considered myself a very patient person – that is, until we had children. I discovered that nothing I had encountered in my life wound me up like children who did not co-operate when I had asked them to do something. And what was guaranteed to make my blood boil fastest was when they got angry with each other. I found myself suddenly flaring up and shouting at them for shouting at each other. It took me a number of years to realise that I was not helping them to resolve their disputes. Indeed my angry outbursts generally made the situation worse and did not set much of a model for sorting things out.

Pressing the pause button on my anger has meant not wading in straightaway. Counting to ten in another room, when fighting was breaking out elsewhere in the house, has often helped me to be more rational.

Removing ourselves from the situation, if only for a minute or two, will often help us to cool down and to get back in control. One mother living in the heart of the city with two children aged nine and seven wrote: 'I sometimes find I just have to walk out of the room, even go outside and gulp some fresh (well, not that fresh …) air. Sometimes I say, "I think we'll stop this discussion here," and go anywhere, or ring up a friend, or say, "I'll talk to Dad about this later." In the car I am likely to put on music – LOUD! Anything to give myself breathing space to calm down.'

Practising self-control when we are angry is a major issue for parents. All of us need to find ways to press 'pause'.

Sila For a while my relationship with one of our children, who was then aged fourteen, became tense and difficult. I didn't understand why until our son eventually said to me, 'Mum, you are always stressed with me.' That brought me up short. When we discussed it, I realised that for him, being around me was like living on the slopes of a smouldering volcano.

I also recognised that my over-reaction, regardless of the particular incident, was tied up with my annoyance at his behaving like a typical teenager, such as suddenly leaving the house without any explanation of where he was going, being monosyllabic on his return, or being unappreciative at mealtimes. I was anticipating his responses even before they happened and sounded constantly critical of him.

In order to help me deal with this better, we came to an agreement that, if I started to raise my voice, he could say, 'Mum, you're getting stressed.' That helped me a lot, as often I hadn't even realised I was doing it, and I then made an effort to behave more calmly with him. Sometimes it meant deferring a discussion about something that was worrying me to a better time.

2. Recognise the sources of anger

Anger at home has many different causes. A mother or father may be feeling the pressures of parenthood, or they may be on a short fuse because of ill health or financial worries. If you feel you are not coping, the first thing to do is to sit down as a couple and look at all the things you are trying to juggle. Make a list and then talk together about your priorities. Are there activities you could drop for a time in order to make life more manageable? Could some of the tidying and cleaning go, even if the house is more messy than you would like? Is a child's activity or club after school, that requires you to take and collect him, absolutely necessary? Could re-designing the house wait for a year or so? Could you cut back on your socialising during the week or at the weekend? (If you are parenting alone, go through your list with a friend.)

Sometimes a small change can make a big difference to the stress levels. Sometimes a bigger change is required. One couple, with two children under three, decided together (after much agonising) that the husband should change his job. He had been working long hours, under high pressure, and earned a reasonably high salary. He moved to a firm where he was not on call at weekends, where he could return home at a regular time each evening and where he was able to see the children in the morning at breakfast. Their income dropped but they both felt that things were far better for him and for the rest of the family.

Another father we know, who works as a doctor, realises that he needs some 'downtime' when he gets home from work as otherwise he will be short-tempered with his children all evening. He and his wife have worked out ways to give each other some time on their own, and their home is much calmer as a result.

When they are old enough, we can tell our children the main stress trigger for us. A friend of ours said to her children, 'I need you all to come straight away when I tell you it's tea time – it makes me SO cross if you don't when I've gone to all the trouble of making it for you.' The children learnt to co-operate with that request and it helped everyone.

Sometimes a family meeting can help us to identify changes that will improve the atmosphere in our home. A single parent with three children said, 'If ever it feels like the stress is making us argue and not manage well as a family, we have developed a system where we sit down together and take time out to talk. The deal is that we all have a turn in saying why we are hurt and how the others can help. No interrupting and no finger pointing allowed. Everyone gets a chance to be heard and someone might even say, "You seem too busy and I just need you to play with me," or something along those lines, and the whole atmosphere always changes afterwards.'

Other sources of parental anger may not be so easily fixed. But recognising what is making us angry will help us to address the source rather than attacking whoever is in our path.

3. Practise apology and forgiveness

Behind much of the anger and stress in our lives are strained relationships and hurt feelings. As parents, doing everything we can to resolve conflict in all our relationships is important for two reasons. First, all our relationships affect our parenting. If we are upset with our boss, our husband or wife, our neighbour or our parents, and we do nothing about it, our children will probably suffer. We often end up directing our anger and frustration at them.

Secondly, we set an example. Children notice whether arguments are resolved or left to fester. Children listen to adult conversations and notice if Aunt Flo is never invited to Sunday lunch any more. They notice that the atmosphere becomes icy when Dad gets back from work. This can worry them and they may even feel responsible for the tensions at home. Or children may witness their parents having arguments, sometimes at high volume, but never see them making up more quietly in another room or later in the evening. The children's anxiety about these apparently unresolved rows can leave them wondering whether their parents are on the verge of splitting up. They need to see conflict being resolved in the home. They will then imitate this behaviour themselves.

Repairing relationships, whether with our partner or another person, involves three steps. The first step is to talk *to* the person who has upset us or whom we have upset, rather than only talking *about* him or her to a third party. The second step is to take responsibility, swallow our pride and be prepared to apologise where we know we have got it wrong. As parents, it will sometimes be appropriate to say to our children, 'I'm so sorry for what I said to you today. Please forgive me.'

Sila I remember a particular occasion when I lost my temper with one of our children when he was about three years old. He would not get into the double buggy beside his younger brother so we could go to the park. I was tired and it was the last straw. Without any warning, I grabbed our son, smacked him very hard on his bottom several times (thankfully I think his coat took the brunt of it) and then strapped him forcibly into his pushchair.

I shocked myself at my loss of control. As soon as I'd done it I knew I had over-reacted and that I must apologise. Amidst his (and by now his younger brother's) crying, I took several deep breaths as I put my coat on. I got down to his level, held both his hands, looked him in the eye

> and said (calmly now), 'I am so sorry – Mummy was wrong to do that.' After lots of reassurances, I then gave him a long hug. I was not excusing his behaviour, but rather apologising for my wrong reaction to the situation.[3]

If apologising is new to us, and we have not seen it modelled in our own family as we were growing up, this will be difficult at first. We must resist the desire to make excuses by saying something like, 'I shouldn't have said such unkind things to you but you asked for it,' or, 'I shouldn't have got so angry but you were being very naughty.'

Saying sorry to our children will not cause us to lose their respect or our authority as parents. In fact, the reverse is much more likely to be true. A family counsellor tells the story of Stephen, a thirteen-year-old boy, who had been causing trouble in his neighbourhood. His parents did their utmost to persuade him to take responsibility for his behaviour. Exasperated, they took Stephen to see the counsellor, who said to him, 'Your parents want you to apologise for the trouble you have caused.' 'No way,' replied Stephen. 'How long is it since you've heard an apology in your home?' asked the counsellor. 'That's the point,' said Stephen. 'Grown-ups never say sorry – it's just us children.'[4]

Being able to apologise makes home a safer place, free from unattainable standards. Who wants a perfect parent anyway? If we model appropriate apologies to our children, in time we will hear them apologising when they have done wrong. The shorter and more direct the apology, the better and more effective it will be. We are communicating to our children that it is all right to fail and that none of us is faultless. This will help our children to handle their own failures. A nineteen-year-old told us, 'Mum and Dad never leave anything unfinished. A week after some issue, you have completely forgotten about it and they will say, "I am sorry about last week." It's taught me that it's never too late or embarrassing to say you are sorry. Now I can't sleep well until I have sorted things out.'

Sometimes parents have to guard against over-apologising. It is easy during a warm moment at bedtime suddenly to regret disciplining our child earlier in the day and to apologise for banning their favourite television programme or whatever consequence we imposed. We confuse our children and do them a disservice if we say sorry for fulfilling our proper parental role of maintaining necessary boundaries.

The third step in dealing with hurt and anger is to forgive those who have offended us. Forgiveness is hard for us all, and we will sometimes have to say the words, 'I forgive you,' without feeling like it at all. In our experience, great freedom comes through voicing our decision to forgive, and generally the feelings will follow. Commenting on the verse in the New Testament, 'Bear with each other and forgive whatever grievances you may have against one another,'[5] the author Beth Moore writes:

> Perhaps nothing is harder than forgiveness. Let's face it. Each of us has been confronted by some pretty overwhelming challenges to forgive. Some seem, well, unforgivable. We argue . . . that all inflicted hurts are not created equally. For instance, sometimes the person who hurt us isn't sorry. Or won't take

> responsibility. Or is in the grave. Or the person might be sorry but refuses to recompense. Perhaps the person simply doesn't deserve our forgiveness.
>
> Then, if we let it, truth begins to eclipse our mound of excuses: we won't be okay until we forgive … Left untreated, unforgiveness becomes spiritual cancer. Bitterness takes root, and since the root feeds the rest of the tree, every branch of our lives and every fruit on each limb ultimately become poisoned. The bottom line is: unforgiveness makes us sick. Always spiritually. Often emotionally. And, surprisingly often, physically.
>
> Please keep in mind that forgiveness is not defined by a feeling, although it will ultimately change our feelings … Forgiveness is our determined and deliberate effort to let something go. To release it from our possession. To be willing and ready for it to no longer occupy us.

She goes on to comment further from the perspective of her Christian faith:

> God is not asking us to let it go haphazardly into the black hole of non-existence. Forgiveness means letting it go to God, practising the mercy He's extended to us.[6]

Forgiving our children does not mean excusing poor behaviour or failing to punish them when they have crossed a boundary.

But they need to know that the slate can be wiped clean and that they can start again without having the past held against them. After the misbehaviour has been addressed and the punishment administered, saying to children, 'We don't need to talk about that again,' and being true to our word, helps them move on to more mature behaviour.

We also need to be able to forgive ourselves. We may regret having said something unkind or having failed to express our love. But going on being racked by guilt, even after we have apologised, will be destructive. We are going to make mistakes.

One friend, after two hours of squabbles and rows between her three children, all under seven, in fury drove them to the outside of a children's home and announced, '*That's* where you'll go if you continue arguing.' Later on she was filled with remorse. She imagined they would all be scarred for life. It took her two months to forgive herself. The children, however, recovered as soon as she had apologised.

Handling our children's anger

Few parenting tasks are more important than helping our children to handle anger, and few are more difficult.

Allow for childish displays of anger

As we have already described, young children, when upset and angry, will express themselves loudly and aggressively. This will include hitting, kicking, biting, throwing toys, screaming, crying and shouting. In a toddler, such behaviour is normal. But if our ten-year-old is still exhibiting the same behaviour, something has gone wrong.

Similarly, a five-year-old, who is angry, is quite likely to lose control and be rude. This is normal childishness. We should certainly correct them if, in their rage, their words and actions are unkind or hurtful to other people, but without shutting them down. An angry child needs to be heard. Only as children are allowed to talk about what has upset them will they learn to channel their feelings properly. One mother told us, 'One of my children buried his anger silently and reacted by filling his pants – I realised there was a problem and I had to get to the source of what was upsetting him.'

So, if our child comes home from school and blurts out, 'I hate Jane/Fred/the teacher,' we should not say, 'Don't be silly! Jane/Fred/the teacher is lovely,' and close down the discussion. It is better to draw out of them why they are feeling this way and then decide if we should take further action. Perhaps they are anxious about the homework they have been set, or they are being bullied in the playground, or they are worried about an activity the following day that they think is beyond their ability.

Just as tantrums are normal for young children, so teenagers are naturally prone to bouts of anger. Like toddlers, they are struggling to come to terms with strong surges of emotion and are pushing for more freedom than they have the maturity to handle. Teenagers, like toddlers, occasionally kick the wall and yell, but are more likely to express their anger through irritating habits directed mainly at their parents. These passive-aggressive responses may include being uncommunicative, moody, rude, forgetful and intentionally inefficient. One fourteen-year-old boy said, 'I blank my parents and I know it really winds them up.'

See it as a process

Children of any age express their anger immaturely. This is a source of major frustration for many parents. It may cause them not to let their children talk about their negative feelings at all. But just as children only start to learn to paint by making big colourful splodges on large sheets of paper, and on everything and everyone else too, so it is only through being allowed to give voice to their strong emotions that they learn to express themselves maturely.

This process of teaching children to handle their anger is easier said than done. The force and power of a child's or teenager's anger can be quite overwhelming and may cause us to give up, or lose confidence in our parenting skills. We must keep our long-term aim in mind: to help our children talk about their anxieties and anger without becoming loud, aggressive, unpleasant, going into a sulk, or retreating inside themselves to the point of isolation.

As parents we have approximately eighteen years in which to train our children how to express their anger, and we will generally need all that time! Sometimes it seems as if they take great leaps towards maturity, only to slide back into behaving like a toddler again. It is important not to lose our nerve.

As they grow up, our role is to teach them that, the more they resist throwing things, lashing out, destroying property or shouting obscenities, the more we are able to listen to them. They learn that talking is better than shouting; that self-restraint is better than losing control; and that discussing a problem is more helpful than harbouring anger, bitterness, anxiety or jealousy. They discover that they cannot manipulate the household and get what they want by going into a mood.

If they do not learn these lessons at home as they are growing up, life will be harder for them and for those they will be close to as adults.

Allow for their different personalities

The way children show their anger will depend not only upon their age and maturity but also upon their personality. One child may let rip, while another keeps up a show of compliance and cheerfulness but is angry and unhappy under the surface. Another may withdraw completely.

Nicky Our own children are very different in the ways they display their emotions. One son is just like Sila – we have always known exactly what mood he is in. As a young child, if he was really angry with us, he would jump up and down on the spot out of sheer frustration, doing a near perfect impression of a pneumatic drill. This would reduce the family to hysterics and make him crosser still. In his teenage years he would relieve his pent-up feelings by kicking a ball hard against a wall.

With another son, we never knew if he was feeling upset unless we managed to pick up a few hints – usually at bedtime, when he was little, and in casual conversations well after midnight when he was a teenager.

Our own personality as a parent (and where we come on the rhino-hedgehog spectrum) means that we will find talking about feelings easier with one child than with another. A parent with rhino tendencies may well clash dramatically with a child of a similar temperament. A quiet child will be crushed or frightened by such confrontations. Meanwhile a parent and child, who share hedgehog characteristics, will be in danger of not talking about feelings at all.

Youth worker and author, Tim Smith, advises parents of teenagers: 'The challenge is to find some appropriate expression of anger. If you don't permit your teens to discover a healthy way to express anger, it will smoulder and grow and find its expression in another, less acceptable way.'

Encourage them to talk

More often than not it takes time to understand a situation from our child's point of view. We can easily assume that he or she is going to be difficult, rude or unreasonable and shut them down. Or we do not even attempt to initiate a conversation as we think there is nothing to be discussed.

Nicky When our children were teenagers, I suddenly realised that I was making assumptions if they vaguely mentioned they wanted to go to a party. I tended to say, 'no,' before having had any proper discussion. I would jump to the conclusion that there was bound to be something dubious if they didn't want to talk to me about the details. I found it took time and patience to draw out of them the full particulars of the situation so we could make an informed decision.

Such discussions prevent anger and resentment building up in our children, as well as helping them to be honest with us. Sometimes our own concerns will make it difficult to listen, especially if the child in question is angry. We may be so upset by the unpleasant expression of anger that we fail to dig down to the root cause. This can simply lead to the child being angrier still. Ross Campbell writes from his own experience as a father:

> When a child approaches you with anger, the normal reaction is to be angry in return. But this response will not resolve the anger. My most unpleasant experience of a child speaking to me in a very inappropriate manner was with [my son] David when he was about thirteen. Thank goodness the phase did not last long.
>
> I would say to myself, 'Good, David, good. Let that anger out.' … The reason I was glad to see it come out was that the more anger that came out of his mouth, the less there would be to come out in lying, stealing, sex, drugs, and all the other passive-aggressive behaviours going on today.
>
> We cannot train them to express their anger in mature ways simply by getting upset and forcing them to stop expressing their anger.[7]

To follow Ross Campbell's advice takes not only self control but strength of character and a willingness to sacrifice. Responses such as, 'Try to explain to me what you're upset about,' or, 'What hurt you most?' shows the child we are on their side and want to understand.

Some practical steps to help teenagers express anger

- Teach them to press the pause button. Say, 'Okay, let's meet in the sitting room in fifteen minutes when we are both calmer.'
- Ask yourself, 'Can I see a reason why my child is angry? Am I over reacting? If so, why?' Remember HALT: is either of us Hungry-Anxious-Lonely-Tired?
- Ask your teenager what is upsetting him. Listen. If possible, help him to resolve the problem. Listening may be enough.
- If the anger is over a boundary you have set, be prepared to negotiate. If you still decide the boundary is reasonable, explain why your decision is for her own long-term good. Do not expect her necessarily to agree with you.
- Address any inappropriate reactions such as swearing, being rude, physical aggression or destructive behaviour.

With teenagers who are clearly angry but are unwilling to talk to you, try to set up non-confrontational situations where they do not feel under pressure to communicate. Find an activity that you could do together that you both enjoy. Allow time during the activity for casual conversation. Listen for clues to possible sources of their anger. If you feel you are not making any progress, and your teenager's anger is being expressed in ways that are self-destructive or harmful to others, we would encourage you to seek professional help.

Help them towards maturity

Encouraging our children to tell us what they are upset about does not mean letting them say or do whatever they like, whenever they like. While we must allow for a process of learning and not expect too much too soon, unhelpful anger patterns need to be addressed. If children have an overdeveloped sense of injustice and get furious with anything and everybody from the playstation to the referee who awards a penalty to the other side, we should not indulge them. It is in their best long-term interests that we help them to develop self-control and to keep their temper when things do not go their way. Allowing children to smash up their room or bash the computer, as a means of self expression, is not going to help.

However, some physical outlet for angry feelings can be very beneficial. One twelve-year-old boy told us, 'I get angry with my brother quite a bit because sometimes we are in a no-win situation. When I get really angry, I go into my room and I punch a beanbag.' Another teenager we know would go for a run to work off her frustration.

Teach them to forgive

Every parent will be familiar with, 'It's not fair.' And children are right. Life is not fair. Either they go through life resenting every person who treats them unfairly, growing angrier and more bitter by the day, or they learn to forgive. That does not mean pretending nothing wounds their feelings. Nor does it mean never telling someone how they have been upset. But it does mean deciding to let go of the hurt and determining not to take out their anger on others.

Children, like adults, find forgiveness hard. But for them the process of letting go will often be quicker. We found we had to talk our children through the simple, but demanding process of saying, 'Sorry,' and, 'I forgive you,' over and over again. It usually occurred when one of them had hurt a brother or sister. We spelled out the wrong behaviour, and then required the child who was at fault to say, even if it was through gritted teeth, 'I'm sorry,' and then the other one to say out loud, however reluctantly, 'I forgive you.' We were amazed at how often this ritual immediately enabled them to play happily together again.

The regular practice of apologising and offering forgiveness over squabbles, big or small, has unparalleled power to dispel anger and to restore harmony, not least within the family.

Conclusion

Anger is normal. It is healthy. It is a part of our emotional make-up. But all of us need to learn to control our anger so that we do not damage ourselves or hurt others. All children will experience situations in life that upset them, disturb them, confuse them, hurt them and make them angry. The best way to deal with these emotions is to talk about them. If children are allowed to do this in their family without anyone thinking worse of them, they will become healthier individuals and they will make stronger relationships now and when they are adults.

Pause and consider

- How many rhinos and how many hedgehogs are in your family? How does this affect disagreements between you?
- What do you and your partner get most angry about? Discuss if you could handle these situations better.
- How easy is it for people to say sorry in your family? What response do they get?
- How easy is it for your children to express negative feelings at home? What could you do to help them express their worries, fears and anger?

Chapter 15

Stress, depression and eating disorders

Our daughter, Kirsty, described the start of her 'A' level year at school:

> In my first term of my last year at school I had a very weird sensation of never quite being able to catch my breath. At the time I thought this was my main problem but looking back I can see that it was panic attacks caused by stress. The pressure was largely self-imposed and a generally high level of expectation at school in relation to 'A' levels, university entrance and the plethora of activities (school newspaper contributions, parts in plays, dissertations, sport, etc) that had continually to be achieved. I enjoyed them all and at the time found it hard to hear that I might be stressed. I remember thinking, if only I could breathe normally, everything would be fine.
>
> I never actually took days off school (unlike my brothers, I always hated the idea of the dreaded 'catching up') but did find myself with Mum in casualty one night with us both wondering if I had a hole in my lung. The hospital tests came out clear

and it was only when a friend of Mum's handed her an article on 'chronic hyperventilation' that this strange sensation of being out of breath began to be explained. It described characters like me who think they are fine and can cope with lots (including other people's problems) until suddenly they can't control the most basic and essential function in life – breathing. While it was re-assuring to have it explained, I still battled with believing that it was caused by stress and not a concrete physical problem that a doctor could find and fix.

No one else in the family had ever struggled with stress and I remember feeling very much the odd one out. The boys thought I had gone completely mad when they saw me sitting on our sofa breathing into a paper bag (a short-term remedy for hyperventilation). However, I always felt totally safe at home and they would manage to make me laugh even when I thought I was on the verge of death! They were always quite rightly very clear that I probably wasn't.

A dramatic shift occurred over the Christmas holidays when we were going away as a family. Mum and Dad said that, even though I had my mock 'A' levels when I got back (the results of which I knew were all important for getting interviews at universities), they wouldn't let me take any work away, saying that my mocks were, ultimately, of less importance than my health.

> Taking off the pressure like this (I thought, 'Well, if I'm not allowed to work, I can't be expected to do well') made all the difference. My breathing went back to normal and I actually did better in those exams than almost any others. The breathing thing does come back sometimes, but, having had help to understand the emotional causes as well as the physical symptoms, I'm pretty good now at controlling it. It's a very good indicator of when I'm putting too much pressure on myself.

As parents we long for our children's lives to be carefree and happy. However, the reality is that children face anxiety, and at times the level of anxiety can result in unhealthy stress.

Healthy and unhealthy stress

As with anger, anxiety and stress have an important purpose in motivating us to take action. For children, some stress is a necessary part of the challenge to growth and maturity, and parents should not try to make their lives entirely stress-free.

But there is a balance. If the challenges become overwhelming, or our children feel unsupported, this might lead to a state of constant anxiety, depression, or an eating disorder.

The same holds true for us as parents. Stress is harmful when it interferes with our daily routines, our relationships and our health. To help our children we must first help ourselves. Unhealthy levels of stress can be contagious.

Clinical psychiatrist, Ross Campbell, has written:

> Anxiety is complex; a good emotion with ill effects ... It's an emotion that says we care ... But anxiety can enslave us. It is fear coiled around us so that we are never free from its pressure. And much of the time we may not even be certain what we're anxious about. The word 'stress' is used more and more often for anxiety. It is usually described as a mental or emotional strain set off by change. We might think of a fear as having an identifiable cause ... Anxiety is something more elusive, something more comprehensive.[1]

Many parents today are under more, and quite different, pressures than fifty years ago. Beth Follini, a 'baby coach', describes the expectations some parents feel they have to fulfil:

> These days parenting is a science, a competitive sport and a vocation rolled into one. It is laced with paranoia about food, education and emotional nurturing. And while some of us feel the fear but do it anyway, others feel worried that they won't be up to the job. The pressure to be perfect is huge. You are expected to be beautiful, to lead an exciting life, be young and have an amazing career. They want to be in the perfect house, with the perfect partner, creating the perfect life for their child. But how many people with children can really do that? Something has to give.[2]

Deciding it is preferable to be a 'good enough' parent, rather than being an unrealistic icon of perfection, relieves the pressure.[3]

Handling anxiety and stress

- Try to identify the cause of any stress. Do you have unrealistic expectations of yourself or your children? Is it fear about the future? Is it caused by a particular set of circumstances?
- Talk about your fears with your husband, wife, or a close friend.
- Put your fears in context by mentally rehearsing all that is going well, and by recollecting your longer term goals. Things often get out of perspective when seen in isolation.
- If you pray, bring your worries to God. As the Bible instructs us, 'Do not be anxious about anything, but in everything, by prayer and petition, with thanksgiving, present your requests to God.'[4]
- Decide what action to take. Anxiety is only of benefit when it causes us to do something.

If you find that you cannot shake off constant and overwhelming feelings of anxiety and worry, you may be suffering from depression. We would encourage you to get medical advice.

Finding support

Few activities in life are more stressful than looking after a young child. Feelings of isolation and frustration can build up so quickly. As we mentioned in Chapter 2, in the past, relief from the pressures of parenthood usually came from other members of the extended family and a settled geographical community. Today a peer group is more likely to provide understanding, support and an outlet for stress.

Sila When Josh, our youngest child, was born, I found myself desperate for a break from the house and the seemingly endless routine of looking after four children. The levels of stress were making me short tempered much of the time.

A single friend of ours, who worked part-time, saw a way to help me and very generously offered to look after the two youngest children for half a day a week. I joined a local exercise class – something I hadn't done before but which I really enjoyed – and those Tuesday afternoons were a lifeline for me. They made me feel life was manageable again.

We need to be honest if we are not coping with our situation. Talking with our husband, wife, partner, a close friend, or doctor (who may be more objective) can help to identify what is putting pressure on us. We may be suffering normal levels of parental stress or we may have become depressed.

Post-natal depression

Approximately ten per cent of mothers experience some form

of postnatal depression. Depression is often described as a hidden illness, partially because it is difficult to recognise and partially because, for some people, there is a stigma attached to its diagnosis. As a result, many women suffer in silence without support. Postnatal depression may last for up to three months – longer if left untreated – and does not always begin immediately after the birth of the baby.

Recognising the symptoms of postnatal depression

Any one of the following symptoms might be the result of a long wakeful night or an off day. But if a mother shows these signs for more than a week or two, professional help should be sought.

- Persistent sadness, tearfulness, obsessive behaviour or setting unreasonably high standards for yourself or your baby.
- Anxiety, irritability, withdrawal.
- Finding yourself unable to leave your baby with others, while struggling to cope with the demands of parenting.
- Dramatic weight loss or gain, comfort eating or no interest in food.
- Low concentration, often finding conversation difficult to follow.
- Lack of interest in yourself or your home. Even the simplest task seems unachievable.
- Feeling worthless or thinking you would be better off dead.
- Feelings of guilt.[5]

If you think you or your partner may be in this situation, getting support is the first and most important step. Speaking with someone who understands will be a huge relief.

There are support organisations that can put you in touch with a person or a group near you. (See the end of the book for a list.) Talk to your doctor, who may prescribe temporary medication.

Your relationship as a couple will also be important. The mother may well be feeling vulnerable after the birth of her child. She will need her partner's understanding, love and care to enable her to tell him how she is feeling. The father will have to go out of his way to show his commitment and support, even if he does not fully understand her feelings. He has to resist the temptation to try to 'fix' the problem. Listening, listening and more listening will be essential. So will other tangible signs of his love, such as giving little presents and treats, organising help and coming home from work earlier than usual, if possible.

Do not underestimate the difference these things can make. Being encouraged by her partner that she will get well again, but without feeling under pressure to do so immediately, is deeply reassuring to many mothers struggling with postnatal depression.

Symptoms of anxiety and unhealthy stress in children

Even young children can experience unhealthy stress, although the signs will not always be obvious. Our child's personality will affect how they respond to it. Some children cry, or become irritable, unco-operative or aggressive. Others behave well but are nervous, fearful or panicky. Young children often have difficulty describing how they are feeling. They are unlikely to say, 'I feel stressed,' or, 'I feel worried,' and are more likely to complain, 'My tummy hurts,' or, 'My head hurts,' or, 'Don't go away.'

A friend of ours described to us her symptoms as a young girl that were undiagnosed:

I remember when I was eight I was sent to a new school in the Easter term. I was the only new girl and I hated the school and was desperate to go back to my old school, friends and familiar surroundings. I felt very alone and really struggled to fit in but I found it hard to tell my parents how I felt. When I did, they would just say it would get better. The teachers said, 'Big girls don't cry,' and encouraged me to get on with it.

It was about this time I developed chronic stomach aches. My parents were really worried and I did the rounds of doctors and specialists. No one could find anything wrong. It was only years later I realised it had been stress … no one diagnosed it at the time. But now it seems so obvious – I was struggling with the change and was ill-equipped to express the feelings inside. The stomach aches were the physical manifestation of the inner turmoil.

Symptoms of stress in young children

- Fearfulness
- Increased crying
- Irritability
- Stomach aches
- Bed wetting or soiling
- Clinging to a parent
- Aggression
- Sudden new habits such as thumb-sucking or hair-twirling

Other symptoms of stress or depression in older children

- Attention-seeking behaviour such as lying, bullying, defying authority
- Moodiness/outbursts of anger
- Crying more than usual
- Feeling a failure
- Regularly not wanting to go to school/problems with relationships at school
- Isolation
- Noticeable changes in school work/unable to focus or concentrate
- Difficulty in sleeping
- Change in eating patterns
- Cutting themselves/self-harm[6]

Causes of stress

Anxiety and stress in children and teenagers have many causes. One particular pressure will be parental expectations.

Elizabeth Hartley-Brewer, child development expert and author of *Raising a Self Starter*, comments on the situation today:

> We have fewer children and a greater self-consciousness about parenting. We invest more time, hope and expectation in our children, which has a positive side, but which also keeps them in the full beam of our attention and aspirations.
>
> We see their behaviour and achievements as a reflection on us. If children do well we take the credit for it, and if they don't we feel they let us down.

Our children can feel a pressure to perform. According to the Office of National Statistics, in the UK one child in ten between the ages of five and fifteen, has mental health problems. The number one cause is the pressure to do well at school.

Parents may be well-intentioned, but unwittingly add to the anxiety in their children's lives.

A teenager, whose father was a scratch golfer, felt that the only reason his father played with him was to coach him to a higher standard. The son's objective was different. He just wanted to enjoy this time on the golf course relaxing with his father. His father was also a successful businessman and, seeing that his son had the potential to do well in life, he continually pushed him to achieve a high standard in his academic work. The son felt constantly criticised and demoralised. He became depressed.

Our children are growing up in a culture of comparison and competition.

"Henry is an artist now. So disappointing..."

The media's focus on celebrity polarises people into seeing themselves as a success or a failure, famous or a nobody, rich or poor, a 'mover and shaker' or a drop-out. The pressure can begin even before they go to school as the advertisers bombard them with the message that, unless they have this toy or that game, these trainers or that game console, they will not keep up. The pressure continues at school with league tables, endless assessments and frequent exams as they compete for a place in secondary school or higher education.

Common sources of stress among young people

- Pressure of expectations from a young age – by school, family, friends or peer group
- Unresolved parental conflict and divorce
- Illness
- Fear of failure – social and academic
- Pressure from advertising and a culture of comparison and competition
- Lack of time with parents
- Insufficient time to play
- Being bullied or excluded at school
- No opportunity to talk at home
- Fear for their own safety through seeing news on TV of terrorist attacks, wars, starvation, knife attacks, etc
- Change – experiencing new and unfamiliar situations through moving home or changing school[6]

Helping our children cope with anxiety and stress

Are there ways we can protect our children from unhealthy levels of stress? Can we help them to handle stress well in a stress-driven culture? As parents we can and we must, not least through our example, as they will absorb what we model. So, the following tips are as much for us as for our children.

1. Avoid perfectionism

Elizabeth Hartley-Brewer writes, 'We're in danger of creating a society hamstrung by perfectionism where the "successful" pay a heavy price in terms of their emotional health, and the "unsuccessful" are socially excluded.'

Teaching our children to accept a balance of success and failure, rather than expecting to achieve perfection in everything, is essential for their emotional health. In order to check our expectations as parents, we should ask ourselves what our own goals and priorities are for them. Are their health and happiness more important to us than academic, sporting or social achievements? Are we more concerned about their building great relationships than achieving great results? Would we rather have an unkind child in the top class or a kind child in a lower stream?

We can easily want to be the 'super-parent' and unwittingly put unrealistic expectations on our children – to be more academic, more sporting or more sociable than they are naturally. Have you assured your children that you do not necessarily expect them to get twelve A*s at GCSE and that they will not have failed if they do not manage to do this? Have you told them it is fine if they prefer to hang out with two friends and not be part of a big crowd? Do they know your love is not conditional on how they perform?

Children are hyper-sensitive to their parents' expectations, and by and large want to please them. We should avoid making comparisons between siblings, or with other children of their own age. Otherwise we can leave our children feeling they are not good enough and that they are not loved for who they are. Keep reminding them that all you expect is that they will do their best.

2. Create enough space for relaxation

Healthy eating, healthy sleeping and healthy play all contribute to reducing stress in a child's life (see Chapter 2). Making time to be with our children each day is enormously reassuring to them, especially when they are little. According to one organisation that deals with stress in childhood, 'A two-year-old child may very well be anxious because a parent isn't there enough to satisfy him or her. For pre-school children, separation from parents is the greatest cause of anxiety.'[7]

To have enough relaxed time, we may need to reorganise our own schedules, as well as to think carefully about our children's. We may imagine they love going to a club or the playground everyday after school, when in reality they find messing about at home more relaxing after a busy day. Too many after-school activities can be highly stressful for children. Debbie Cowley, from the *Parenting Education and Support Forum*, says:

> When the school day is over, we ferry them on an exhausting round of extra-curricular classes designed to help them realise their potential and make them shining all-rounders. We can't pretend this is just creative recreation. Music and dance lessons often lead to the stress of more examinations and grades.

Laura Kelly, a teacher at a large comprehensive school, has observed, 'Parents want their children to shine not just academically but also creatively and socially. There is more of a tendency to see every aspect of life as something to "get right" rather than just for pleasure.'[8]

Dare to opt out! Some friends of ours said 'no exams' to their daughter's piano teacher. This is counter-cultural in their peer group, but they are convinced that children need not, and should not, be examined in everything they do. Children need space and time to chill, relax, mess about and even be bored, whether they are six or sixteen. George Marsh, head teacher of an independent junior school in London, advises, 'I try to get parents to see that it would be better if their child stayed in playing at least two nights a week, spending time with parents, rather than being out at endless aspirational classes.'

If we ourselves are constantly wound up, our children will sense and share our stress. Just being around for them, without engaging them in activities every minute, is usually enough to release their pressure valve. Observe how each child relaxes. Do things for fun, not just to improve. Play tennis for the sake of doing something together, and if the ball spends most of the time in the next door court, say, 'Well at least we're getting double the exercise!' Resist always turning games and activities into a coaching session.

3. Talk to children about their fears

Creating natural opportunities for good communication is a part of healthy family life. Among the other benefits, they enable us to draw out from our children what is worrying them. Sometimes they will tell us exactly what is causing them anxiety and we can reassure them we have understood. (Reflecting back their words, as we described in Chapter 7, is particularly helpful.) Then we can work out a plan together so that they know they are not alone in their fears. So, if they are anxious about exams, we could help to plan a revision timetable. If they are worried about going on public transport, we may be able to find a friend to travel with them.

If they are under a lot of stress, go one step at a time. Do not try to deal with all the problems at once. So, if they are struggling with school work, focus on one subject, and help them to think of some simple steps for improving next term. Try to find out what is worrying them most. We may be surprised. Sometimes all they will need is our reassurance.

4. Help your children to have a healthy view of success and failure

We can take the sting out of failure by talking about our own mistakes and showing that life still goes on. Our children's mistakes are disappointing for them, even painful, but we must not allow failure to equal shame. Also, do not try to rescue your children every time they get something wrong. It is tempting to try to fix their problems for them. So, if they lose the key of their sports locker, miss the team training, and are consequently dropped from the Saturday match, we may be tempted to ring the coach to try to change his mind. That will not help. Children have to learn from the experience, take responsibility for their mistake, and think of a better way of looking after their key.

5. Think about how you praise

Praising our children – for working hard, for making progress, for trying something new, for being a part of a team or for simply taking part in a competition – gives them a healthy sense of achievement and encourages them not to define success by having to come top.

When a young child shows you her painting, instead of simply telling her it is brilliant, respond to it and ask questions about it. Say something like, 'You've used lots of red here and I like those gold dots there. Is the lady smiling?' Children want our attention and interest, not a mark out of ten. With an older child, we might say, 'I like the title of your project. How did you come up with the idea?' This type of praise shows them we are really interested.

6. Ask open questions

Open questions, such as 'What did you like about this or that?,' encourage more than a one-word answer and help children to express their feelings. If a child has done well, we might say, 'How did you do it?' and, if they were not so successful, we can ask, 'What do you think happened?' or, 'Is there something you could do differently next time?'

7. Keep adult conversations for adults

Young children can pick up bits of adult conversation and then worry unduly about situations they do not fully understand. Even if our work situation is dire or our finances are in a critical state, it is best to discuss them when the children are out of earshot. If they do hear, talk about the conversation and alleviate any anxiety.

With older children, we will need to use our discretion about how much we tell them. They are likely to pick up undercurrents in our home and may feel more anxious if we keep them in the dark about what is going on. We need to consider carefully what is helpful for them to know. Whatever we decide, if we are going through a hard time, we should not look to them to meet our emotional needs.

8. Change the behaviour not the child

If we are trying to motivate our children to do their best, rather than attacking their character, it is better to suggest some action they can take. So, if revision for exams is not happening, instead of saying, 'You're hopeless! You're not going to pass one exam like this,' try to find a way of helping them. We have put some suggestions below.

Making exam revision more manageable

- Make a large wall calendar, broken up into morning, afternoon and evening. List what has to be revised. Then enter realistic goals in each space. Create variety and insert breaks.
- Divert them from viewing revision as 'one huge task'. Break the job down into smaller pieces so they are not overwhelmed. They will feel better once they have begun. Fifteen minutes a night is a good starting point for even the most obstinate 'revision refusenik'.
- Give encouragement whenever possible. Exam pressure can mean that the tiniest negative comment may result in meltdown.
- Give little gestures to show you care. Provide favourite snacks. Offer loads of sympathy that, yes, exams are tough, but this season will not last forever.
- A timetable (in bitesize chunks), treats, and lots of encouragement are much more productive than nagging.[9]

Recognising the signs of depression

Mood swings are very normal teenage behaviour and should be treated as such, frustrating as they are for parents. However, persistent negative feelings about themselves and about life in general could well be a sign that there is a deeper problem.

As parents we have to tread the difficult path between being over-anxious about our children and yet being aware of the struggles they are facing, so that we respond quickly when something is seriously wrong. The daughter of some parents we know became depressed in her teens. Her mother described to us how it began:

> When my daughter started showing signs of depression, I did not 'read her' at all. And I wish so much I had. She began sleeping erratically, showing huge mood swings and suffering from low self-esteem. Her eating patterns became haphazard and she would easily get into panics or become very worried about how she looked. Her room was a chaotic mess. My reaction at the time was to 'fix it', to tell her to get her act together, to stop worrying and to realise how fortunate she was. I think I got swept along in thinking I had to perpetuate the perfect family scenario. It is easy to look back and regret deeply, but at the time we just did not see what was happening. We assumed she was all right – just rather stressed. Weeks flew by and we were not really communicating properly with her.
>
> It was not until she became deeply depressed and had a complete breakdown that we grasped this was not normal teenage trauma, but serious clinical depression. We realised to our shame that we needed to treat her and the whole situation totally differently. It has been a very hard time for us all – but, with the right care and help, she is on the mend.
>
> Now, I would advise anyone whose children are showing signs of inner stress and turmoil, to

> look out for the signs, to see the whole picture, to take the time to talk and to find out what is really going on. Do not to assume all is fine and, if necessary, do not delay in finding some expert professional help. Appreciate the pressures on young teenagers and be there for your child. Just be there and accept them.

If we suspect depression, the first thing to do is to listen and to try to discover what our child is feeling. If suicide is mentioned, we should always take it very seriously. We should immediately seek professional advice, both for our child and for ourselves. Medication may be prescribed together with counselling.

Eating disorders

Eating disorders are a complex subject. The temptation is to label sufferers with neat definitions, but there is no clear and simple category. An eating disorder is a serious psychological disorder and we would recommend getting professional help as soon as possible.

At the same time, building up our children's confidence through showing our unconditional love not only helps prevent eating disorders, but also acts as a channel for healing. We saw a recent advert on the London Underground that read, 'Radiate confidence this summer.' It showed a tanned, slim young woman in a bikini. Underneath was the name of a Harley Street medical clinic that specialises in cosmetic surgery. As parents, we must do everything in our power to help our children to understand that who they are is determined by their character, and not by their appearance –

whatever the rest of the world is telling them. Feeling good about themselves on the inside is what builds real confidence.

The facts about eating disorders

There are three main categories to which we will refer.[10]

1. Anorexia nervosa

Anorexics control what they eat, slowly starving their body, sometimes (though rarely) to death. Anorexia is all about control – controlling food, controlling weight – as sufferers feel that everything else in their lives is out of control. The symptom, therefore, is the relentless pursuit of the thin body. But that is the outward working of the inner struggle, as the person seeks to escape into a world where nothing else matters but being thin. This obsession makes them forget other problems. By not eating they can feel numb. That is what they want.

Typically, the onset happens in early to mid teens, but increasingly younger children are presenting some of the symptoms of anorexia, such as always feeling full or often feeling sick, finding it tricky to swallow, or having persistent tummy aches.

Perfectionism and competitiveness are common traits in anorexics. They have exceptionally high standards and, if they fail to meet those standards, they punish themselves. Breaking their own strict, self-imposed rules leads to self-hatred. They deprive themselves of basic needs, perceiving them as luxuries. Anorexics bury themselves in tasks, not only because of the value they place on high achievement, but because it gives them less time for eating.

The starvation can cause a dramatic personality change. A young girl who was once sweet-natured and gentle can become unbelievably difficult and selfish. The brain is affected, thinking becomes impaired, and they start to see the world in black and white. They also develop a false perception of their body so that they see themselves as larger than they really are.

Early warning signs to watch out for include: avoiding going out for meals; arranging to meet people after meals; constant drinking of mineral water or fruit teas; becoming emotionally withdrawn; weight loss (or remaining the same size when they should be growing) and, for girls, the stopping of, or delayed start to, having periods.

2. Bulimia nervosa

Bulimia often begins slightly later in the teenage years and can follow on from anorexia. The sufferer eats huge amounts of food in a short time, known as bingeing, followed by getting rid of it inappropriately, known as purging. Common methods of purging are vomiting or using laxatives. Purging is the attempt to get rid of not only the food, but also their feelings. They want to spit out their emotions as they feel unable to deal with them. The person may also purge to prevent weight gain.

Bulimics do not know how to handle their feelings, so anxiety or stress are experienced as a compelling urge to binge. The eating takes their focus away from the problems, and after purging they feel calm. But nothing is solved.

Bulimia is a condition shrouded in secrecy. Of all the eating disorders, it is the hardest to spot as the person can be of a normal weight and do a very good job of appearing to cope on the outside. But inside there is a hatred of self, shame, and an intense fear of being found out. They feel weak and pathetic, unable to control the urges that push them on. 'If people knew the real me,' they tell themselves, 'they wouldn't like me and would run away.' They have a deep desire to be known, understood and cherished; but their feelings tell them that they are bad, ugly, undeserving and that they will never win.

Signs to watch out for include: regular sessions in the loo after meals; frequent escaping from meals with excuses that they have already eaten, they are full or will eat later; food disappearing from the fridge or cupboards between meals, or the potential sufferer constantly smelling of toothpaste.

Parents should be aware, however, that bulimics will go to great lengths to maintain secrecy. They become masters at covering their tracks, and may try to hide their bulimia through techniques such as replacing the food that they have consumed.

3. Compulsive overeating

This condition is similar to bulimia except that there is no purging, as the sufferer wants to feel full. It is often called 'comfort eating', because sufferers are seeking comfort from hurt, disappointment or stress. They overeat in order to try and squash down their emotions so as to avoid dealing with them. Like the bulimic, they cannot separate their feelings from the need to binge, and they binge until they feel uncomfortably full. This kind of eating becomes a secret habit and is accompanied by feelings of guilt, shame and depression. This in turn leads to more bingeing. The result is a huge increase in weight and the distress of feeling out of control.

Sometimes, people with this condition are grazers rather than bingers, eating constantly throughout the day. They do not eat because they are hungry. They are trying to fill the emotional void inside.

The causes of eating disorders

Eating disorders are not fundamentally about image. They are the aftermath of unresolved inward emotions that express themselves in different outward forms. Certainly the cult of the celebrity supermodel and the current perceptions of the ideal female and male forms do not help. But increasingly, medical professionals are realising that the major causes are emotional issues springing from childhood, from trauma, and from developmental problems.

Eating disorders are an outward symptom that the sufferer feels the need to escape from a world of anxiety and depression that threatens to overwhelm them.

Every case is different. The disorder normally starts with a gradual build up of painful life experiences, which usually include not feeling loved and accepted. There will be a catalyst such as facing exams, moving home, parents divorcing, illness, death of a loved one, or some other trauma that causes the teenager to feel that life is out of control. So they turn to food as a way of retaining some control. It often starts with a seemingly harmless diet.

When the effect of the diet becomes noticeable, people may comment on how well they look. This makes them feel good so they aim a little higher and set off on a dangerous path. It can feel like quicksand. They are sucked into patterns of thinking and behaving, which they feel powerless to break out of. Some sufferers also have the urge to self-harm, to misuse alcohol or drugs, and may become suicidal.

The growth in the number of people diagnosed with an eating disorder is partly due to an increased awareness of the conditions. More significant reasons are the increase in family breakdown, the loss of time for close family relationships and the greater stress of life today.

Finding help for eating disorders

If you suspect you have a child with an eating disorder, do not delay in getting help both for the physical symptoms and the underlying emotional causes. Eating disorders quickly become a way of life. The earlier the diagnosis and treatment, the quicker and more successful the recovery is likely to be.

One parent with a child who has suffered with anorexia for five years said to us:

> We should have got help much sooner. We'd got to the stage where the whole family was broken down and I couldn't take advice from anyone any longer. It was beyond us. I was pushing everyone away – every other member of my immediate family, my sister, my mother – I was fighting with everyone. My advice would be, get professional help and stay with it until you get the help you need. And don't be too proud to go into group therapy yourself. Actually, it was essential for me.

A friend of ours, who runs healing courses for people with eating disorders, said to us recently: 'I often see people in their twenties, thirties and forties, who have never dealt with their eating problems. It sometimes takes twenty years to surface and come to a course like ours. Eating disorders normally start in the teenage years but, if undealt with, can last a lifetime.'

If you think your child is suffering from an eating disorder

- Do not panic. It is frightening, but help is available and recovery possible.
- Communicate. Allowing and helping children to talk about their feelings shows support and understanding. Take time to listen and try not to interrupt.
- Gain, or re-gain, their trust. Rather than talking about food, talk about their feelings.
- Better to focus on mood changes than weight changes. Be empathetic.
- Make sure your child understands you care and that you are not trying to take control, fix things or criticise.
- Do not confront. Life is difficult for them and they may react more aggressively and dig their heels in. Be as relaxed as you can. If the conversation gets tense, end it and try again at a better time.
- If verbal communication is too difficult, think about writing a note and suggest they reply with a note.
- Consider if there is a friend, relative, godparent or trusted teacher to whom they might talk.
- Be careful to ensure that a sufferer does not feel talked about behind their back. Ideally, the other person (godparent, etc) should talk to the sufferer about symptoms they have noticed themselves, and not be acting solely on 'insider information'.
- Help them to see a doctor. This may well be the first and most difficult step on the path to recovery.
- Get help yourself.
- Patience is essential. Recovery is going to take time. Developing an eating disorder is a gradual process – so too is the healing process.
- Do not spend energy blaming – either yourself, your child or others. Concentrate on the root causes.
- Children with eating disorders, as with all addictions, become adept at lying and manipulating. Do not allow them to control you or to destroy all the other family relationships.

Reducing the risk of eating disorders

It is never too early and it is never too late to ensure our children know our unconditional love and to build up their confidence. We have looked at the practical ways we can do this in Section 2. The material in Section 3 is also relevant to reducing the risk of eating disorders, as it explains the need for clear boundaries. These help our children feel safe as they face the world in which they are growing up.

With regard to eating, our own attitudes to food and to dieting will help our children develop a healthy approach. A woman, who had an eating disorder as a young woman, described the influence on her of her mother's attitude to food:

> I remember from quite a young age being aware that my mum had this odd relationship with food. She went on all kinds of different diets and ate some very strange meals – huge bowls of soup, or salad, and not much else. She'd be on these strict diets, but then I would find her hiding in the spare room furtively eating chocolate buttons … I guess it is no surprise that I developed my own complex relationship with food and eventually needed treatment for an eating disorder.
>
> I've worked through my own issues, and now that I have children of my own, I am really aware of what they learn from me about food and eating.

Nancy Alcorn, author of *Mercy for Eating Disorders*, advises parents:

> Educate yourself and then your children about the dangers of trying to alter body size and shape through dieting. As far as food goes, make sure they eat a wide variety of foods for a balanced diet, consumed in at least three meals a day, around the same time each day. Never skip meals. Never force your child to 'clean her plate'; this gives the child a sense of not being in control of her own food as well as possibly forcing her to eat when she is not hungry. (This can destroy your child's ability to discern the feelings of hunger and fullness.) The parent should decide what the menu is while the child determines the amount consumed. Avoid dividing foods into 'good/bad, safe/unsafe, fattening/low-fat' categories.[11]

Exercising as a family should also be a normal part of life, so that children grow up knowing that exercise is for health and fun, not just about weight and appearance or getting rid of fat and calories. Have fun engaging in sports with them such as biking, swimming, going for walks or playing football.

Helping children develop their own identity

Eating disorders are on the rise amongst adolescent boys as well as girls. Teenage boys are increasingly aware of their image, which can lead to obsessive body building. They need their parents' regular affirmation and reassurance about their natural size and shape.

For some children, entering puberty and adolescence is

frightening. Hormonal changes can cause new and often uncomfortable thoughts and feelings. They fear the loss of their childhood and staying small and childlike feels safer. This is a key time to instil positive beliefs about their changing bodies and their emerging sexuality.

Both mothers and fathers have a big part to play in helping a daughter find her own identity as she becomes a young woman. To do this she must separate from them. She does not have to leave home, but girls often have to push their mothers away in order for the separation to happen and to become independent.

This can be a difficult time for mothers. They have spent all their daughter's life giving her everything she needed and keeping intimately involved in every aspect of her life. Allowing this separation to take place, while still putting in the necessary boundaries, is a juggling act for every mother. But, unless a teenage girl is allowed to develop her own identity, controlling her size and weight can become her identity.

Fathers also play an important role in this separation process. Many fathers talk about feeling uncomfortable with their daughter's emerging sexuality. They do not quite know how to relate to her any more, so they pull away. Girls who felt very close to their fathers when they were little – whose fathers played with them, read stories to them and sat them on their knee – now find their father withdraws, just when they need his affirmation the most. A father needs to remain involved, to help his daughter feel beautiful, loved and cherished.

A father enables his daughter to feel like a woman in her own right through constant affirmation, through engaging her in conversation, through appropriate physical affection and through showing an interest in her school work, boyfriends, hopes, dreams, aspirations – and other aspects of her life (even if they are of no interest to him at all).

Conclusion

We all hope our children will not suffer from undue stress, depression or eating disorders. But, although we do our best to protect them, there are no guarantees. There are many different pressures and influences on our children. If we realise they are suffering, being frozen into inactivity by a sense of guilt or regrets will not bring them the help they need.

Actually, as parents we can help them to manage stress in such a way that they will be equipped to handle it successfully in childhood, in adolescence and into adulthood – and often, through these tough experiences, the whole family will grow.

Pause and consider

- What do your children get most anxious about?
- Which steps outlined in this chapter do you think could help them cope with their anxiety or stress?
- Are there any activities that you could drop to take off unhelpful pressure?
- Where would your children turn if they were very anxious about something?
- What is your family's attitude to food and dieting? Would you want to change anything?

Chapter 16

Sex and sexuality

Parents – especially fathers – have largely abandoned their responsibility for teaching their children about sex, OFSTED said in a report yesterday. Instead they have left them to glean what they could from teenage magazines in which the underlying message was that sexual activity was the norm, perhaps contributing to Britain having the highest teenage birth rate in Western Europe.[1]

John Clare
Journalist

Sooner or later, your son or daughter will make their own choices about when, where and with whom they have sex. If you want these choices to be informed and responsible, you need to teach them and talk to them about sex in a positive, natural and guilt free way.

Steve Chalke
Author

I think I should have been told about the emotional side of it. How it can screw you up, how you can get involved with people who don't want to know you.

Faye, aged 20

Embarrassment can easily stop us telling our children the truth. A seven-year-old boy was set a homework assignment to write about his family history. As soon as he got home he asked his mother, 'Where did I come from?' 'Well,' replied his mum, not quite ready to give a full explanation of the facts of life, 'a stork brought you and left you under a gooseberry bush.' The boy continued his research. 'Where did you come from?' he asked his father.

His dad, also caught off-guard, followed the party-line, 'A stork brought me and left me under a gooseberry bush.' Next, the boy approached his grandmother with the same question. Thinking her grandson too young to learn the truth and, anyway, it was not her place to tell him, she replied similarly, 'A stork brought me and left me under a gooseberry bush.'

The boy digested this information and began his essay, 'There has not been a natural birth in our family for at least three generations.'

For some parents it is not embarrassment that stops them talking about sex. It is more that they do not know what to say. But in today's culture there are few topics that are more important to address. In a survey of twelve and thirteen-year-olds, only twenty per cent of boys and thirty per cent of girls cited their parents as their main source of sexual information, while in a separate study of eleven to fourteen-year-olds, seventy-five per cent said they wanted their parents to talk to them about sex.[2] Sex education must begin at home.

Why talk to our children about sex?

Helping them to face the pressures

Our children come under pressure on three fronts. First, they will face a pressure from within. The onset of puberty can lead to startling changes, bewildering to parent and adolescent alike. A twelve-year-old's disdain of the opposite sex can turn overnight into a fascination of this newly discovered species!

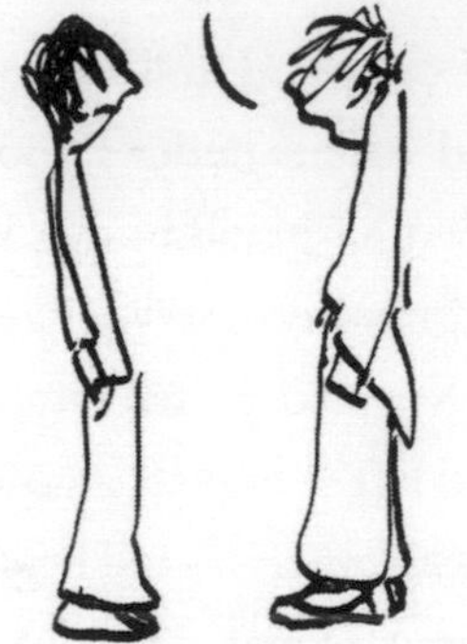

Sexual desire, at one time completely absent from their thinking, can suddenly absorb all their waking thoughts and govern their dreams.

Secondly, they will face pressures from the culture around them. Western society has become marked in large measure by unrestrained hedonism, individualism and consumerism. Each of these has affected our culture's approach to sex. Without parental guidance, our children will be unprotected from these harmful trends.

Attitudes towards sex

- *Hedonism* puts the pursuit of pleasure as the highest value in life, ahead of love and faithfulness, and sex becomes part of the quest for the elusive 'feel good factor'.
- *Individualism* fuels the question, 'How am *I* going to give expression to *my* sexual desires?' Sex becomes self-orientated, divorced from its purpose of forming an enduring and intimate relationship with the potential to create life.
- *Consumerism* creates and then feeds off the mentality, 'If it's not working, throw it away and get a new one.' This mentality is applied not only to material goods but also to people. Sexual relationships come to be governed by short-term values and short-term goals.

Thirdly, there is peer pressure – everyone else is doing it (or so their classmates boast) and they do not want to be the odd one out. An article in *The Week* commented on how much harder it is for teenagers today to stand against the expectation that they ought to be sexually active:

> Our children are growing up in a culture that bombards them with messages about sex. They listen to their peers, to whom sex seems cool and grown up. They watch pop videos full of sexual references, adverts which assume that sexual activity is the key to happiness, TV programmes in which everyone leaps from one bed to the other … Our teenagers flounder about in a mire of sexual confusion. From as young as twelve, they are expected to be sexually aware and body conscious. Nearly a third of British under-sixteens have had

> sex … Today's young people are victims of a savagely 'free' culture which no longer gives them permission to say no … They must be given the self-esteem to resist peer pressure.[3]

Our children need our support and our guidance. Just because it may be awkward, or we feel we are sailing into uncharted waters, we cannot afford to avoid discussing this vital aspect of their growing up. And, if *we* feel talking about sex is new territory, imagine how *they* feel.

Helping them to aim for the best

We live in an age that has cheapened sex and commercialised sexual desire. Our children need to hear from us, not only about the mechanics of sex, but also about the mysterious beauty of making love. As we teach our children the positive nature of sexual desire and sexual intercourse, they will more easily understand the negative consequences of physical intimacy outside the context of a loving, committed relationship. By being open with them, we help them to delay.

In answer to a plea for help from a woman who discovered her thirteen-year-old daughter was having sex, *The Times* columnist Dr Tanya Byron encouraged the mother to talk to her daughter about the consequences.

> Puberty is by no means a maker of emotional, psychological and social maturity sufficient to enable a young person to think through the implications of having sex … we are still a society that is remarkably prudish about talking honestly to our children about sex and a number of us believe that if we talk about it they'll do it. This is as dangerous as stuffing them full of sexual images at a young age.
>
> Do you believe that sex at 13 is a risk to her? If you do then explore every way you can to get her to think about her behaviour … there are times as parents we need to act in the best interests of our children whether or not they want us to. And for what it's worth, I am happy not to sit on the fence and say unequivocally that I have yet to meet a 13 year old who is emotionally able to have a sexual relationship that will enhance their life and their long-term sexual development.[4]

The UK, like many countries, protects children by setting the legal age of consent at sixteen years of age. The Sex Offences Bill (2003) states that all sexual acts that involve at least one person under the age of sixteen constitute criminal activity and, if the other person, man or woman, is over sixteen, they could be charged with statutory rape.

Some parents take the view that, when their children are sixteen, they are old enough. Our own view is that sex is best kept for marriage, and we will explain our reasons later in the chapter.

Whatever our beliefs, we must work out how best to explain them to our children, and take the time to do so. We need to tell our teenagers that they will not be living a suppressed and unfulfilled life if they are not sexually active. They, like everybody, need to learn how to control their sexual desire so they do not hurt themselves and others through ignorance and misuse. Passing on clear values will help to protect them from meaningless one-night stands, sexually transmitted diseases and eroded self-esteem, and motivate them to want more meaningful and enduring relationships.

Helping them to see through the myths about sex

There are a number of current and pervasive myths about sex which, from our perspective, need to be exploded.

Myth number 1: Sex is mainly about satisfying our own desires

The media today is a major influence on society's attitudes and values. Despite showing increasingly explicit sex, few films portray a sexual relationship within the context of a long-term committed relationship. More often we see a strong physical attraction between a beautiful woman and a good-looking guy resulting in instantly fulfilling and amazing sex. In real life, however, not all relationships begin with fantastic sex. And, anyway, every lasting sexual relationship has to be worked at in a spirit of mutual honesty and trust over many years, long after the initial infatuation has died down.

We may be the only ones to tell our children that sex is ultimately fulfilling only in the context of a loving and committed relationship, that it must be other-orientated, and that it is not principally about the satisfying of our own desires but rather about the giving of ourselves in love and faithfulness to another person.

Our children need to know it is possible – indeed it is healthy and normal – to exercise restraint and self-control. Sexual intercourse does not have to be the end goal of every relationship with the opposite sex. Our responsibility is to help our children know the truth and to aim for what we believe to be the best.

Myth number 2: A variety of sexual partners provides good experience

If our children only learn about sex through the media, they may think that the more partners they have, the better. They will fail to understand the potential power of sexual intercourse to join a man and a woman at the deepest levels of their being. We must explain that there is more than a physical joining that takes place through sex; that there is a deep emotional, psychological and even spiritual union that is formed. This is described in the Bible as a man and a woman becoming 'one flesh'. Couples who sleep together and later split up, tear apart this 'one flesh' bond. This can cause intense pain, leaving wounds and scars that are difficult to heal. We want to protect our children from being hurt and from hurting others in this way.

Encouraging our children to keep sex for marriage is not to spoil their fun, but is a recognition of the best context within which to build a strong, intimate relationship. Author, Philip Yancey, writes:

> Marriage provides the security we need to experience sex without restraint, apart from guilt, danger, or deceit. Teenagers worry that they will miss out on

> something if they heed the Bible's warnings against premarital sex. Actually, the warnings are there to *keep* them from missing out on something. Fidelity sets a boundary in which sex can run free.[5]

Myth number 3: Protected sex makes sex okay

The high number of pregnancies amongst unmarried teenagers in the UK stems, in part, from the incomplete and misleading messages children have received about sex. Sex is divorced from its potential to create new life with all the responsibility that accompanies having a child. The 'safe sex' message taught in many schools suggests that, if teenagers use a condom, they will be able to avoid unwanted pregnancies and sexually transmitted diseases. Neither is entirely true. First, because condoms are less than eighty-five per cent successful when used by sexually inexperienced teenagers, and, secondly, because some sexual diseases, such as herpes, can be caught through sexual intimacy without having intercourse.[6]

No contraceptive is 100 per cent effective, even when used by adults. And the consequences are not easily dealt with. Herpes can last indefinitely, and chlamydia, if not detected, can lead to infertility. Meanwhile, tens of thousands of unwanted pregnancies end in abortion each year in the UK as teenagers attempt to undo their mistakes. But many of those who have aborted their child struggle with deep feelings, not only of sadness for a lost child, but of guilt for their part in ending a life. These, often suppressed, emotions can have harmful results such as depression, suicidal tendencies, drug or alcohol abuse, promiscuity, dramatic personality changes or difficulties in forming close relationships. In our view, 'safe sex' means abstinence outside marriage.

Myth number 4: Pornography is harmless fun

With the extensive availability of pornography on the Internet, more people than ever are affected. This is mainly men, though increasing numbers of women are being drawn in through the popularity of chat rooms, sometimes with explicit and unrestrained sexual conversations. People justify their interest in pornography by saying they are not causing harm to anyone. In fact, the pornography industry damages everyone involved.

Pornography is highly addictive. It promises enjoyment and satisfaction, but in practice causes people to become disgusted with themselves and deeply unsatisfied as they crave ever more sexual stimulation. Pornography destroys many relationships by causing feelings of betrayal, jealously, mistrust, resentment, disgust and deep hurt. Far from providing sexual freedom, addicts find themselves trapped in a secret and isolated world.

For adolescents, in a time of intense awareness of their own sexuality, pornography separates sex from its rightful context of love and commitment. In essence, it is the ultimate consequence of hedonism, individualism and consumerism. Boys learn to see women as sexual objects to arouse and then satisfy their sexual desires without the complication of forming a relationship. Addiction to pornography can later on seriously affect their ability to form and sustain a loving marriage.

The availability of pornography through the web has made it imperative to address the subject with our children before they start to look at it, unintentionally or intentionally. Some friends of ours discovered to their dismay that their eight-year-old son, while using the Internet alone in his room, had been searching for pornographic sites. Many children now have Internet access on their mobile phone. Monitoring Internet use, blocking pornographic material through a web browser and locating the computer in a communal area of our home will all help to protect our children. (We cover practical steps like these in Chapter 18.) They, like us, can never 'unsee' what they have once seen, nor totally erase the images from their minds.

Myth number 5: Living and sleeping together helps couples decide if they are right for each other

Cohabitation, either before or as an alternative to marriage, is widely accepted as normal in Western society and in some other parts of the world. However, living together lays weak foundations for marriage, and statistics show that couples who do so are more likely to split up than those who do not.[7] Some have not had long enough to test the depth of their friendship before starting a sexual relationship. They can then easily drift into marriage rather than see it as a decisive moment of commitment. Others feel trapped – moving in together makes it harder to break up, even if one of them is uncertain about the long-term future of the relationship. A woman, who married young and was soon divorced, told us, 'We fell into bed together at university. We got married a few years later. I see now how living together clouded our judgment. We were totally unsuited to each other.'

As parents, we will want our children to choose their marriage partner wisely. After all, it is one of the most important decisions they will ever make. Keeping sex for marriage will help them to do so.

Myth number 6: Sex is unfortunate and embarrassing

Some parents portray sex to their children as an unfortunate and embarrassing fact of life. Some avoid talking about it altogether in the hope of discouraging premarital sex. But these negative messages undermine a healthy view of sex for children entering adolescence as they try to make sense of the increasing power of their sexual feelings.

Those who have been sexually abused may only be able to think about sex as something negative. If, as an adult, you struggle to see marital sex positively, we would encourage you to get help to address this.

How do we talk to our children about sex?

1. Little and often

Sitting our children down at some magic age and giving them the one 'big talk' or bombarding them with a list of 'dos and don'ts' is not the answer to sex education. Knee-jerk reactions to what they do or say will be equally ineffective. Much more effective is the 'drip feed' method of information over many years. We do not pretend this is easy. Many parents wanting to fulfil this responsibility feel poorly equipped to do so. But we know our children better than anybody else, and can be confident that we are in the best position to pass on our beliefs and values about sexual matters.

Talking little and often as the opportunities arise, perhaps when a TV programme or a newspaper article introduces the subject, or through stories we hear of the way people behave (whether appropriately or inappropriately), gives children lessons for life. A teenager, who became a father through a one-night stand when very drunk, opened our own children's eyes as to how far-reaching the consequences can be when sex happens outside marriage. It made way for several very constructive conversations with each of them on different occasions.

Sometimes opportunities will arise out of our children's questions. A friend told us of a conversation with her twelve-year-old daughter:

> Kate said to me the other day, 'What would you do if I was pregnant?' As we were on a long car journey, I said, 'Okay, let's pretend and do a role play.' So I did the, 'Thank you for telling me,' and 'How are you?' and, 'Who is the boy?' etc. Then I asked when the baby was due. 'October.' So I said she was to stay at school until the end of the Summer term when she would get ready to have the baby. She could look after it until the next September and then go back to school to do her GCSEs. I would look after the baby in the day, but she would do nights and weekends as I was too old to do it all. By this time she looked horrified!
>
> Then we talked about her managing to get into uni, bringing some lovely young man home and there would be this gorgeous six-year-old child. We talked about the adult consequences of adult decisions. It was one of the most important conversations that we have ever had and she has repeated it to her friends. The whole thing was in no way planned or thought out. It just happened.

Talking regularly in shorter chunks gives our children time to think, ask questions, formulate their own opinions and prevents the subject of sex becoming over-intense, or a 'big deal'. Giving a lecture, or bombarding them with too much information in one go, can put them off. One mother we know wanted to be very open with her children. When asked a question on a car journey about some aspect of sex, she launched into a detailed description of orgasms. Feeling rather pleased with herself at her twenty-first century openness, she was rather taken aback to hear one of her children say, 'I didn't want that much detail, Mum! Please stop.' It can be even more awkward if we talk about sex from too personal a perspective. Teenagers are typically embarrassed by the thought of their parents *dancing* together, let alone making love.

Of course we will not be the only people from whom they learn. Other sources of information could be school, a youth group, helpful magazines, books or DVDs, which we can then discuss with them. Especially important for our own children were their youth group leaders and other young adults, who spent time in our home, who shared our values and who acted as good role-models. Some were students when we first met them, and our children watched them as they dated, got married and had their own children. As teenagers, our children discussed things with them they would not have wanted to talk to us about.

2. Starting at a young age

The sooner we start talking about sex, the better. But the information should be appropriate to their age. A three-year-old who asks how his newborn brother got out of his mummy's tummy does not need all the facts of life – just an explanation of how the baby squeezed out through a passage between his mother's legs. A five-year-old, who wants to know how babies are made, can be told that a man puts his seed into a woman, which then joins together with an egg inside her and that grows to become a baby. But she is too young to comprehend why a couple would want to engage in sexual intercourse. An eleven-year-old, who says he has been looking at pornographic images on his friend's mobile phone can (and should) be helped to understand why that is inappropriate, but does not need all the facts about the porn industry.

It is helpful to discuss some issues ahead of time, such as bodily changes at the onset of puberty, so they are prepared when they reach this new stage. For one seven-year-old boy, a freshly moody and spotty teenage cousin gave rise to helpful talks with his parents. He also regularly started checking his legs for the appearance of dark hairs! Girls, who understand about their mother's periods as they are growing up, are less likely to be anxious about when they will start theirs. In fact, this can be seen as something to look forward to – a step into adolescence. Boys, too, are better off being told the truth about menstruation before the topic is a source of embarrassment to them. One five-year-old boy, with two sisters at least six years older than him, discovered a tampon in the bathroom. He immediately searched out his mother to ask why there was a stick of dynamite in the house! The term stuck and made discussing the subject much easier in the ensuing years.

3. Taking the initiative

One friend told us, 'My parents left a book, called *Susie's babies*, strategically in my brother's and my bedroom. It was a story about gerbils mating and having babies. Neither of us had any idea that this was for our own sex education and, instead, started asking if we were about to get a new pet.' A more direct approach will probably yield better results. Finding books appropriate to different aged children and to teenagers can help us to open up a conversation and can build understanding of both the facts and our values about sex.

Some books, and particularly magazines, that older children might want to read may not hold our values. Should we let them? One parent's solution was to allow her daughter to buy a teen magazine, but then initially to read it together and discuss the contents. Whatever we decide about what we allow them to read, the values we pass on will generally be the stronger influence in the long run.

Sexuality raises many moral and cultural issues. Only by thinking through what we believe will we be able to have open discussions about topics, such as homosexuality and pornography, that will help our children to develop their own standpoint in a confused and tough peer group culture.

Topics to discuss

Sooner or later our children will need information on:

- Accepting their changing body
- Understanding puberty
- Knowing how to behave appropriately with the opposite sex
- Learning to accept themselves as sexual beings
- Feeling comfortable with their masculinity or femininity
- Understanding masturbation and wet dreams
- Knowing the dangers of pornography
- Learning about sexual attraction
- Understanding gender confusion and homosexuality
- Avoiding inappropriate sexual language (eg, understanding that using the 'f' word denigrates 'making love' to a swear word)
- Being aware that ways of dressing or dancing can be sexually arousing to the opposite sex

⇨

- Seeing sex as an expression of love and commitment and not just a physical act
- Valuing their virginity
- Appreciating the place of sex in marriage
- Understanding the physical and emotional consequences of casual sex outside a committed relationship
- Equipping them to have healthy boundaries and to know how to say 'no' when they need to

We are not recommending passing all of this on in one go!

Nicky Many of the family conversations about sex arose naturally as our children were growing up – through discussing where younger siblings came from, seeing animals mating, reading stories or watching TV programmes.

However, not everything we needed to talk about came up spontaneously. Sometimes we just had to bite the bullet. When each of our boys started travelling to school by public transport at the age of eleven and had the opportunity to make a detour into a newsagent, I looked for a good opportunity to talk about the lure and the longer term effects of pornography – whether through magazines, films or the Internet. To make the conversation easier for them (and me), I chose a moment when I was in the car with one of them on our own. Sitting side by side is less intense than face to face, and bringing up the topic when we were not too far from home meant he knew the

> chat need not go on for too long. In fact, with one of the boys, I sat in the car talking for over an hour, parked outside our house.

Fathers need to continue to raise the subject of pornography from time to time throughout their son's adolescence. Accountability to a father can be exactly what a son needs to help him handle a strong sexual drive and to learn the value of self-discipline with his eyes and thoughts. In our eroticised culture with its encouragement to lust, the benefits of being in control of our desires, rather than our desires controlling us, need to be explained and discussed. In families without a father, another trusted male adult who can talk about sex from this perspective may help to fulfil this role.

4. Affirming our children's sexual identity

Giving our children a positive view of their sexuality includes affirming their masculinity or femininity. Even before our children are born, we should keep any disappointment about whether we were hoping for a boy rather than a girl, or vice versa, to ourselves. We may well relate more easily to a son or to a daughter, but our children's confidence in who they are is helped hugely by having their gender affirmed by their father and their mother as they grow up.

As children approach adolescence they need much affirmation. So often the opposite happens. A child arriving at puberty becomes gangly and unsure of him or herself, quite different from the sweet and cuddly little child we have known from birth. Parents can easily withdraw both physically and emotionally. A father may struggle with his son if he feels threatened by the competitiveness of the young man's masculinity, or he may not know how to respond to his daughter's developing femininity. But boys and girls at this stage continue to need the presence and affection of, ideally, both a mother-figure and a father-figure. This strengthens their own gender identity and gives them the confidence to make friendships with the opposite sex while maintaining proper sexual boundaries. Nothing helps them to delay sexual intimacy as much as knowing they are loved and accepted.

During the pre-teen stage, the difference between the mother and father roles becomes heightened. The father (or father substitute), while acting as a role model for his son, provides for his daughter an example of a healthy relationship with a man. As we have written, it is crucial for a father to remain engaged with his teenage daughter in every aspect of her life. Through spending time together and telling her of his love and pride in her, he will help her to be confident in her womanhood.

A mother (or mother substitute), meanwhile, has a dual responsibility. She must allow her children to separate from her while remaining available to give advice and emotional support throughout adolescence. She is a role model for a daughter while, for her son, her presence helps him to know the differences between the sexes and to learn to treat women with respect and care.[8]

5. Guiding teenagers

We should certainly have discussed all of the topics raised so far in this chapter by the time our children are teenagers. If they are already in their teenage years and we have not begun, we should start from where we are and take every opportunity to talk. They will have many questions, voiced or unvoiced.

How far can they go with the opposite sex in terms of touching or kissing? How do they say 'no' to having sex, so they do not slide into doing something they later regret? How do they overcome their shyness and tell a boy or a girl that they fancy them? How do they know if they are in love? Should they start going out ('dating') as a young teen? What if they feel an attraction to someone of the same sex?

If our teenager tells us that he or she has strong feelings for a person of the same sex, the worst thing we can do is to get angry and stop any further conversations about the subject. It may have taken them great courage to tell us, and they will need us to listen and discuss the issue sympathetically. We should let them know that such feelings in teenagers are not uncommon and are by no means an indication of their sexual orientation as an adult.

Find out the age of the other person and if the feelings are reciprocated. If they are, and the other person is several years older, we should do whatever we can to prevent them spending time together, particularly alone. As part of our discussion with our teenagers, we should make a clear distinction between their feelings, which they cannot prevent and are likely to pass, and sexual activity, which is likely to leave lasting scars and they can refuse. Other parents may take a different line, but, if we are to guide them, we need to be prepared to debate such issues with our teens. Sometimes that will be at inconvenient moments and usually when we want to be asleep in bed.

Some of the topics we need to discuss will ideally involve a mother speaking to her daughter or a father to his son. Again, we would encourage single parents with a child of the opposite sex to find support from a trusted friend of the same sex as their child.

Sila Many were the occasions when, having run myself a deep, relaxing bubble bath at the end of a long day, I would find I was joined in the bathroom by our daughter. Some of our best and most open conversations happened at these times. Often the only reason for stopping was the risk of my developing hypothermia.

Most of us will need to overcome a degree of embarrassment, particularly in discussing issues like wet dreams and masturbation. With boys, masturbation is most easily and effectively addressed in relation to pornography. Making a teenager feel guilty about masturbating will be detrimental, not least because almost every teenage boy masturbates from time to time. It is much more helpful for them to understand that some form of sexual release is natural, hence wet dreams. Teenage boys should know they do not need to be embarrassed by marks on their pyjamas or sheets. However, we can also explain that masturbating can all too easily become a habit, often fuelled by pornography, which can then become obsessive.

This will lead to a distorted view of sex, as a solitary activity, that will inhibit natural and unselfconscious relationships with women.

It is important for daughters to understand that boys are aroused more quickly and easily than girls, particularly through what they see. As young teens, girls will often be unaware of the effect they have on boys through sexually alluring clothes and sexually charged dancing. Ignorance of this difference puts them in danger of being taken advantage of by men.

Sila I remember as a teenager getting dressed up to go to 'a barn dance' with a bare midriff, a lot of bare leg and not much on my top half! My father took one look, was furious and told me to change, without explaining why. As a bolshy fourteen-year-old, I refused, but agreed in the end to wear an unbuttoned shirt over my top, thinking it could be removed after my mother had dropped me off at the party. My only thought was to look as cool as I possibly could – with no real understanding as to the effect on the opposite sex.

It didn't take long for me to discover; I found myself being chased behind the barn by the father of the girl holding the party. That was definitely *not* what I had had in mind. With the panic of having to extricate myself from the situation and my father's words ringing in my ears, the experience taught me a lesson. As a mother, I decided with our own daughter to explain in more detail the reasons for thinking carefully about how she dressed.

6. Helping them to relate naturally to the opposite sex

Our child's desire to have a boyfriend or girlfriend may happen sooner than we anticipated. As the author, Penny Palmano, observes: 'The age at which teenagers become attracted to the opposite sex appears to get younger and younger. When I was thirteen I was still going to marry my pony …!'[9] The moment they become interested will vary, depending on when they reach puberty. This will be somewhere between nine and fifteen years old, and it will be different, not only for girls and boys (the average age for girls is eleven and three-quarters and for boys just over thirteen), but also uniquely for each child. Their personality, their peer group, their parents' attitudes, what they read in magazines or see on TV and films, as well as their physical maturity, will all determine how soon puberty begins.

Relating to the opposite sex becomes a delicate and sensitive area for most teenagers. They are moving into a whole new, almost adult, world and can easily feel vulnerable and awkward. Their first 'relationship' will probably not be smooth-going and they may be painfully aware of their own inexperience. Our job is to respect them and guide them sensitively. Laughing things off does not make them disappear. Our children will simply take their feelings into their bedroom or to their friends, and not open up to us. Of course, they may do that anyway. We have a difficult path to tread as we simultaneously respect privacy while inviting, but never forcing, dialogue.

Relationships need practice. Alongside some clear guidelines and parameters, teenagers need space. An ongoing commentary with our fifteen-year-old of, 'Oooh! We saw you two being all lovey-dovey last night,' can be demeaning. And saying, 'So Laurie's your girlfriend. I thought it was Julia you fancied,' can devalue a new relationship. Think of teenagers as young adults. Treat them and their relationships with respect. Refrain from asking too many questions, and err on the side of restraint. For example, 'Are you and Jamal just good friends?' is less threatening than a barrage of: 'What have you been doing with Jamal?' 'Have you kissed?' 'Are you in love?' and so on.

The expectation foisted on many young people is that they need to be paired up and, only then, have they somehow arrived. Teenagers are desperate for approval. Being seen to have a boyfriend or girlfriend can send the message to their peers that they are attractive and popular. We can help our children to feel under no pressure to jump too quickly into a 'going out' relationship, and encourage them to get to know the opposite sex in a group of friends. That might then naturally lead on to asking one of them out on their own in due course. We explained to our own teenagers that having a boyfriend or girlfriend should not lead to them cutting themselves off from their close friends or becoming an 'exclusive' pair and spending all their spare time alone together.

Sila One of our sons, aged thirteen, took a shine to a gorgeous twelve-year-old girl and he asked us if he could take her to see a film. We said, 'Yes, that's fine,' but suggested they went with some of his other friends (both girls and boys) so it didn't make the event too intense for either of them. He disagreed and said he wanted it to be just the two of them. So, after more discussion, Nicky and I agreed with him which cinema they would go to and the timing of when they should come home.

All went fine. They duly returned and I drove her back to her parents. In the car on the way home, our son reflected on how the evening had gone. He said he didn't think he'd ask her out again on her own as he thought she hadn't liked the film, and they'd been decidedly short of anything interesting to talk about afterwards. He'd experienced the downside of too exclusive a relationship too soon.

Helping young teens with 'going out'

At the point when our children want to start to go out with a boyfriend or girlfriend, here are some ways that can help to prepare them – and us:

- Discuss with each other, and then with your son or daughter, whether they are old enough and ready to start 'going out' on their own.
- Have their boyfriend/girlfriend to your house for meals so that you get to know them and they get to know you.
- Do not be embarrassing! Do not try to sound cool and trendy. Do not grill the boyfriend/girlfriend with a million questions. Encourage the rest of the family to act normally.
- Be careful not to sound disapproving of their friends. It is the quickest way to alienate teenagers and cause communication to shut down. More than likely they will stop bringing their friends home. Even if you do not like them, do not show it.
- When they first go out with a girlfriend/boyfriend, rehearse with them your guidelines and what you expect in terms of the physical boundaries. Impress on them that it is *their* responsibility to be clear about these with the other person, and the onus is on them to uphold these standards for both their sakes. For example, in our family:
  – we encouraged them to keep sex for marriage.
  – we did not allow them to sleep in the same room as a boyfriend or girlfriend.

⇨

- we did not want them staying over at a boyfriend or girlfriend's house if it was just the two of them alone together with no parents around. The same applied in our house.
- we trusted them to make good choices in their physical relationship based on the advice and the values we had imparted to them. We would rehearse our guidelines again if and when we were worried that they were feeling under pressure to cross a boundary.
- we warned them that alcohol could impair their judgment.

- If you are seriously concerned that a relationship is having a negative influence on your child's behaviour or moods, have a quiet, private conversation. Ask them what they feel about this friendship. Draw them out and listen. Together, work out a positive way forward.
- Talk to them about abusive relationships. Warn them of people who might try to use them for their own ends – sexually or emotionally. Keep an eye open for this – you may feel it is unlikely, but it does occur.
- If a boyfriend/girlfriend relationship does not work out, encourage them to end it well; not by sending a text or over the phone, but face to face. Help them to be clear and kind. It is always much better in the long run, and ultimately will cause less pain for the other person.
- Be around for them if and when a relationship comes to an end. Be supportive and give them lots of hugs, even if they ended it. They may be only fifteen, but they can still feel broken hearted. Reassure them that time heals emotions.
- Give practical advice about what to do in the meantime. Thinking they can move to being 'just friends' again straight away is unrealistic. So, help them to agree on how long not to meet, phone or text. Even if they feel sorry for the other person, it will be easier in the long-term.
- Explain that having a boyfriend or girlfriend can be an expensive business!

7. Sex and alcohol

The UK's high rate of teenage pregnancies is linked to excessive drinking. Whatever line we take with alcohol (and we address this further in the next chapter), our teenagers must know clearly that drinking too much leads to a loss of control. This can cause them to do things they may deeply regret. Fathering a child or becoming pregnant is much more likely when drunk, even for children who have grown up with strong values and clear sexual boundaries. Educate your teenagers about 'date rape' drugs, and warn them to guard their drinks against interference if they do not trust the people they are with.

How to talk to a teenager who wants to sleep with a boyfriend/girlfriend

- The fact that your son or daughter is prepared to discuss this subject with you means you have a good underlying relationship.
- With older teenagers, you are not making the decision for them. Rather you are helping them to make the best decision for themselves. If they are under sixteen, you are very much involved in the decision.
- Set aside time for an unhurried conversation. Listen. Find out *why* they want to sleep with their boyfriend/girlfriend. Are they feeling under pressure to do so? Are they worried the relationship might end if they do not? Do they just want to know what it is like? Are their friends also sleeping with their boyfriends/girlfriends? Or are they so infatuated they are finding it hard to resist going all the way?
- Be sure they know that sex is more than a physical act. Talk about the joining that takes place and the much greater emotional pain if and when the relationship comes to an end.
- Ask them if they know the 'sexual history' of their boyfriend/girlfriend. If their boyfriend/girlfriend has previously slept with other people, there is a chance they have a sexual disease unknowingly, such as chlamydia or genital warts. Explain the effect that sexually transmitted diseases can have on a woman's fertility, whether you are speaking to your son or your daughter.[10]

⇨

- Do not be afraid to encourage them to aim for the best, particularly if you think that the ideal is to keep sex for marriage. Show them you recognise this can be really hard and requires self-control, but that it is possible, and you do not want them to have regrets if and when they get married.
- Talk to them about contraception. Explain to them the reasons for your views. Be sure they understand that no contraception is 100 per cent effective. Talk about the consequences of an unplanned pregnancy and of becoming a parent. Tell them about the lasting emotional and psychological effects of abortion on both men and women.
- Point out that they cannot take their virginity back, having once lost it. Are they sure this is the person they want to give it away to rather than to their husband or wife?
- Similarly, if they have previously slept with a boyfriend/girlfriend, we can encourage them not to make this a pattern for their future relationships.
- In order that they do not end up having sex against their better judgment, discuss boundaries – such as not sleeping in the same bed, not getting drunk, not arousing each other with heavy petting.
- Let them know they can keep coming back to talk to you about sex and that your love and acceptance of them are not conditional on their decisions, even if you disagree with them.

8. An unplanned pregnancy

How should parents respond to an unmarried teenage daughter who tells them that she is pregnant? Or to a son who announces his girlfriend is pregnant and he is the father? Tempting though it may be, this is not the moment to launch into a lecture about why sex is best kept for marriage, or an attack on her boyfriend, or accusations of their self-centredness.

A friend said to us, 'I remember hearing an expert, who has helped a lot of people through a crisis pregnancy, say that we should all put a cushion on a chair and pretend that it is our daughter/son coming to tell us she/his girlfriend is pregnant, so we can sort out our reactions in case it ever happens. His main words of advice were: "DO NOT OVER-REACT!" I cannot tell you how important that phrase has been for me as a mother.'

The way we react will affect both the outcome and all the relationships. Unless we have thought through our response ahead of time, most of us will say and do things we regret later. Above all, our daughter or son will need support and guidance. That may start with our initial words being, 'Thank you so much for coming to tell us,' or, 'We love you, and we can get through this together.' Taking time to come to terms with the situation will help parents to face the future more calmly and to talk through the different options. If it is our daughter, she may be able to bring up the child on her own, with the support of the father, or with our help. (We would not recommend putting pressure on them to get married, as a convenient solution, if they are not both ready for this step of commitment.) Or they may decide to have their child adopted. We would suggest getting advice from a crisis pregnancy centre.[11]

We would never advise abortion, first because of our own beliefs regarding the sanctity of life from the moment of conception, and secondly because of the emotional and psychological effects for the mother and, though less well-recognised, for the father.[12]

9. Leading by example

Whatever our own sexual history, as parents we will want the best for our children. We are not being hypocritical to set standards for them that we failed to keep ourselves. Rather we are helping them to learn from our longer experience of life. We may well wish to share some of our own regrets, but this needs to be appropriate to their age. If a child is too young, hearing about their parents' fallibility may damage their security. As a young teenager, knowing about their parents' mistakes may provide justification for not setting high standards with their own sexuality. At the right age, however, children will appreciate their parents' honesty, and our openness will deepen our relationship with them.

The example we give will be at least as powerful as anything we say. If we are parenting together, being physically affectionate in front of our children and guarding our relationship from the temptation of an affair will give them a model of faithfulness. Sooner or later they will hear about other parents splitting up, and they may wonder if we will be next. Assuring them, with our words and our actions, that we will stay together helps to allay their fears and contributes to their sense of security.

If one of you has had an affair and your children know about it, you will need to talk to them about what has happened and help them to handle it. Whatever they say, they are likely to be deeply angry, as they will feel that their world has been torn apart. Children are likely to show signs of insecurity at home, their schoolwork will usually be disrupted and, if not addressed, their reactions could cause them to become promiscuous later on. The anger needs to be expressed and worked through rather than dismissed and shut down.

Listening, and showing you understand how hurt they feel, will be more helpful than justifying your actions or putting all the blame onto your partner. At an appropriate moment, saying sorry to your children for your part and showing them that you are working towards forgiveness will help them to come to terms with what has happened. However, do not expect this to happen instantly, or even quickly, and in some families we have seen that the professional help of a family therapist has been valuable for both adults and children.

Keep loving and keep talking whatever happens

You might have a son or daughter who, against your best advice, has started sleeping with a boyfriend or girlfriend, or has become promiscuous. Or you may have a teenage daughter who has had an unplanned pregnancy. Such situations can cause parents to feel a failure and to take the blame on themselves, but you still have an important role to play.

We know a number of parents who have offered their child and their grandchild a home, thus providing emotional and practical help, and easing the financial burden. This has been costly. But their support has made a huge difference, and has led to rich relationships within the wider family.

We hope the following three points will help parents facing a similar situation to keep a sense of perspective. First, guiding our children in terms of their sexuality is not easy and we must not be too hard on ourselves. We are not the only influence on them. While in the long term our values are likely to be the most enduring, in the short term our teenagers are being encouraged by the prevailing culture to give full expression to their sexual urges.

Secondly, parents cannot, nor should they, supervise their teenagers' every move. We have to take the risk of letting go, trusting, and, if we pray, praying regularly that our teenagers will make good choices. We can influence those decisions, but we cannot make them.

Thirdly, when they act against our advice, it is not the end of the world and certainly should not mark a change in, let alone the end of, our relationship with them. Sexual relationships matter, not least because each sexual encounter affects people beyond the couple themselves. But they are not all that matters, and we must keep them in proportion. One man spoke to us of the time when, aged seventeen, he started sleeping with his girlfriend and told his mother as much. She exploded with fury and verbally attacked him. He said that since that moment he had never been open with or close to his mother. He is now in his thirties.

We have been full of admiration for parents we know who have done what they can to encourage their children to aim for the best, trying over the years to explain the reasons behind their ideals. And then, when their children have failed to keep to those standards, despite their own disappointment, they have been there to help them with the consequences of their choices.

Conclusion

Sigmund Freud once wrote that delaying gratification is a sign of maturity. On that principle, we live in an increasingly immature society. Teaching the value of waiting and the importance of self-control (hard though it may be) is a part of parental training.

A friend of ours described an occasion that inspired her to pass on to her children the value of delaying their first sexual relationship:

> Before I became a Christian, I had been to a lot of weddings. They were generally heart-warming affairs full of beautiful dresses, kind words and

> good wine. However, I shall never forget the first wedding I went to where I knew for certain that the wedding day marked the beginning of the couple's sexual relationship. There was something different in the air: a perceptible lightness, a feeling of awe, a sense of fragility, preciousness and purity. The look in their eyes as they made their vows is a look I shall describe to my children.[13]

When parents leave the door of conversation on sex and sexuality open to their children from an early age, embarrassment soon gives way to honesty. Children who are encouraged to speak openly about sex will be confident to raise their questions throughout their childhood and their teenage years. They may not always agree with our views. They may push hard with a different approach. But, more likely than not, at critical moments they will turn to us for support. And, best of all, our children will hear advice from their chosen source – us.

Pause and consider

- When are the most natural opportunities to talk to your children about sex?
- What do you consider to be the most important values about sex to pass on to your children? Has this chapter raised questions that you need to think through yourself?
- What could you do to create a positive and open environment in which your children could discuss relationships and sex as they go through adolescence?

Chapter 17

Alcohol and other drugs

My parents had a very different upbringing to what I have today … it's like we grew up in parallel universes. They were from Ireland and grew up in secure homes in the middle of the countryside with no cares in the world. I live in inner-city Birmingham, with peer pressure, school stress and lots of other things to deal with. I think most people start drinking alcohol around the age of 13 … There isn't a definite age that most people try drugs. I am nearly 16 years old and I have never tried any, but I know plenty of people who have. This really depends on who you hang around with and how much will-power you have to say no.[1]

Kaytee, aged 15

It's hard for busy parents to become well informed, but they need to know what's going on out there. If parents are informed, teenagers can talk to them about things.

Kirsty, aged 28

We were in the middle of a family discussion. Our two older children, aged ten and eight, were quizzing us about heroin addicts, curious to know why people would continue to take a drug that was so destructive. We were trying to explain, in language they could understand, the physical and psychological aspects of addiction and how hard it is to break a habit. There was an unusual attentiveness until the worried voice of our five-year-old suddenly interjected, 'I think I might be addicted to sweets.'

While open to misunderstanding, discussion about drug taking and drinking can begin at a young age. We might think that talking about these subjects will create an interest that will encourage our children to experiment. Research reveals that the reverse is much more likely. Giving them the right information equips them to make wise choices, to go against the tide, and helps to protect them against misinformation from their peers and from those wanting to take advantage of them.

A common response from parents today is, 'My children know more than I do.' While that may be true, it is no reason to leave the job of talking to our children about alcohol and drugs to others, such as teachers or a local police officer visiting their school. Having confidence in the positive role we play as parents is important.

At the end of the day, even with all the information our children need, the best protection is a good relationship with us. Children, who know they are loved, who know boundaries have been set for their own good, who feel understood and who do not doubt their own self-worth, are least likely to develop an addiction. They are better able to say, 'No,' when they want to and need to.

Of course there are no guarantees. Many teenagers from stable, loving homes will experiment. They want to know what it feels like to drink too much or to take illegal drugs. But for the overwhelming majority, where there is a good relationship with and positive role-modelling by parents, parental values will be a far stronger influence preventing them from forming a habit detrimental to their health and future.

In this chapter we will look at how we educate our children about alcohol and illegal drugs such as cannabis, ecstasy and cocaine. Before we start, it is worth recognising that, if we ourselves take illegal drugs or drink too much, our children are likely to imitate us, whatever we say. If, on the other hand, we back up our words with a consistent lifestyle, our children will probably follow our lead.

Why drug taking and alcohol abuse are so prevalent among teenagers today

As part of a drugs awareness evening for parents of teenagers, the presenter asked why some of them drank alcohol. These parents, mainly in their forties, talked about social expectations, relaxation, enjoyment, dealing with stress, breaking down inhibitions, liking the taste, having developed a habit and so on.

She then asked the same group why they thought some teenagers drank excessively or took illegal drugs, and the answers were very similar. That insight helped those parents to understand and talk more helpfully with their teenagers.

However, there are a number of other factors that have led to the increase in binge drinking and drug taking amongst teenagers in the UK, as in other countries, today. These factors include:

1. Relativism

A fundamental shift in our Western culture from absolutism to relativism has gathered pace over the last fifty years. Previously our society was based on the understanding that there are absolute standards for our behaviour, set for us by authority figures, with consequences for breaking them. Relativism involves no such clear boundaries.

Rather, individuals choose for themselves what is right or wrong, normally using their own feelings as the final arbiter. A pop icon of the 1990s, Noel Gallagher, outlined his philosophy of life when his group Oasis was at the height of its success: 'If it feels good, then do it.'

In a culture based on individual freedom of choice and a wide scale rejection of authority, tolerance becomes the highest value. This has both encouraged teenagers to ignore boundaries set for their behaviour, and undermined the confidence of many parents to impose rules on drugs, alcohol or anything else.

2. Accessibility

A second reason for the increase of drug taking and alcohol abuse is their easy availability, combined with teenagers having greater spending power than previous generations. Teenagers today offer a lucrative source of profit to those marketing drugs and alcohol. Having access to too much money can expose them to temptation, as the parents of one teenager discovered:

> We give our children a monthly allowance and Claire usually saved most of hers but, after a few weeks of the change in her behaviour, I opened one of her bank statements. Several withdrawals had been made from ATMs in nightclubs. She had taken out £500 in the space of four days.
>
> She'd stopped seeing her school friends and was socialising with some girls she'd met on nights out in Harrogate. I've met some of them, too, and they aren't deadbeat drop-outs; they're bright girls, into their shoes and their handbags. But they like drinking too much and staying out late in clubs.
>
> The changes in Claire, the cash withdrawals and her sometimes extreme behaviour made us fear she was using drugs. Our fears were confirmed when our cleaner caught Claire and a friend smoking cannabis and saw a bag with more of the drug in it. When we confronted her, Claire claimed it wasn't hers, but eventually she admitted that it was – and that 'her friend' was a dealer.[2]

Meanwhile, the advertising of alcopops, targeted to include the UK teenage market, is helping to create alcohol dependence at a younger age today. A report on teenagers' drinking habits found that it is binge drinking among girls that has increased most dramatically:

> The 2003 Salvation Army Alcohol Awareness Survey showed that 22% of girls aged fourteen to

> seventeen binge drink – compared to 19% of boys – with drunkenness often leading to unprotected sex. Among teenage girls, 60% said their first alcoholic drink was premixed, like alcopops. Only 40% knew that pre-mixed drinks had a higher alcohol content than beer.[3]

John Dalziel, a spokesman for the survey, said, 'Because of the marketing of the premixed drinks to teenagers, they're very attractive. They're well packaged, they're pretty, they're fashionable and they're mixing all their favourite childhood drinks like milk, lemonade and Coca-Cola with spirits.' Karen Zailckas, a former binge drinker and author of *Smashed: Growing up a Drunk Girl* writes, 'What's so dangerous for girls these days is that the drink goes down too easily. You used to have to acquire a taste for alcohol. Now you can have all the new fizzy concoctions you want, and not even realize you're going over the edge until it's too late.'[4]

3. Insecurity

Linda Blair, a clinical psychologist, lists three pressures on teenagers which makes them susceptible to alcohol and drug abuse:

1. More than almost anything else, teenagers want to be accepted and liked – by their parents, yes; but at least as much, if not more so, by their peers.

2. They live in a chaotic world of unpredictable hormone levels, an unrelenting demand for sleep, and numerous academic and social

> pressures, and they are trying to find out where the limits lie. That is why they argue with you. That is why they take risks.

3. Few teenagers estimate personal risk accurately.[5]

According to a consultant psychiatrist dealing with teenage drug problems in London, 'Most teenagers today take drugs because they're there – an instant route to feeling better about themselves.'

The teenage years have always involved a degree of self-questioning and insecurity. But, for many, that uncertainty has increased considerably through having less time with their parents, either as a result of longer working hours or due to family breakdown. They are therefore particularly susceptible to the pressure to conform to the behaviour of those around them. Karen Zailckas observes, 'For many young people, it's a vicious cycle. You want to be a social success, but you don't yet have the accomplishments or the self-assurance to shine on your own. So you turn to alcohol to create the illusion of success, and the illusion can't be sustained without drinking to excess.'[6]

Those who feel insecure about themselves and their identity discover that, for a while at least, alcohol, like 'recreational drugs', breaks down social barriers.

Be equipped with the facts

Getting informed as parents is a crucial step. Knowledge on the subjects of alcohol abuse and illegal drugs will do three things. First, we will be able to have productive conversations with our children. Secondly, our children are better equipped to make good choices if they are armed with the facts. Thirdly, knowledge dissipates much of our fear.

Alcohol

We recognise that parents living in countries where the law is different to the UK will have to handle the subject differently. In the USA, for example, no person under the age of twenty-one is allowed to buy alcohol. Some states allow minors to drink alcohol under adult supervision in their home, while others prohibit any consumption by those under twenty-one. In other countries the minimum age is eighteen, or alcohol is banned altogether. Meanwhile, in France, sixteen-year-olds are able to buy wine and beer in cafés and restaurants.

We can only comment from our own experience within the UK, while appreciating that parents in other cultures and countries will have different approaches. Most of the statistics and articles we quote are of UK origin. We are citing a culture where under-age binge-drinking has become a social and health issue that we cannot ignore, both for school-aged children and students at college or university.

We are also aware that for varying reasons some people abstain from drinking alcohol altogether. (Even within a wider family, people may have opposing views.) If you yourself do not drink, your situation as a teetotaller is in some ways no different to those parents who drink in moderation. The reality of the world our children are growing up in today is that alcohol is easily available to them (whatever the laws) and they need our help to make right choices in how they approach its usage.

The following information will help us as parents to guide our children towards a healthy, responsible approach to alcohol – whatever standpoint we come from.

Basic facts about drinking alcohol

- Alcohol is a depressant – it appears to be a stimulant because it dulls those parts of the brain which usually make us behave with constraint.
- In whatever form it is drunk, alcohol has a similar effect on the body. Those who think they will be unaffected if they stick to beer or cider and avoid spirits are quite wrong.
- Fizzy drinks (eg, champagne, sparkling wine or carbonated drinks) will affect a person more quickly than still drinks because the alcohol enters the bloodstream more quickly.
- Drinking alcohol on an empty stomach affects a person more quickly than drinking with a meal.

⇨

- Generally, the same amount of alcohol will affect light people more than heavy people because it becomes more concentrated in the blood.
- The same amount of alcohol will affect a woman more than a man, regardless of their weight, because men have a higher body water content, so the alcohol becomes more diluted.
- Children and young people, who are still developing, will appear intoxicated on a smaller amount of alcohol than adults. This is partly because their bodies are smaller and less able to absorb the alcohol, and partly because they are not familiar with its effects.
- There is no way of sobering up quickly – black coffee, cold showers and fresh air can make a person feel less sleepy, but they do not help the body get rid of the alcohol at a faster rate.
- The alcohol content of drinks is measured in units. There is approximately one unit in each of the following – half a pint of ordinary strength beer; one small glass of wine; one 'pub measure' (30ml) of spirits. One can of 'superstrength' lager contains as much alcohol as four pub measures of spirits.
- According to UK government guidelines, a healthy adult male can drink three to four units per day and a healthy adult female two to three units, without harming their health. The sensible drinking guidelines for adults apply whether a person drinks every day or less frequently. It is not okay to save up units for the weekend. Binge-drinking is very risky and is responsible for most of the problems associated with drinking alcohol.
- Mixing alcohol and other drugs, whether illegal or prescribed medicines, can be dangerous, and even fatal.[7]

The law

Whatever line we take with alcohol, and wherever we live, as parents we will be in a stronger position to guide our children if we are clear about the law. The law is there to protect children from alcohol abuse.

The law regarding drinking in the UK

- It is illegal to give alcohol to a child under five – even at home – except on the orders of a doctor.
- It is not illegal for a child over five to drink on private premises, eg in the home.
- Children under fourteen are not allowed in a bar during opening hours, unless the bar has been granted a children's certificate. They are allowed in other parts of licensed premises at the discretion of the licensee.
- Young people aged fourteen or fifteen may be in a bar but they must not buy, be bought, or drink alcohol.
- Young people aged sixteen or seventeen may buy, or be bought, certain drinks in a bar, but only in a separate eating area and only for consumption with a meal. Permitted drinks in England and Wales are beer, cider and perry (an alcoholic drink made from pear juice). The law in Scotland also allows the purchase of wine.
- It is illegal for anyone under eighteen to buy alcohol from an off-licence.[8]

Health risks

Besides the short-term dangers of risky behaviour and accidents through being drunk, there are long term health risks of alcohol abuse such as liver cirrhosis. A person's emotional health can also be affected. A twenty-five-year-old called Nick described why he gave up alcohol at the age of twenty-two:

> I started drinking with friends at fifteen or sixteen and that progressed to drinking heavily when I was at college. British universities have a culture of drinking from which it is difficult to escape. My behaviour when drunk was obnoxious. It affected relationships with friends and girlfriends.

> My academic work suffered and my mental health went to pot. I started to feel depressed, guilty and angry for allowing myself to get into that state.[9]

Guiding our children about alcohol

Jonathan Leake, science editor of the *Sunday Times*, commented recently, 'For parents it is one of the great dilemmas of child-rearing. How do you teach your children to deal with alcohol? Should you ban it altogether – and risk making it seem more attractive – or let your youngsters try a little wine at family meals in the hope that they will learn to drink responsibly?'[10]

Some parents decide that not allowing their children to drink any alcohol until they are legally allowed to buy it for themselves will be the best protection. A recent study from the *National Institute on Alcohol Abuse and Alcoholism* in the USA found that, if young people have their first taste of alcohol before the age of fifteen, it sharply raises the risk of becoming alcohol dependent in later life.

Meanwhile, other research in the UK shows that teenagers, who start to drink away from their parents, are more likely to abuse alcohol. Professor Mark Bellis, from Liverpool John Moores University's public health centre, said:

> We were looking at young people who drink, because by the age of fourteen the majority of young people are already drinking. The question really is, 'Are they learning to drink from their parents in a socially responsible environment or are they learning behind the bushes in a park or in a bar where they shouldn't be in the first place?' The chances are, if they are in

> the latter position, they are learning to binge drink, they are hiding their drinking, and they can't talk to their parents about it. What we found was that the children who were being provided with some alcohol at home with their parents were less likely to do these most damaging types of drinking.[11]

(The same research also found that the more money teenagers had, the more likely they were to become problem drinkers.) Some parents argue that learning to drink alcohol as part of a social gathering over a meal is a healthy and open introduction.

Whether parents hope their children will remain teetotal or aim to teach them to drink in moderation, they will need to have thought through what they will say. When children start going to parties where alcohol might be available, it is well worth talking to the other parents to find out their policy on what they allow or disallow. The more that parents can work together and agree a joint approach, the better protected their children will be.

Some children do not like the taste of alcohol and will show no interest. In this case we can support them by giving them the words to say when offered an alcoholic drink, such as, 'Could I have something soft instead please?' Placing their hand over the top of their glass is also useful if someone tries to serve them.

Other children are keen to try alcohol. Parties where alcohol is being served may be the first real testing ground for how they will handle it. If you allow your children to drink alcohol after a certain age – or you know that they will probably do so anyway whatever your view – you will need to equip them with some practical advice. Recommend that they alternate an alcoholic drink with several soft drinks. Rehearse with them what they might say. For example, 'I'm really thirsty – I'll start with a coke please.'

Above all, drill into them two non-negotiable rules. One: never to drive a car if they have drunk any alcohol (even if it means leaving the car at some distance from home and having to retrieve it the next day). Two: never to get into a car driven by someone of their own age group who has drunk any alcohol. Embarrassing and inconvenient though it might be to refuse a lift in such circumstances, make it clear it could be a matter of life and death.

Let them know that, if they are within range, you would rather go and pick them up, whatever time of night it is. Suggest that, if they are going out with their friends, they take it in turns not to drink alcohol so as to be able to drive.

If we discover our teenager has drunk too much, the way we respond will affect their future behaviour. Shouting, getting angry and generally over-reacting will usually make things worse. Staying calm and suggesting that we talk when they have slept it off is more helpful. If we get heavy and give them a lecture, we will probably shut down all communication.

Most teenagers will get it wrong at one time or another. They need to know we are still there to love them and guide them despite their mistakes.

Illegal drugs

The facts

Parents need to be informed. That might mean finding out the facts about different kinds of drugs, including the immediate effect they have on the body and the longer term consequences. One twenty-year-old said that, despite being offered drugs throughout her teenage years, she did not talk to her parents about it. She thought they knew nothing about the subject and would be shocked and anxious.

There are many helpful and reliable sources available with up-to-the-minute facts. While not giving an exhaustive description of the different drugs, the following basic information will help to protect our children against misinformation from the media and their friends.

1. Cannabis

Cannabis is the most widely used drug in Britain. It is relatively cheap and easily available. A variety of cannabis called 'skunk' is a particularly potent form, generally made from a blend of three commercial strains selected for their strength. The main active compound in cannabis is THC (short for tetrahydrocannabidinol), a psychoactive substance that affects the mental state. Skunk contains an average of two to three times more THC than ordinary 'weed'.

The research today is unequivocal that cannabis can affect a person's mental health and emotional stability. One mother tells her tragic story:

> As a child, Guy was the liveliest, most happy-go-lucky boy that a mother could wish for. He was mischievous, charming and always on the go; if there was a tree to be climbed, he was there. He loved music, he loved life.
>
> In 2003, at the age of sixteen, he started experimenting with cannabis. I assumed it was just a phase he would grow out of and, to some

> extent, turned a blind eye. But within six months my ebullient boy was transformed into a quivering, paranoid wreck, who was bombarded by voices in his head and who rarely left the house. A year later he committed suicide.
>
> Five months after he started using the drug, doctors diagnosed him as suffering from cannabis-induced psychosis. He stopped smoking it immediately, but the damage was done.
>
> I was stunned to learn that cannabis could be so harmful ... Although it has been around for years, I had never heard of skunk, the superstrength variety that is now increasingly available. It bears almost no relation to the resin sold 10 years ago, containing 25 times the amount of THC. Had I known, I would have acted differently. I'm convinced that it was skunk that ultimately killed Guy.
>
> Again and again I think about how different things could have been, and I would urge all parents to be vigilant and to arm themselves with information about strong cannabis and its effects.[12]

As part of the campaign to legalise cannabis some have argued that smoking a joint is no different to having a drink or two. With regard to the short-term effects they are largely correct. The difference, however, lies in the recovery time. The human body is able to eliminate alcohol from the blood stream at the rate of one unit every hour (half a pint of beer or a small glass of wine each representing one unit).

By contrast THC is fat-soluble and stays in the body for many weeks. According to Professor Heather Ashton, Emeritus Professor of Psychopharmacology at the University of Newcastle:

> Elimination is extremely slow, so slow that complete elimination of a single dose takes about a month. Clearly with repeated dosages of cannabis, even once a week, high levels of cannabinoids can build up, continue to reach the brain, and exert long-lasting effects. This slow elimination is important because cannabis exerts many other effects apart from purely pleasure.

Therefore, while there is some comparability between alcoholism and drug addiction, an occasional drink and an occasional joint are not on a par.

Professor John Henry, clinical toxicologist at St Mary's Hospital, London, states, 'Anyone who uses cannabis more than twice a week is likely to lose their drive and focus in everyday life, to become withdrawn socially and less able to think coherently, to concentrate and study.'[13]

2. Ecstasy

Ecstasy is a drug that became popular in the early nineties within the rave culture. People started taking it so they could dance all night. Rosie Leach, aged sixteen, interviewed by *The Times* in June 2007, spoke about the culture she finds herself growing up in:

> I became aware of drugs around the age of 12 in personal and social health education lessons. Then, about a year and a half ago, friends began talking about other friends taking drugs – we were 13, 14 – usually weed, and a lot were smoking cigarettes. That was about it until just before this Christmas when some started taking pills.
>
> When I asked why they did, they said that taking Ecstasy gave you the same feeling as drinking but it was mainly cheaper and you didn't have to queue for ages at the underage bars for drinks; it was quicker to get a pill.[14]

Many do not realise ecstasy is a Class A drug. Users put themselves at risk of dehydration, irrational behaviour and becoming addicted. Possession carries a jail sentence of up to seven years and, in the eyes of the law, giving an ecstasy tablet to your friends is 'supplying', which carries a jail sentence of up to life imprisonment and a hefty fine.

3. Cocaine

Cocaine and crack cocaine are powerful stimulants and highly addictive. Professor John Henry warns, 'Users are taking a risk every time they snort cocaine, no matter how long they have been using the drug. It's a form of Russian roulette. The truth is this: you can die or suffer permanent physical damage the first time you take cocaine, the fiftieth or the five hundredth.'[15] Journalist, Leah Hardy, reported this story in the press:

> It's Thursday night. Anabel and her two girlfriends are huddled in the loo at a friend's house party. Three innocent-looking lines of white powder are expertly snorted, one after the other. It's a great night, thinks Anabel – the music is cool, the right people are here, and she is having a good time. But as the girls open the door, Anabel suddenly begins to feel a pain in her chest. It's as though someone is crushing her. She goes to take a deep breath, but can't. Panic sets in, her eyes widen and her legs begin to buckle.
>
> Last December, Anabel, now 30, spent the rest of that night in the emergency department of a London hospital. She had taken cocaine regularly ('at least every weekend, and probably once during the week') for four years and was shocked to discover that her 'habit' had aged her heart to that of an unhealthy 50-year-old. Twelve months on, she is still under the close supervision of a cardiologist.[16]

Cocaine is particularly dangerous when used with alcohol. Anabel says that most of her friends still take cocaine, despite her experience. 'I've gone on and on about the dangers, but you know how it is – they can't resist that mood lift, the stamina and the mistaken feeling of social confidence it gives. Even the two friends who took me to A&E that night still take it once in a while. But once is one time too many.'[17]

Guiding our children about drugs

If we are to help our children, first and foremost we must develop a relationship of trust with them. Nineteen-year-old Max says, 'Some people do drugs as a reaction to overprotective parents. Mine weren't overprotective or hysterical. They informed me of the dangers and trusted me to come to my own conclusions.'

Our children need to be equipped with good judgment, self-control and strength of character. Teach them when and how to say, 'No, thanks,' for those situations where they need to make the right choices. Talk through with them likely scenarios at school, or at parties when they are encouraged 'to try' something. This will help arm them against peer pressure.

One of our own children found the most helpful way to respond was simply to say, 'Thanks, but it's not my sort of thing,' and then, if he could handle it, to continue to engage in conversation with whoever had tried to persuade him. He wanted to make it clear he was rejecting the drugs, not the person.

As children become more independent, continuing to talk about drugs and alcohol is important. We can help them to realise that, even if they try a drug once, they do not need to continue to take it. And the way in which we talk will make a big difference. If we expect our children to listen to our views, we must be sure to draw theirs out of them. If we are dogmatic and draconian, they are more likely to go out and do exactly what we are insisting they do not do. A light touch will help them feel safe enough to open up, ask us questions and talk about the situations they and their friends are facing.

However, some teenagers will decide to take drugs, even if we have tried our best to equip them to make good choices. We can easily believe we have failed as parents or feel judged by others, but we must not be too hard on ourselves. There are many factors in our children's lives, such as their peer group, their desire to experiment, the influence of their friends, the media and their personality, over which we have little control.

Tips for talking to children about drugs

- Know your facts. Read up on the risks and statistics of drug use and know which drugs do what.
- Do not try to scare your children by exaggerating.
- Find out their school's policy on drugs and, if necessary, get involved to encourage a tough stance.
- Set clear guidelines where you feel it is important. Make sure they know they are responsible for their actions. Establish clear boundaries of what is acceptable behaviour and tell them the consequences for crossing them.
- If they get into a difficult situation, suggest they use you as the reason why they have to be home. They might say, 'My parents won't let me go out for the rest of the weekend unless I'm home by midnight.' It is also well worth giving them each a fallback £20 note – only to be used if they cannot get hold of you, or their planned lift has ended up taking drugs or drinking alcohol, and they need to get a taxi home.
- Know their friends. One of the key signs that your teenager is at risk of getting involved with drugs is if their friends are. Know whom they are spending time with. Invite their friends to your home. If necessary, help them to widen their friendship group.
- Listen to them; really listen. This should start from birth. Eating a meal together every day, turning off the radio in the car, bringing them a cup of tea/coffee/hot chocolate when they are studying, all create opportunities.
- Listen to them; really listen. This should start from birth. Eating a meal together every day, turning off the radio in the car, bringing them a cup of tea/coffee/hot chocolate when they are studying, all create opportunities.

⇨

- If you suspect your child is taking drugs, the first step is to talk with them. Your immediate emotional responses will probably be anger, fear, disappointment and panic. This is not a good state of mind in which to approach him or her. Wait until you have calmed down and are able to show care and concern, rather than only wanting to give a punishment.
- Make sure your children know you love them unconditionally. Otherwise they might only tell you what they think you want to hear. Showing them you believe in them is the best way to ensure they will feel confident enough to open up. Also, if they feel confident, they are much more likely to resist drug taking of their own free will.
- If they have been taking drugs and show no signs of stopping, try hard to persuade them to get professional help.[18]

Conclusion

As the strapline for FRANK, a UK anti-drugs campaign, puts it, 'Drugs are illegal; talking about them is not.'[19]

It is easy to feel overwhelmed by the culture in which our teenagers are growing up. The real life stories are not to frighten you as a parent but rather to enlighten you to the reality of the world our teenagers face, sometimes daily. The good news is that, as parents, we are still the main influence.

Pause and consider

- Have you read a book, or done research online, to be equipped with up-to-date facts about drugs?
- Have you had a discussion jointly as parents as to the boundaries you need to make for your teenagers regarding alcohol and drugs?
- Do you avoid talking about them, give your children lectures about these topics, or allow them to discuss the issues with you?
- Do you know your children's friends?
- Can your children tell you the pressures they face with these issues?
- How could you help your children rehearse some typical scenarios they will encounter?
- Are you approachable enough for your children to tell you of any mistakes they have made?

Chapter 18

Money, TV and the Internet

'Everyone else in my class has one.'

'If I don't get those Nike trainers, I might as well drop all my friends now.'

'Eastenders IS my life.'

'I couldn't live without Facebook.'

'Dad, I need £20. Now. Please.'

One of my rules when we take a family vacation is that you can't take any technological stuff. It's amazing. You think that your children would be clinging to you crying, 'Dad, I really need my iPod! You're ruining my life!' Within a day the kids will actually be reading a book, playing a game and going outside to have fun with their siblings. Imagine.

Robin Williams
Actor

Today's culture is giving parents tough new challenges to manage. We may well feel out of our depth with the trends that are shaping our children's attitudes: aggressive brand advertising; the desire for more and more new 'stuff'; the obsessive playing of computer games; the hours spent online.

Our children may be developing an identity based on the labels they wear, the mobile phones they possess, or the persona they present in the world of cyberspace. Online relationships may be in danger of replacing real-life relationships.

Andy Grysell, who interviewed a cross-section of teenagers for a TV documentary, said, 'People have been talking about virtual reality for a long time … but it's happening. Someone's virtual life on *MySpace* can now take priority over their real life.'[1]

We may long to turn the clock back to protect our children from these influences. A report on the six part TV series, *Teen Angels,* said:

> It's every teenager's worst nightmare to be stripped of any access to TV, the Internet, game consoles, and even mobile phones. But for Chris and Marie Ellis, the parents of 16-year-old Anni and James, 13, it was the solution to months of despair.

> Anni was a persistent truant, James was permanently in detention at school, and family meals were characterised by furious rows. Their home was stripped of all electronic equipment [for a fixed period] … Mr Ellis, 56, said losing his TV was enough to make a grown man cry.
>
> The results are life-changing, with the family made to rely on board games and conversation. James, it emerges, was desperate to spend time with his father but did not know how to ask. Anni says she truanted as a cry for help after her mother, 42, was diagnosed with skin cancer. Previously stroppy James even spends an afternoon playing golf with Mr Ellis, who was normally attached to his TV remote control.
>
> Anni admits, 'Before, I used to think about spending time together and I'd think [sarcastically], 'Oh great, a whole day with my family.' 'Now,' she says, 'it's the listening that makes the difference.'[2]

While occasional breaks from the technology that rules our lives are healthy for all of us, ultimately we must try to show our children how to live within the modern world with its temptations and opportunities.

Money, money, money

Adopting a healthy attitude

In a world dominated by a consumer culture and by brands, demonstrating a healthy attitude towards money and possessions has become hard for everyone. Teaching our children is not easy, as one father of four children recounts:

> My nine-year-old daughter Hannah asks, 'Can we get a PlayStation 3 for our birthday?' I patiently explain how Mummy and Daddy do not believe in gaming consoles. The kids have cable TV, the Internet, PC games, Tamagotchis and other gear and can barely sit still to read for 20 minutes. 'How can you not believe in something that millions of people own?' asks Asher, 12, our resident logician and mathematician. 'Do you mean you don't believe the PlayStation exists, like you don't believe in the tooth fairy? Or do you mean you want your children to be practically the only ones in the whole town who don't own a gaming console, and can't join in probably 50% of normal conversations that happen with other normal kids with normal mums and dads?'
>
> 'Yeah!' said Barak, who is also nine. Jared, Barak, and Hannah are triplets. 'Why are we the only ones who don't have GameCube or Xbox? Why? Why are you and Mummy so mean?'
>
> Barak's jaw quivers as he drives himself towards tears. 'How come we can't get a convertible?' adds Jared, the third triplet.
>
> I cannot fathom why the kids are suddenly anxious about our lack of a high-priced sports car, especially since, with six in the family, we couldn't

> even ride in one together.
>
> 'You never took us to Disney World either!' Hannah says. 'Or Hawaii,' Jared says. 'We'd be willing to overlook a lot of that if we just had one PlayStation,' Asher says. 'I could show you a website that has free shipping.'
>
> I stare at my oldest child, and feel the countervailing waves of pride and exhaustion crash over me. If Asher plays his cards right, he could grow up and negotiate peace treaties. Or run a religious cult.[3]

The pressure of what to buy for our children (what they 'need' or 'must have') starts before they are born. Whether or not we have the money, we still have to decide how to respond. Do we buy it now? And then, as they grow up, do we tell them they have to wait for a birthday? Or would it be better if they saved up for it? But perhaps the overriding question is, 'What kind of values are we passing on about money and possessions?' Indulgence or frugality? Being grateful or making demands? Generosity or selfishness?

Bill and Melinda Gates could buy their children anything they wanted, give them huge allowances and take them regularly to five-star hotels. However, because of their vast wealth, they have had to think very carefully about the attitude to money they want to pass on to their children. So they have worked out a policy that they try to keep to. Their children are expected to help around the house. They are given only a modest amount of pocket money, which they can save up if they wish or spend straight away. And they wait to get presents on their birthdays and at Christmas.

Sue Palmer in *Toxic Childhood* writes, 'Most parents believe that possessions shouldn't hold such importance in their children's lives but beset by a combination of pester power and the very reasonable desire to protect their offspring from social exclusion, they see no option but to hand over money to purchase a place in the in-group.' And as Martin Lindstron, in his book *BRANDchild*, observes, 'As formal religion in the western world continues to erode, brands move in to fill the vacuum.'

Advertisers are targeting children as young as three to create a desire for particular brands of toys, games, types of foods and activities such as going to Disneyland or going skiing. As they get older, the list grows to include shoes, clothes, computers, music, games, iPods, iPhones and so on. Teenagers are especially susceptible. They are desperate to be accepted by their peers – to belong. They need the image presented by the brand to feel part of the 'in crowd'. And, compounding the issue, our 'have it all' culture encourages people to take on debts to buy what they or their children want now, and to pay later.

Sometimes we find it easier to throw money at our children rather than teach them to wait or to use their pocket money wisely. The consumerist society in which we live constantly feeds us the message that instant happiness and peace are better than delayed gratification. One mother reflected, 'My daughter banged on and on about getting a digital camera. In the end I got her one. But as soon as I did, I wished I had got her to save up for it instead – or even gone halves with her. She is seriously "high maintenance", and I can see we have allowed that.'

It requires thought and imagination to find ways of enabling our children to have fun without spending lots of money, to teach them the value of money, to help them understand that, one day, they will have to earn what they spend, and to encourage generosity. Some friends of ours spoke about the way they have helped their children to have an outward looking attitude:

> We started them off with very small amounts of pocket money and we explained to them that they should divide it into a 'save some' pile, a 'spend some' pile and a 'give some' pile. They each have three money boxes – or funky wallets. We tried to teach them to manage their money wisely right from the start, something that we felt we hadn't quite started out in life with ourselves. We talk to them a lot about giving and about areas they can give in. It's exciting when they've got a fundraising thing on at school and they want to use their 'give some' pile. It may be a smaller amount than their classmates, but it is their money that they have chosen to give.
>
> We want them not to be the centre of their world and to try, somehow, to see the needs of the world, the needs of others, and to try to look outside themselves.

Other families we know save up for a family project such as sponsoring a child's education in a developing country.[4] In one family with two young boys, the parents have helped their children give away some of their toys and books before Christmas to other children in their own neighbourhood who would not otherwise have received any presents.

Nicky Our aim with our own children has been to try to teach them two attitudes towards money – generosity and responsibility. We started by giving them pocket money from the age of five, and an allowance once they became teenagers.

The allowance was to pay for presents, going out with friends, clothes (apart from basic necessities), and anything else they wanted to save up for. We tried to gauge the amount so that they had enough to give them some independence, but not too much so that they would still have to make real, hard choices. We wanted them to learn to keep account of how much they had left to spend each month, before they were bombarded with alluring invitations to have a credit card.

We found one of the most effective ways to help our teenagers to take responsibility was insisting they earned their own money when they wanted to travel with friends after doing their GCSEs and on their gap year. They learnt to value every pound they earned, to save up for several months and then to budget their spending while they were away. (Admittedly, we did need to bail one of them out when he ran short of funds on the other side of the world!)

Ways to teach children about money and possessions

- Talk together as parents about what sort of values regarding money and possessions you want your children to grow up with – they may be very different from those of your own childhood.
- Talk to your children about brands and the power of advertising, which can make them want things they don't need.
- Think about peer pressure – on you as well as on them – to have the latest fashion item, gadget or expensive holiday.
- Teach your children wise attitudes towards money and possessions. More is not, necessarily, better.
- Where possible, involve children in your own consumer decisions, and listen to their input.
- Give them pocket money/an allowance and encourage them to divide it between saving, spending on themselves and giving away to others in greater need.
- Discourage impulse buying; help them to plan ahead.
- Help them to become responsible with money. If their allowance is for buying clothes, make sure you do not end up buying the clothes yourself because they have spent it on other things. Resist adding to their allowance on demand.
- Be as positive as you can about how they have chosen to use their own money.
- Talk to them about the consequences of getting into debt.
- Encourage them to appreciate and take care of their possessions.

Sila Even though we taught all our children the same principles, we noticed as soon as they started to have money of their own that each one had a very different approach. I suppose this was inevitable due to their unique personalities. One of them spent everything straightaway and was then happy to go without for the rest of the week or the month. Another

> spent practically nothing and saved the rest with no particular goal in mind. The third saved up for months and then spent all his savings on something he really wanted, whilst the fourth was more guarded and always seemed to have funds in hand.
>
> Each of them has had to learn different lessons about balancing giving, spending and saving. Sometimes, as they were growing up, we had to stop one of them criticising another for handling money differently.

If our own financial position becomes very difficult, or if we run into debt due to unemployment, illness, an accident or family breakdown, it is much better to get help than to bury our head in the sand. Anxiety about the future can be crippling and will be felt by the whole family. Getting advice will help our children believe there is a solution and not to be frightened by the situation.

Passing on values

Although extremes of wealth or poverty will clearly affect our children's lives enormously, in the long run it is not how much or how little money we have, but the attitude we display towards money and possessions that counts. Of course parents, too, have to work out how to deal with the pressure of their own peers. If we give the impression that that we must go on our dream holiday or that we must have the latest designer clothes, a flashy car and trendy gadgets, our children will follow suit. On the other hand, if we demonstrate to them that happiness and fulfilment do not depend on money and possessions, those are the values we will pass on to them.

Practical tips for handling money

1. *On brands.* One mother told her children she would pay for a pair of jeans for each of them but, if they wanted designer jeans, they had to save up and fund the difference. Often they did not bother and then discovered that designer jeans were not such a big deal amongst their peers anyway.
2. *On waiting.* Having to wait to acquire something usually engenders more happiness in the long term. Equally, if children have worked to pay for it themselves, the sense of achievement adds to their enjoyment of it. When teenagers want something over and above the limits of their allowance, encouraging them to find ways of earning money – through doing extra household chores, babysitting or working part-time in a shop – helps them to appreciate the value of what they have worked for. Telling children they have to wait for their birthday, or work in order to earn enough for an air ticket, makes them more appreciative of what they have.
3. *On budgeting.* One way of helping big-spending teenagers is to get them to write down everything they have spent over two weeks so they know where their money is going and where they can cut back. One girl discovered she was often paying for her friends who had 'forgotten' to bring any money. Keeping accurate notes helped her not to give away what she didn't have.

TV and DVDs

Wholesome entertainment or negative influence? Good relaxation or harmful inactivity? Family bonding or individual isolation? Do we let our children watch what they want for as long as they want, or should we censor the content and limit the quantity? Most parents feel they should put in some boundaries, but knowing where can be difficult.

Allowing children to watch limitless TV and DVDs keeps them quiet for hours. Stopping them usually leads to noise and complaints. So how much is too much? And what should we stop them watching altogether?

Quantity

Dr Aric Sigman, a psychologist trying to persuade the UK government to issue national guidelines to protect children from too much TV, argues that spending hours slumped in front of a small screen is 'the greatest unacknowledged health threat of our time'.[5] He recommends the following limits:

Child's age	Amount per day
Under 3-years-old	no screen exposure [clearly difficult if there are older siblings]
3 to 7-years-old	30 to 60 minutes
7 to 12-years-old	60 minutes
12 to 15-years-old	90 minutes
16 + years-old	2 hours

We are not suggesting that sitting a two and a half-year-old down to watch a suitable DVD to help him wind down after nursery school, while Mum feeds the baby, is going to damage him – particularly when this is done within the context of an active family life with plenty of exercise and time outdoors. Actually, such an arrangement may benefit everybody. These figures should be taken as guidelines for the ideal limit and we must remember the context. The average child in the UK today watches between three and five times that amount, while adolescents watch an average of seven and a half hours a day. Dr Sigman linked the 2007 UN report that British children are the unhappiest and unhealthiest in the developed world to the statistic that Britons read the least and watch the most TV of any nation in Europe.

Health risks for children if too much time is spent in front of a screen

- Obesity – the result of too little exercise.
- Sleep disorders – over-stimulating the senses causes sleeplessness.
- Poor concentration – the development of brain cells governing attention span is impaired.
- Difficulty in reading – a result of poor intellectual stimulation while young.
- Short-sightedness – staring at a screen can cause eye damage.
- Behavioural problems and autism – these can be linked to a lack of social interaction.
- Increased cholesterol – the result of an inactive childhood.
- Lowered immune system – through suppression of production of the key hormone melatonin.[6]

Limiting TV to a set amount of time each day for each family member, depending on their age, benefits not just each child, but family life. Children will be helped most if the parents also control how much they watch. As Dave Veerman writes in *Help! There's a teenager in my house*, 'This will lead to healthy discussion and decision making, and perhaps even to conversation and alternative family entertainment.'[7]

Content

Nicky When our children were young, we wanted to protect them from frightening images that could disturb their sleep. Images on screen are very powerful for a child. Even children's cartoons can be frightening, and it is worth watching some to see if you think they are suitable for your child's agegroup. Sometimes we got it wrong. We remember one of our children's reaction to watching a cartoon of Baba the elephant's mother dying, and we realised how deeply involved with the story he had become.

The films we let our children watch regularly, when they were young, were ones in which the heroes and villains were clearly distinguished and the heroes came off better, while the villains had their comeuppance. These simple storylines helped to develop their moral compass. Of course, as they got older, the stories had more subtly nuanced characters, showing the heroes as flawed and the villains with redeeming features. These simple storylines helped to develop their moral compass.

We were also aware that news programmes were often full of frightening and graphic images, and so, when our children were young, we only watched the news on TV after they were in bed.

Sila I have probably had as many discussions with our children about the effects on them of watching certain films and TV programmes as any other topic. Nicky and I wanted to protect them from scenes of violence or sex. So we generally followed the guidelines of the film censors and the 9 pm TV watershed as to what was suitable for their age. They regularly protested that all their friends were (apparently) allowed to watch almost anything.

I found I developed a mantra which went, 'You don't know it. You can't see it. But it affects you,' which they would parody back at me as soon as I started on what they considered my hobbyhorse!

We wanted to protect their subconscious minds and did not want them to become desensitised by seeing too much too soon. We were concerned that, if they regularly watched scenes of violence, each time they would be less shocked and need more violence to keep up the excitement. Similarly, with sex, what they saw they could not unsee, and the images could potentially spoil their own sexual relationships in years to come.

With other TV programmes, such as the soaps they enjoyed, we tried to watch them ourselves occasionally so as to know what was being said, particularly about relationships. Many of the storylines reflected short-term values and short-term relationships, but they led to some interesting discussions.

Ultimately we wanted to help our children become responsible and be able to regulate what they saw, either at home or at the cinema. Controlling what they watched in other people's houses, when they were visiting or staying overnight, was much more difficult. When they were younger, we would sometimes ring the other parents ahead of time to discuss what we allowed or did not allow and why. We also gave our children some lines that they could use if they did not want to watch something – such as, 'Films like that give me really bad dreams,' or, 'My parents would be really cross with me if they knew what we were watching.' Encouraging them to put the blame on us helped their street cred.

We have never allowed our children to have a TV or DVD player in their bedrooms. Despite their impassioned pleas of how beneficial their own TV would be for their entertainment and education, and despite the fact that loads of their school friends were allowed one (or so they said), we stood firm. Apart from encouraging separation from the rest of the family, it would also have made it much more difficult for us to control both the quantity and the content of what they saw.

Computers and the use of the Internet

Computers and the Internet are a mixed blessing. Few people doubt their huge potential benefit. But they also pose a serious question to us as parents. How do we teach our children to communicate safely online? The Internet can offer an escape from reality. With its easy accessibility, potential for anonymity, secrecy and lowering of inhibitions, it also offers a dangerous sense of intimacy with strangers.

Surfing for information, online relationships, computer games and using chat-rooms can all become obsessive and unhealthy. IAD (Internet Addiction Disorder) is now a recognised disease:

> A recent study at Stanford University School of Medicine in California found that more than one in eight Americans showed signs that they could be suffering from some form of Internet addiction.
>
> At China's first officially licensed clinic for Internet addiction at the Beijing Military Regional Central Hospital, children as young as twelve are being admitted. They had abandoned school because they were spending so much time using online games and virtual chat rooms. They arrived suffering from depression, nervousness, panic, fear, agitation, unwillingness to interact with others, sleep disorders, the shakes and numbness in their hands.[8]

So how do we help children to use computers and the Internet safely and constructively?

Computer games

With proper boundaries, the right computer games can provide a lot of good entertainment – although the educational benefits are generally limited. One father, with four children aged seven to fourteen, wrote:

> In our family, we have a rule that the children cannot play games on the computer during the week. At the weekend they can have an hour a day (either computer games or Playstation), provided they have completed their homework and music practice and done their chores etc. It is an earned privilege rather than an assumed right. For one

> boy who is a reluctant reader, we laid down that, if he read a book for an hour, he earned an hour of computer games; our daughter got the same reward if she practised her music for one hour. We found that this was a useful incentive.

When our own three sons clubbed together and bought themselves a Playstation, we restricted both the type of game and the time they played on it. Anything with too much violence or a hint of the occult we did not allow. We also encouraged games where two of them could compete, such as playing golf, snowboarding or racing cars, as this included interacting with each other rather than just with a screen.

Inappropriate content

Inappropriate content, including pornography, is easily found through a search engine. Sometimes it is unsolicited, such as when a pornographic advert appears on a page. Generally the embarrassment of being caught is one of the best deterrents to viewing it deliberately. One family decided, 'We make sure we have the computer in a public place. We definitely don't allow computers in the bedrooms.'

Parents need to be able to check what the computer is being used for. This has become more difficult with wireless broadband, laptops and sophisticated mobile phones with Internet access. But it has become even more important. We need to be able to talk to our children about our concerns and explain how and why we are monitoring their computer usage. We also need to set up effective filters, not least on laptops.

Ways of controlling and monitoring computer content

- Content filters should be on (eg, *Google Safesearch* settings). This stops the computer receiving anything with explicit sexual references.
- Use an ISP (Internet Service Provider), which filters and classifies content and allows parents to set controls. It explains how to block access to inappropriate sites.
- Monitor browsing history and temporary Internet files, in order to see what sites children have been visiting. (For teenagers, this should only be done after discussion as otherwise this could undermine trust.)
- Check the recycle bins. A sure sign that something may be up is if the recycle bin is empty, and the browsing history and temporary files have been deleted. This cannot be done accidentally.
- If viewing inappropriate sites has become a problem, install a programme like *Covenant Eyes*, which sends you a monthly list of all the websites visited on that computer. Tell your children it is in place. It will help them to be accountable to you.
- Have spam files automatically deleted so they cannot even see unsolicited mail.

Mobile phones

As increasing numbers of mobile phones can access the Internet, many children today succumb to the temptation of downloading pornography. If they need a mobile phone, our advice would be to find a basic model that does not even make this a possibility. You will probably meet with considerable resistance. But you will be helping to protect them from temptation and potential trouble. It will also be less attractive to potential thieves.

Peer to peer (P2P) file sharing

Current computer programmes such as *Limewire*, *Gnutella* and *Trustyfiles* allow users to link up directly to millions of other computers in a file sharing network. They can browse and download files from these other computers, while in return the files on their computer are also available to be accessed by all users.

These programmes are used mainly for breaching copyright on music, film or computer game downloads, but also for downloading inappropriate content (mostly pornography). There are absolutely no content filters that can be put in place and no history of what the user has downloaded. Our only advice is to check whether these programmes are loaded on your computer and to monitor media files (music and video) often.

Instant messaging

Instant messaging has rapidly become one of the preferred modes of communication for ten to fifteen-year-olds. Most parents do not want to discourage their children from communicating with their friends in this way. However, there can be a downside. One parent writes:

> One issue for us has been our children using Messenger while doing homework – decreasing the quality of their work and probably increasing the incidence of cheating. We are also concerned about the way children tend to take on a much bolder and more sexually expressive tone. They tend to be more flirtatious and more risky when they use this form of communication. They can start to present a different person to their real self and write things they would not say in person.
>
> For some, messaging becomes obsessive. It's almost as if our teenagers have gone out with

> their friends, without physically leaving the house. Our main control is time limits – they are not allowed to go on Messenger before 8 pm and not until they have done their homework; so they can only do thirty to sixty minutes a day max.
>
> In our family, we have also agreed with our teenagers that they can only use Messenger if the programme is set to record their message conversation. We have explained our concerns and reasons. We very rarely view the actual conversations, but using this facility allows us to set and monitor how long they spend online.

Often, messaging can include using webcams so that the messages are exchanged with a live image of the other person on the screen. This is another good reason for having the computer in a public space (and turning the webcam to the wall when not in use as it can be accessed externally).

Personal web space

Social networking sites such as *MySpace*, *Facebook* and *Bebo* are a combination of chatting, blogging and posting photos. They present a wonderful opportunity for children and teenagers to make contact and communicate with people around the globe. But the dangers are as real as the benefits. It can be very difficult for them to manage their personal web space. Friends of theirs may take photos using their mobiles and put them on *Facebook* or reveal private conversations in a message for others to read. Paedophiles and sexual predators also use sites like these to meet children whom they 'groom' to disclose personal information, so that they can then meet up with them and abuse them. According to one newspaper article, more than 50,000 sexual predators are online at any one time.[9] Children need to be warned and protected so that they do not inadvertently make themselves a target.

One newspaper article recommends, 'Cyberspace is full of sites that allow kids to chat with their friends, but they also open the door to strangers. Tell your child to add a "private" feature (usually free) to the home page to block out personal info. As a rule, kids should chat only with people they know.'[10]

One couple also placed these restrictions: 'We have decided to allow our children to have personal webpages, but our rule is that we are able to look at their webspace. They need to put content, photos and language on it that they are not embarrassed for us as parents to view and that are appropriate to their age. We have also emphasised the importance of not giving away addresses and postcodes or other personal information like phone numbers.'

Apart from the safety aspect, our children should know that whatever they put on the net stays as a record, and that potential employers often check their webspace before offering them a job, even though in some countries this is illegal.

Gambling

With its easy accessibility online, widespread advertising and addictive draw, gambling is becoming an increasing problem amongst children and teenagers. In order to draw people in, some sites allow newcomers to choose between 'playing for money' and 'playing for fun'. When playing for fun, it is easy to win a lot (as the odds are biased towards the player), making them think they are good at it and encouraging them to play for money. Some casino and racing sites also offer a free first bet to get the dabbler started.

The *International Gaming Research Unit* suggests that three and a half per cent of eleven to fifteen-year-olds in the UK have a gambling problem. Some teenagers have become addicted to using Internet auction sites such as *eBay*. Schools are discovering that pupils have been online all night and are coming into classes exhausted. To feed these addictive habits, many of them need to get hold of considerable amounts of money – either their own or from a non-legitimate source – while children who have money to spare are more open to temptation to gamble or place bids.

As parents, we should talk to our children about the dangers. Gamblers may be 'in credit' occasionally, but even the best of them end up losing money – often more than they actually possess. We advise seeking professional help if you think your child may already be hooked.

Internet safety

- Be involved – discuss and share your concerns. Let your children tell you what they feel about computer use.
- Be informed – keep up-to-date through websites such as blogsafety.com that advise on safe social networking.
- Be consistent – as parents, agree the rules first.
- Be adaptable – the goalposts in this area are moving very quickly.
- Be computer literate – learn at least the basics for monitoring computer usage if you don't already know.
- Be discreet – do not read what they write privately to friends unless you have cause for concern.

Conclusion

The world is changing fast. We can easily feel bewildered, and even intimidated, because our children know more than we do. But our children still need our guidance. They may pick up with great speed how to navigate the latest computer program or work the latest gadget. But that does not mean they necessarily have the maturity to use them wisely or within proper limits.

Talking with them about handling money, TV usage and Internet safety helps us engage with their world. We can acknowledge our own areas of ignorance, when appropriate, and allow them to teach us – perhaps watching their favourite soap with them or listening to them explain why they enjoy a social networking website. This helps us work out what boundaries to set for their welfare.

Our aim, as with all the other topics in this section of the book, is to help them develop self-control, so that they learn to monitor their own usage. And the very process of tackling these subjects with them can help to build a relationship of trust between us.

Pause and consider

- Are there any signs of your children being out of control with money, TV, and/or the Internet?
- What values about money and possessions do you want to pass on to your children? How can you pass these on?
- How could you help your children to take responsibility with money?
- Is the TV a positive or negative influence in your family life? If negative, how could you change that?
- What action could you take to monitor Internet use?
- Are there any more filters you need to add to your computer at home?

Section 5

Passing on our beliefs and values

Chapter 19

Establishing a family identity

Whenever it's someone's birthday in our family and we sing 'Happy Birthday', the birthday person always stands on a chair and conducts us all.

Heather, aged 14

When driving to my nan's, we have to go through this tunnel. Every time we drive through it, my dad has to beep the horn once for every family member in the car or for all the family members who aren't in the car. I don't know when or how it started, but we do it every journey now.

Jen, aged 15

We don't have any traditions, but it would be really nice to have some because they bring people together and they sound fun too.

Jamie, aged 13

The benefit of traditions

Traditions give our children a sense of belonging within our family. Traditions can be great fun as well as building stability and rhythm. Our traditions might be having different 'house rules' for *Monopoly* from everybody else; always having egg on toast with bacon and baked beans for Sunday night supper; each year getting up at 4 am to go away on our summer holiday; having a competition in the car to be the first to spot the sea; Dad tossing pancakes and hitting the ceiling on Shrove Tuesday; going for our walk on Sunday afternoon; eating twelve grapes, one for each chime of the bell at midnight, on New Year's Eve and so on. Families unite around traditions. Some may last for years and years – others will die out as the children grow up.

Christmas and other religious festivals are occasions when traditions flourish. We know a family who keep a special evening around Christmas to get together to watch the same film they have watched every year for the last twenty years. The film is not a classic, but for them it ushers in the Christmas season with all its associated feelings. Each year they have the same food and drink, and they still laugh and cry at the same scenes that they now know by heart. Or it may be birthday traditions that are most valued. In one family with six children, they have always had birthday breakfasts in their parents' bed – all eight of them – with presents and the birthday child's favourite food and drink.

Traditions can be especially important for those parenting on their own. A friend of ours wrote, 'As a single parent, when my children were still deeply unsettled by the break up of my marriage, reinforcing traditions was a saving grace. Even when things got really tough, the children looked forward to birthdays, Christmas, holiday places that never changed, picnics in the rain, bedtime stories and so on.' When she then married a man with three children from his former marriage, the challenge was to combine two different sets of (sometimes conflicting) traditions. Dropping any of them met with considerable resistance from the children in whose home they had been established. But knowing how important routines were for their new family, the parents made compromises, let some go and made a point of establishing some new ones.

While the majority of family traditions will be enjoyed by children, as the sociologist and author Tony Campolo writes, 'Participants do not have to *like* a given routine for that routine to have a positive psychological effect upon them.'[1]

We remember hearing the Chief Rabbi in the UK, Jonathan Sachs, reporting on a survey amongst Jewish children who were asked what their favourite and least favourite times in the week were. For least favourite, many had answered the Sabbath customs they had to observe (not being allowed to watch TV, having to sit for longer at the table on Friday evenings and so on). For their most favourite, many of the same children put Friday evenings. When asked why, they said it was the time in the week when they knew they would be together as a family. It was not what they would have chosen to do on a Friday evening, but it was what they ended up enjoying the most.

Sila As a child growing up in the Scottish countryside, some of my family's routines I liked, others I definitely did not. One of the ones I grumbled about most was going for a walk after lunch on Sunday afternoons, often in the pouring rain and normally up the near vertical hill right behind our house. I would have much preferred to stay in and watch TV. Now, looking back, I can see how those walks were regular 'family time' all together. And I suppose it caused me to grow up believing that a bit of bad weather doesn't have to stop you being outdoors.

We have brought up our own children in the city, so the traditions they will remember will be more urban: the Saturday morning expedition to the local shop to buy milk and pain au chocolat for breakfast; the excitement of going to the noisy, overcrowded swimming pool on Saturday afternoon; the Sunday afternoon games of football in the park with another family (with the dads confined to goal, initially because they were too big to play midfield and latterly because they were too slow) and the annual Christmas treat of going to a pantomime with their grandparents.

Of course, too much routine can adversely affect family life, particularly if it prevents spontaneity and creativity. One man associated family meals as he was growing up with his father grilling him every evening about his school work, and he came to dread the next mealtime.

However, amidst all the relentless demands and the unpredictable storms of life, healthy traditions and rituals give children a sense of continuity and security. Through keeping them, children remember more of the good times in their upbringing than the bad. And they are one of the main ways that we pass on values and beliefs to the next generation. Tony Campolo asserts:

> Those families that have a great deal of ritual are usually the ones that are the most solid and secure. They seem better able to impart to their children the values and truths which they believe to be of ultimate significance … Rituals are good for families, and instituting rituals makes family life more fun for everyone.[2]

Establishing family traditions

The fun element of building traditions is that we can use them to create our own unique style of family life. It is worth each of us thinking how the traditions and rituals in our own childhood affected us.

Think through the traditions and rituals in your own family as you grew up connected with:

Birthdays	Christmas	Bedtime
Summer holidays	School holidays	Other festivals
Mealtimes	Family games	Weekends
'Family time'	Doing chores	Seeing cousins

If you are parenting as a couple, discuss together which ones you remember from your upbringing and decide which ones you would like to perpetuate with your children. Are there new ones you would like to initiate?

Traditions can continue through many generations, and what we do now may well be taken on by our children's families.

Sila Bathtime games had been a feature of my childhood, so it became a natural thing to pass them on. One ritual I remember as a child was when my mother covered her hands with soap and blew huge bubbles through them. There would be lots of 'oohs' and 'aahs' as we watched them float up towards the ceiling, sometimes popping on the way, sometimes making it all the way up accompanied by our excited cheering.

I found myself repeating this same game with our own children. Many a time I would be hurrying to get bathtime over and done with, and one of them would say, 'Blow a bubble, Mummy, pleeeeeeeease!' not only for the sheer fun of seeing the bubbles, but also to gain a bit longer in the bath.

Annual traditions

Annual rituals within a family help to give shape to the year, highlighting special events and marking the different seasons.

Nicky I grew up in the English countryside where my parents had created a small farm out of the few acres around the house. This provided many rituals, some of which involved the whole family and which undoubtedly drew us together.

One annual tradition was 'dressing' a hundred turkeys in the week leading up to Christmas. Each member of the family had a different job, from drawing out the innards to sewing up the wings, depending on our age and strength. Then the turkeys had to be delivered around the local town. Some years they were bigger than usual, and my parents told stories of how husbands were required to sit on them to make the overweight bird fit into an oven.

With the hard work and the customary racing against the clock, tempers inevitably got frayed. On more than one Christmas Eve my parents vowed they would never breed turkeys again, but we kept it up for ten years. It contributed to a rich store of family memories that are still often recounted when we get together.

Sila In my family, every Easter we would paint hard-boiled eggs with bright patterns and have races rolling them down a grassy bank. And every summer for our week's holiday we went to the same beach in Scotland. We stayed in the same small hotel, jumped on the same sand dunes, paddled in the same pools, drank the same fizzy lemonade and played the same games. The very familiarity year by year created huge amounts of anticipation for weeks beforehand, and lots of happy memories that have stayed with me ever since.

One man told us about his annual family Christmas gathering: 'Each year all the cousins would come together for a day of eating, games, charades, staying up too late – and we loved it. It gave us all a sense of belonging to a wider family. We still do it. At the last count there were fifty-two of us.'

Night time traditions

The easiest rituals to create, and often the most beneficial of all, are around a child's bedtime. The bedtime routine can easily seem to busy parents, tired at the end of the day, to be purely functional – we are simply trying to settle our children down for sleep as quickly as possible. But, for children, they can give a deep sense of comfort and security. A five-year-old we know, tucked up in bed, said to her mother quite spontaneously one evening, 'I love you more than sweeties and chocolates!' Since then they have said it to each other every night.

With Josh, our youngest child, a longer sequence developed. It was a dialogue, repeated every night with whoever was putting him to bed. Its final form was:

> 'Night-night.'
> 'Sleep tight.'
> 'Sleep well.'
> 'I love you.'
> 'See you in the morning.'
> 'Have fun.'
> 'Goodbye.'
> 'I'm waving.'
> 'Have a nice supper.'
> 'I agree.'

The last line was added when he learned at Sunday School that 'Amen' means everyone is agreeing with the prayer. With a child's mastery of delaying tactics at bedtime, this jingle had to be said three times, word perfect, getting faster each time – before we could turn the light off and leave.

Such rituals at night are very powerful. Tony Campolo writes about these bedtime traditions:

> A child may have had a shattering day. He or she may have been scolded by a teacher, suffered

> unbelievable humiliation at the hands of some bully, or been rejected by a friend. Who can tell what really goes on at school? Asking a child what happened at school on a given day will usually elicit the answer, 'Nothing.' And yet that child may have been wounded emotionally.
>
> The good thing about ritual is that it can put a child's shattered world back together again. A ritual before the lights are turned out can convince a child that the world is still in order and that everything is OK.[3]

Friends of ours sometimes ask each of their children at bed time to say their 'best thing' and their 'worst thing' about their day. This helps to draw out the child's feelings, positive and negative. A tradition like this of talking last thing at night may continue for teenagers even after they have become seemingly independent. Questions or concerns will often come to the surface just as we are about to say, 'Good night,' and the conversation that follows can bring them a greater sense of security and peace.

Reading stories

Story time was another popular tradition in our family. It was an opportunity to be close to our children. Our habit was to read stories on our bed, which was a Japanese futon on the floor so there was no danger of the younger ones falling off and getting hurt. We would snuggle up with pillows and duvets. If we were busy later in the evening, bath time was shorter or we read less. But we decided it was important to try to stick to the routine of a story each night.

On those evenings when chaos reigned, when no one wanted to settle down and there was endless pushing, fighting and crying, we discovered that treating story time as a privilege gave us powerful leverage. The threat of, 'There will be no story if you don't quieten down and stop messing about,' meant they risked missing out on something they really enjoyed. We had to be careful not to use this threat too often and to be prepared to carry it through when necessary.

Another story-telling tradition when the children were smaller took place on our summer holiday. The weather was sometimes cool enough in the evenings to warrant a fire. With the children in their pyjamas, we would sit round it and they would plead for another chapter in order to stay up longer. This family time created powerful memories for them and often led to fascinating discussions all together.

Family traditions

We include here a list we compiled by children. Some are unique to their family. Others will be common to many families. But they are all significant.

Family traditions

- 'Opening our stockings at Christmas all in one bed'
- 'Feeding the chickens'
- 'Eating as much ice cream as we liked on the last day of our holiday'
- 'Fancy dress for Christmas supper'
- 'Celebrating each other's achievements'

⇨

- 'Playing lots of games'
- 'Bedtime stories'
- 'Making Sunday lunch a special occasion'
- 'Washing up together'
- 'Driving to Scotland on Christmas Day and having smoked salmon sandwiches in the car'
- 'Games at Sunday lunch'
- 'Taking family videos on holiday and reliving them months later'
- 'Always making birthdays a priority, usually involving themed parties'
- 'Getting into our parents' bed on Saturday mornings with my brothers and sisters'
- 'Having a fondue on the last day of the school holidays'

Retaining flexibility with traditions

Family life must be allowed to evolve and traditions should serve us, not vice versa. Many of us will feel a sense of nostalgia for rituals that have been dropped. This is part of moving on and allowing children to grow up. But some traditions will be appropriate for every age group and will continue.

Sila There is one game I grew up with that my family has never tired of playing. It is, as far as I know, unique to our family. It's called 'cards in the hat'. It originated in my father's family and involves a top hat, belonging originally to my grandfather, that can be flattened. The hat is extended and is placed about twelve feet away from a low stool – young children with shorter arms are allowed closer. Each person is required to sit on the stool and then tries to throw fifteen playing cards one at a time into the hat, which involves a certain technique and gives no advantages to youth.

One of my most vivid and lovely memories of my father the year before he died is him playing 'cards in the hat' at his eightieth birthday party. He had to be lowered down onto the stool by two grandsons and then lifted up again at the end of what turned out to be the winning hand – twelve out of fifteen cards landed in the hat. His older sister, aged eighty-two, was also present and she needed no lowering onto or lifting up from the stool! This is one tradition that I'm convinced will be continued by whoever inherits the hat for generations to come.

Conclusion

Traditions not only provide fun. They also pass on important values. Some homes maintain a tradition of offering hospitality – regularly inviting people who would otherwise be on their own to Sunday lunch; having people to stay, even if that involves a mattress on the floor; putting together a hamper at Christmas for a family who would otherwise have nothing special to eat; sending a box of toys to children in a developing country. Traditions like these will pass on the value we attach to showing kindness to others and sharing what we have.

Our own weekly tradition of going to church as a family has been very important in passing on our most fundamental beliefs and values to our children.

It is worthwhile thinking about the traditions that we are establishing. Does a routine of several hours of television each evening really have a good effect on our family? On the other hand, watching a favourite programme or a DVD together as a family can turn it into a special event.

Writing down a list of our daily, weekly and annual traditions will help us to identify the positive from the negative. We can then continue the ones that build up our family life and cut out those that demean or isolate one or more members of the family. Positive routines and traditions create powerful and enduring memories for our children. They reflect our own family's values and define who we are, where we belong, and what distinguishes us from other families.

Pause and consider

- What daily, weekly and annual traditions contribute to giving your family its own identity?
- Are there any traditions you should drop as they are unhelpful?
- Are there any new ones you would like to introduce?
- Which ones do your family enjoy most?

Chapter 20

Dealing with the big questions

Saturday morning: we're curled up on the sofa and Louis, 2¾, is crestfallen. 'Where's Bambi's mother?' he asks, rather anxiously. One minute he watched entranced as Bambi and his mother glided across the icy meadow and then – kerbang – she disappeared, dispatched by the hunter's bullet. Then we see Bambi's tiny, gawky frame engulfed in a blizzard, the ultimate image of infant abandonment. Not an easy scene for any young child to assimilate. 'When is she coming back?' he asks, turning to me. Oh dear, where to begin? We've just finished our Coco Pops; isn't it a little too early for a lesson on the fleeting nature of life? Cheers Disney.[1]

Emma Cook
Journalist

Children's questions are often shockingly direct. Two days after the funeral in the middle of tea, they ask, 'Where's Granny now?' Or suddenly out of the blue, 'Do you hate anybody?' Or as we are tucking them into bed, 'Why can't I see God?' Or as they start to think about the differences between girls and boys, 'Can I wear a skirt please?' (as Herbie, aged four, said to his mother recently).

They require real answers, not a quick brush-off. Telling them that the family dog is 'asleep', when in reality he has died, merely creates problems and distrust for the future. Children need truthful answers that will help them to build a framework of beliefs and values to guide them throughout their lives. As parents we can only answer their questions and teach them how to make wise choices if we have a framework for our own lives.

The big questions usually come when we least expect them. We're tired, distracted, late for school and suddenly our child wants to know why we get old.

Our own convictions come from a Christian worldview. Yours may be different to ours. But it is important for all parents to work out what they believe as inevitably their parenting will be affected by their beliefs. Our faith has shaped our outlook and our family. We have found the teachings of the Bible to be a strong and practical foundation upon which to build our family life.

Some key questions

- What's the point of life?
- Do I matter?
- Why do so many bad things happen to people?
- If I mess up, is there forgiveness?
- What happens when we die?
- Why do some people believe in God and others do not?
- Why are some people starving while others have more than they need?

In this chapter we will look at how these truths have informed our long-term aims in parenting and what we have wanted to pass on to our children.

Giving a framework for life

As well as answering their questions, our children need a structure for building an understanding of the world in which they live. There are four powerful themes in the Bible which not only answer fundamental and important questions about life, but also, when applied to daily living, make our home an encouraging and healthy environment for our children.

1. Creation

This first theme, the origin of human life, addresses two closely related questions: 'What's the point of life?' and 'Do I matter?' The Christian answer to the first question is that life is ultimately about our relationships. Each individual has been made for a purpose: to live in a loving relationship with God and with others for ever. This perspective gives our children (and us) a healthy view of life. Relationships are what truly matter – not where we live, not which school we go to, not how many exams we pass and not whether we are the cleverest, sportiest, or best looking person among our peers.

The priority of relationships means that people are more important than possessions, loyalty of greater value than success, and love more enduring than money. A poignant illustration of this was the last phone calls made by people in the Twin Towers as the 9/11 tragedy unfolded, telling family members how much they loved them.

One of the UK's most successful designers, Sir Paul Smith, has built up a global multi-million pound fashion empire, yet remains beguilingly down-to-earth. He said in a recent interview:

> One thing I hope to do is to touch people, to just be a nice bloke. I've got 600 people working for me and I know nearly all of them by name; people get a very positive feeling from that. Having time for people, being calm and seeing other people's point of view is vital for long-term relationships with friends, staff or loved ones … So many people are obsessed with money and greed but it doesn't bring happiness.[2]

The answer to the second question, 'Do I matter?' is fundamental to our understanding of ourselves. The knowledge that each of us is a special part of God's creation, made in his image, with a unique combination of gifts and personality, assures children that their life has value, not for what they contribute or achieve, but for who they are. This is how God sees each child, and our role as parents is to reflect God's love, so that we live out the message, 'I love you, not for what you do, but for who you are.'

Competition is an inevitable part of the society in which we live. We cannot, nor should we, try to save children from it. Rather, our aim is to equip them to be good winners and good losers, to work or play as part of a team and to live confidently in a competitive society without constantly comparing themselves to others.

However, as parents it is easy to be competitive for our children. Many parents will identify with the mother of a six-year-old who admitted that, when her child brings a friend home from school for tea, she finds herself stealing a glance into the friend's folder to see what reading book she is on. We want our children to do better than others, to be the best, to come top of everything. We become fearful or even frenzied that we will fail to get our children into top league schools or they will not get into a team, or be chosen for the lead role in the school play.

Nicky I remember one of our children aged eleven telling me proudly that he had got 76% in a maths test. To my shame, I wanted to ask, 'Where did you come?' hoping he was in the top group or even better had beaten everyone else by a wide margin. But it was clear he wasn't thinking in those terms and I realised I had to resist enquiring.

For Robert, a former university tutor, it was through his own experience of God's unconditional love that his relationship with his daughters started to change:

> Prior to doing an Alpha course[3], my relationship with our two wonderful daughters (who are 19 and 17) was slipping south. My rude awakening occurred when our second daughter received her 'AS' results. Not only did I feel proud, I felt justifiably proud. That was until she stated, with much emotion, that I only loved her when she did well. The sails, as you can imagine, deflated instantaneously. I knew there was a deep problem but I did not have the tools to comprehend or to deal with the challenge. At the back of my mind was the feeling, 'Well, after all, the girls are doing well, aren't they?'
>
> We arrived at Alpha with me as one of the world's great sceptics. On week three, Nicky Gumbel, the leader of the course, spoke of how proud he is of his children. Nicky recalled a discussion with his daughter following the disappointing results of a French test, in which he said, 'Darling, I love you because I love you.' (He went on to say, 'That is how God loves each one of us.') That cracked, indeed it destroyed, my armour.
>
> We returned home and I said those very words, 'I love you because I love you,' to our daughters. In fact, I started to live those words. My wife, Margaret, told me later that our eldest hugged her and cried that her dad had started to change for the better.

We will damage our children if they believe that they must earn our love. If we set impossibly high standards for our children, they may doubt that they will ever be good enough and may give up trying. And those who cannot remember their parents saying to them, 'I love you and I'm proud of you,' will often struggle to accept God's unconditional love.

The biblical view is that every individual has intrinsic value through being created by God, and that we all have a unique opportunity to be a force for good on those around us, including helping those less able or less fortunate.

One way we have tried to help our own children gain this sense of a God-given purpose to their lives is by telling them that they have a choice: they can either be an influence for good on the people around them, or they can allow themselves to be moulded by others and simply follow the crowd.

2. Sin and evil

The second biblical theme – the inherently flawed nature of human beings – answers the question, 'Where did it all go wrong?' The Bible traces the origin of war, injustice and pain right back to a primeval choice by humans to live for themselves rather than in a relationship with God. This is the principal point of the story of 'the Fall' in Genesis. The human race throughout history has shown this same inclination towards self-sufficiency rather than dependence on God. We are all inclined to be selfish – to focus first and foremost on our own needs, our own opinions and our own desires rather than those of others. And it is part of our fallen nature to rebel against authority if it prevents us from doing what we want.

Every child is born with this bias towards self-centredness.

Ask any parent! Sometimes to their dismay they see their innocent little babies, with their angelic smiles, displaying an alarming determination to get their own way. Children must be taught to act unselfishly. A newspaper article attributed the increasing incidents of violence by teenagers in the 1980s to the legacy of over-permissive parenting. According to the article, parents have for too long followed the advice of the late Dr Benjamin Spock. Writing in the 1950s and 1960s, Spock stated, 'Thou shalt not thwart a child,' to which the journalist added poignantly, 'until Spock recanted later – too late for some'.

The Old Testament book of Proverbs underlines this need to teach children right from wrong: 'Train children in the way they should go, and when they are old they will not turn from it.'[4] Training involves ensuring there are consequences for their behaviour from a young age – pleasant consequences for good behaviour, unpleasant for bad. Unless they have clear guidance, children grow up without a moral compass and without caring about the consequences of their actions on others.

Children themselves feel the need for boundaries and they will push against them to discover where they lie and how firm they are. When we put appropriate restrictions on our children's behaviour, we contribute to their sense of security. As we wrote in Chapter 13, with teenagers there needs to be more discussion, clear explanations and sensible negotiations. But they still want and need boundaries. One fifteen-year-old boy expressed this when he said to us, 'My mum lets me do what I want, go to any party I like, stay out until any time. I wish she would say "no" sometimes.'

Every child needs to be taught lovingly, but firmly, that they are not the centre of the universe; that they cannot be a law unto themselves and that antisocial behaviour will ultimately be detrimental to themselves as well as to others. Understanding that every human being has a flawed nature enables us to take a more objective and realistic view of our children. In addition, it sets us free from false expectations in our parenting. Despite our very best efforts, we will never turn out perfect children. Not even close.

Sooner or later children will discover that life is not fair for themselves or others. They are likely to ask, 'Why did God allow this person to suffer or that home to be burgled or that person to die in a car crash?' Of course there is no simple answer as to why one person may have suffered more than another, but an understanding of the Fall will help them not to expect the world to be perfect or fair.

3. Redemption

The third biblical theme answers the question, 'Is God on our side?' When we have messed up, is there forgiveness? Is there a way back? Is there hope for our future?

The story of the Bible answers with a resounding 'yes'. God

offers us a new start through the cross, which lies at the heart of the Christian faith and is the symbol and instrument of God's mercy. On the cross, God took upon himself all the consequences of our selfishness so that we might be forgiven and restored into relationship with him. Although none of us deserves it, his love and forgiveness are offered freely to us all. Christian relationships centre around experiencing God's grace towards us – his love, forgiveness, encouragement, patience and faithfulness – and then seeking to show these same qualities to each other. As Jesus said to his disciples at the Last Supper, having just washed their feet, 'Love one another as I have loved you.'[5] This is the greatest kind of love – loving sacrificially – and it sets us and our children free from only showing love to and helping those whom we think deserve it or have done something for us.

We have friends who practised this kind of unconditional love towards their son when he was arrested for dealing drugs. They stood by him in the midst of his shame, keeping him going through the long and anxious months as he waited for his case to come to court, and then helping him to get established in a new career. We know another couple who, having always encouraged their children to keep sex for marriage, welcomed their teenage daughter back into their home when she became pregnant by a boyfriend who was not ready for the responsibility of parenthood. Their open-hearted generosity played an important role in the early stages of their grandchild's life.

Both those couples were acting consistently. These were the values they had lived by, even before their children were born. Practising this theme of 'redemption' in a home means creating an atmosphere where apology and forgiveness are a regular feature of life. Children can learn to say sorry and experience the reality of forgiveness at a very young age.

Without this, they can easily lose hope. And, as well as being forgiven, they learn to forgive others – including their parents, when we get it wrong. They discover that they can end up closer to the very people they fell out with as a result of this process of restoration.

4. The future

The fourth biblical theme answers the questions, 'What happens after we die?' and, 'Is there any hope for the future?' How do we enable our children, as they grow up, to look beyond the next birthday, the next exam, the next pay cheque, the next promotion – in a word, to have a long view of life?

Most topics of conversation are now discussed openly and freely. But one subject remains largely off limits – the question of death and what happens afterwards. Most people find it uncomfortable, or even frightening, to face these questions themselves. Many parents therefore avoid raising them. Children, however, are curious about death and may talk about it at inconvenient moments. A four-year-old suddenly asked his mother recently, 'If I fell down and died, would you get a new me?'

Peter Norman, an educational psychologist and bereavement counsellor, advises:

> Children can cope with bad news much better if parents are completely honest from the outset – and this covers the spectrum from Snow White to natural disasters in the news or even suicide.

> Honesty is about building trust with a child.
>
> Even with murder and suicide, you can't protect the child from what's happened. They will find out somehow, eventually. Now that we live in a sanitised society, we feel that children can't face these things. They can cope with more than we think. The danger is that if you don't tell children the truth, if they feel they're being shielded, it can undermine their confidence in coping with distressing events in the future.[6]

Questions about death and dying can often be addressed most easily through reading a book together, appropriate to our child's age. We may also have to tell them that there are some questions such as, 'Will my goldfish be in heaven?' to which we do not know the answer.

God's plan for us and for our children is to spend our lives now and for eternity becoming more and more like him and growing in our experience of his love and goodness. Parents with a toddler who has high decibel tantrums, or a teenager whose sole means of communication is grunts and sighs, will need eyes of faith to imagine this.

Christianity is fundamentally a message of hope, enabling us to look forward to the future with confidence. We know that Jesus Christ has conquered death for us, and that, despite the failings of humanity, our flawed and broken world will be put together again by God, its creator. Knowing God's love and forgiveness through a relationship with Christ, we have nothing to fear – either now or in the future.

Nicky I was reading a bedtime story from a children's Bible to Kirsty when she was six years old. She suddenly asked me, 'Daddy, what will heaven be like?'

Wanting to give her a proper sense of excitement, I tried to describe how wonderful it will be. I told her that there will be more and more good things to discover, that she will meet Jesus face to face, that he will probably give her a great big hug and they will talk about all the different parts of her life here on earth. As I talked, Kirsty's eyes grew wider and wider. When I had finished she exclaimed, 'Oh Daddy, I can't wait to die!'

I wasn't sure that this was healthy in a six-year-old and wondered if I had gone somewhat over the top. While I was still considering how to correct any imbalance, she added, 'I know! It's really good to be alive and then even better when you die.'

I doubt whether she remembers the incident, but I have never forgotten her words. That is the Christian perspective we hope that all our children will have throughout their lives.

Sometimes our child's question may be more personal and immediate. One mother, whose three-year-old son had been diagnosed with leukaemia, asked her, 'Am I going to die?' It took her breath away. She had not rehearsed how she would answer that one. She had a neighbour who she knew would be wise about the best thing to say. Her neighbour came round and answered the boy's question, 'Yes, we're all going to die. I'm going to die and you're going to die; we just don't know when that will be. But God knows.' That little boy is now a healthy twenty-eight-year-old with a deep confidence in God's care.

Keeping an open mind

Parents who hold on to this big picture are more likely to keep a close relationship with a child by not insisting on rigid rules that are not central to their faith. Allowing our children to question, and even disagree with our beliefs, will encourage open and healthy debate within our home.

This becomes especially important for teenagers. We might, for example, be against tattoos, but we have to debate with our teenager, 'Are they inherently wrong?' or just not a part of our own background or culture.

Keeping an open mind, within a framework of belief, helps children to learn tolerance and to relate to those who hold different views.

Conclusion

When applied to daily family life, the four themes in this chapter will help us to build a home founded on unconditional love, appropriate boundaries, forgiveness and a sense of hope. These in turn create a healthy and safe environment in which children can be comfortable in their own skin and become emotionally mature. They create in children an innate sense both of their own self-worth – that they are loved for who they are – and of the value of every other human being. Such children are likely to develop into outward-looking adults who respect others and do not take themselves too seriously.

Practising these principles as parents will help us neither to abandon our children to the fashionable views of the current culture, nor force them into a straightjacket of legalism. They guard us against an over-intensity that would tend to put our children off. If we pass on our beliefs in an atmosphere of love and encouragement, most children will want to know the source of their parents' views, and, more likely than not, will end up making our fundamental beliefs and values their own.

Pause and consider

- Could you list your top five values?
- What are you doing to pass your values and beliefs on to your children?
- What else could you do?
- Are there 'big questions' your children are asking that you need to think through for yourself?
- Are you and your partner approachable and open to their questions?

Chapter 21

Building a child's spiritual life

I think God is really useful for when you've got something that you can't talk to anyone else about.

Michael, aged 7

My parents saw when I needed to make my own choice about faith. They never lectured me or enforced their faith on me.

Tamara, aged 19

Mum and Dad were living out their faith as I grew up, so I took it for granted that God existed.

Julia, aged 23

I wish I had known what my parents believed in.

Bill, aged 43

Parents, do not exasperate your children; instead bring them up in the training and instruction of the Lord.[1]

St Paul

As parents we play a fundamental part in building the spiritual lives of our children. None of us remains neutral, whether or not the spiritual side of life is important to us. All of us provide a model through what we say or don't say, do or don't do.

Personally, we have wanted to show our own children that the Christian faith affects every part of our lives, and is just as relevant for ourselves as for them. We took the view that only as they saw the 'real thing' being lived out around them, as opposed to an inaccurate caricature, would they be able to make an authentic choice for themselves.

Passing on beliefs and values

We cannot guarantee our children's future beliefs or lifestyle. But certain things we do can affect the whole direction of their lives. You may not be parenting from the same belief system that we have. The following principles are ones we have tried to put into practice.

Our home environment

Make it loving

> *Our faith has been the fundamental thing that we have tried to share with our children. We have tried to pass on the values of being kind, thoughtful, caring, loving each other, them being honest with each other and us being honest with them. They have appreciated that we haven't tried to set ourselves up as perfect, but we have tried to do the best we can and to be real about our failures.*
>
> **Michael & Mary-Claire**

> *Several years ago we sat down and thought about what we wanted to pass on to our children, and the thing that we came up with was that they might be 'God-confident'. We also want them to be self-confident and have that sense of trusting themselves as well as trusting others.*
>
> **Adam & Heather**

Our faith is more easily caught than taught. It is what our children see that will impact them most. The relationship *between* us as husband and wife, or between us and any other adult, says a huge amount to children about the validity and attractiveness of our beliefs.

However many times we pray, say grace, read the Bible and take them to church, if we, who claim to be Christians, are unkind and disrespectful to each other, Christianity will not be up to much in our children's eyes.

Young children form their basic understanding of God's character from their parents. (This is hardly surprising. Initially we are, in their eyes, all-knowing, all-powerful and, if not ever-present, at least likely to turn up when they yell for us!)

Children thrive in an environment they enjoy – where they are free to be individuals and not made to conform; where there are boundaries but not legalism; where there is more thankfulness than complaining; where there is plenty of laughter and good-humoured teasing; where everyone listens to and learns from each other; where there is more encouragement than criticism; where there are apologies and forgiveness and many opportunities for fresh starts.

When children experience that kind of love from their parents, they flourish emotionally and are less likely to reject God's love.

Keep it light

> *The most helpful thing regarding faith was my parents letting me make my own decisions and giving me space to find God for myself – to discover, to validate my faith. They were always there as a reference point to fall back upon; they were always willing to guide me with questions I had.*
>
> **Jack, aged 22**

A healthy, happy home is one where children are not 'boxed in', where there is space for each of them to find their own faith in their own time and in their own way. If we have more than one child, it is important not to typecast them, perhaps by making out that one is more spiritual than another.

Children are like sponges. They absorb our attitudes and the ways we live out our beliefs and values. Children are turned off by any sort of spiritual control, intensity or heaviness.

They are attracted by a spirituality that brings a sense of freedom, love and security.

Examples of spiritual values to model

- Keeping a light hand on our possessions through sharing what we have and giving things away, because we know that life lived to the full does not depend on how much we possess.
- Treating all people, whatever their role in life, with kindness and consideration as we believe everyone has been made in the image of God and is loved by him.
- Forgiving others because we have experienced God's forgiveness ourselves.
- Seeking to trust God regarding the future, as the Bible tells us we can bring all our anxieties to him.

Reading the Bible

> *It's important to remind teenagers about being a Christian but also important not to nag them all the time saying, 'You must read your Bible every night' – it's harder than they think.*
>
> **Lottie, aged 16**

We do not own our children. Our role, and our privilege, is to have a few short years in which to train them for life and to model to them what we claim to believe. The Bible puts our parental responsibility like this, 'Love the Lord your God with all your heart and with all your soul and with all your strength. These commandments that I give you today are to be upon your hearts. Impress them on your children. Talk about them when you sit at home and when you walk along the road, when you lie down and when you get up.'[2]

A mother with an eight-year-old son, Jim, describes how she recently reached a new stage in talking with him about God:

This year, we decided to read together a new children's version of the Bible. The night we started, we read the Creation story and Jim looked rather troubled throughout. 'Do you really believe that?' he said. 'I mean, a talking snake, an apple … it sounds more like a kind of fairy tale to me. When you hear the scientists explain things, it just sounds so much more *likely*. This really makes me question the whole thing. In fact, that Creation story makes me doubt that God is real.'

I look at my watch – this is not going to be quick. I told him that I have asked similar questions. We then talked about what kind of literature Genesis is and the different kinds of truth contained in a poem and a bus timetable. We discussed the fact that Genesis is more about *who* and *why* rather than *how*, that science has an important place within a God-centred understanding of creation. That led on to a conversation about the likelihood of a God-less creation: could the world, with all the complex and delicately balanced conditions required to sustain life, really just be an accident with no designer behind it? And which was more likely? That *someone* created something out of nothing or that *nothing* created something out of nothing?

At the end, he seemed to feel satisfied, especially by the discovery that questions can exist alongside faith, and that it is all right for him to voice his doubts.

We may not always have the answers for our children and it is best to admit this, and to take time to think about the questions ourselves, to seek advice from others, to search the Internet or read a book. Then we can talk about the question with them on another occasion. This helps them to know we value their questions, and do not always have an easy answer.

Our nightly routine when the children were under ten included reading a short section from a children's Bible and then saying a prayer with each of them. What and how much we read depended on their ages.

There are many wonderful books of biblical stories retold for children in contemporary language that remain faithful to the original: parables re-told in contemporary language, biblical stories recounted through the eyes of a child or an animal, the Christmas and Easter stories as activity-style books, as well as an increasing number of children's Bibles.

Children learn more effectively about God's standards through the biblical stories than through lists of rules. Reading these stories together will occasionally result in conversations with our children that will affect their thinking and their choices in the future.

When our children were over ten, our daily pattern – until they each left school – was to try to read a verse or two from the Bible over breakfast and then say a short prayer for the day ahead. The whole procedure lasted about two minutes. Some days time did not permit even this much, and, when we did fit it in, it was hard to tell if they took in anything at all.

Nicky For quite a long time, each morning I would read one or two verses from the book of Proverbs. One morning, after we had had four days on the trot of warnings against adultery, Benj enquired whether I thought our neighbour's wife was currently the chief temptation for his eight-year-old younger brother! (At which point I realised he was listening after all and skipped on a bit the following day.)

Sila When our children became teenagers we gave them their own Bibles in a modern translation. (We chose the New International Version.) We never insisted they read it every day, but they knew that we did and from time to time we have talked of how important reading the Bible is to our relationship with God.

Prayer for our children

Both my parents never missed an opportunity to pray for us and with us.

Jim, aged 25

Over the years I have seen so many prayers for my children answered – small things, big things. When they have gone through tough times, it has been such a relief to pray for them and it has helped me not to worry.

Cynthia
Mother of four

The third main ingredient for passing on our faith is prayer. The prospect of modelling the Christian faith is daunting, but we are not alone – we are working with God in shaping our children's characters and values. He works with us and through us to fulfil his purposes for our children. At the end of the day nothing that we do for our children will be more important than the prayers we pray for them. We cannot start praying too soon. The meeting between Mary, the mother of Jesus, and Elizabeth her cousin, when John the Baptist 'leaps in her womb',[3] shows that even unborn children can respond spiritually. Equally it is never too late to start praying.

Our own practice has been to thank God each day for the gift of our children, whatever is going on in their lives and ours, and then to try to turn our deepest longings for each child into a prayer. We have discovered that, as we pray, we become more aware of what is most important for them now and in their future. Meanwhile, the very action of praying relieves us of some of our fears about our children's welfare and gives us a longer perspective when something has gone wrong. A couple we were talking to recently said to us, 'We can easily find ourselves spending ages discussing a situation we're worried about, such as whether our children are making friends at school. Often it's far better to stop talking and pray!'

To know that God ultimately cares more for our children than we do is both humbling and a relief. We can entrust them to him. Of course there are no guarantees of how they will turn out, but knowing that our heart's deepest desires are a dim reflection of God's desires helps us to worry less and pray more.

What to pray for

Nothing is too big a problem, or too small a detail, to bring to God in prayer. We can pray for our children's friendships, for their health, for their progress through school, for their safety, for their future marriage partner. (If you have a young child and this last topic seems a little early, consider that the majority of children will get married one day, and that their marriage partner may well have already been born. Our prayers could be helping to shape the character of that person.)

We can ask God to bring people across our children's paths who will influence them for good. We can pray for their response to God's love. We can pray for the formation of their character, and that they will increase in what the Bible describes as 'the fruit of the Spirit': 'love, joy, peace, patience, kindness, goodness, faithfulness, gentleness and self-control'.[4] We have found this list particularly helpful in praying for and with our children. Often we thank God for a quality one of them has displayed or, where we see a lack, we ask him to increase that attribute in them.

When to pray

Many different situations give an opportunity for prayer. We can pray on our own. We can pray with others – our husband, wife, relative or friend. We can pray when stuck in a traffic jam or en route to work. We can pray while washing up. We can pray when a child comes suddenly to mind – often we will find out that this has been at moments of potential danger or temptation, and the Spirit of God has prompted us to pray for their protection. A mother told us she found herself one afternoon feeling an urgency to pray for her daughter, Kate. Unbeknown to her, Kate had just been knocked off her bike and was in an ambulance.

We can pray to know God's desires and plans for our children.

Nicky On the day when we were due to hear whether our oldest son would be offered a place at a new school, I remember reading a verse from one of the psalms which said, 'The Lord will fulfil his purpose for me; your love, O Lord, endures for ever – do not abandon the work of your hands.'[5] The thought that God has plans, and a special purpose, for each child was both comforting and inspiring. Since then I have often prayed that God would fulfil *his* purpose for each of our children.

Praying for ourselves

Throughout our parenting we have also known the necessity of praying for ourselves. There is no more important job than parenting; and our own experience, like that of most parents, has been to feel very inadequate for the task. After twenty-nine years of bringing up children, we could not imagine doing it without the experience of God's love in our own lives, encouraging and directing us, and assuring us through the Bible that we can call upon him for his help at any moment. We have often found ourselves praying for more wisdom, more energy, more patience and more self-control.

Sila Over the course of our marriage we have tried to spend a few minutes each day praying together. We simply ask each other, 'What would you like me to pray for you today?' and then turn the answer into a prayer. When our children were all under the age of ten, my main request was pretty much the same every day – for more physical strength and more patience. Many times I felt strength and help coming from God, along with the support I felt from Nicky as he was prepared to pray the same prayer again and again.

Sometimes I've sensed God nudging me to change my behaviour towards our children and to act differently. I'd found myself thinking it was the children who were the problem and it was they who needed to change, when actually the problem was me and I needed to alter my approach. I've often had to look to God for that help or have asked Nicky to pray for me.

A friend of mine told me she often texts her husband during the day if there's something she wants him to pray for, either for herself or for their boys, and it makes all the difference.

Teaching our children to pray

One of my parents prayed with us every night before we went to bed and we had time to talk about stuff. I remember going through the 'Our Father' with Dad – a line each night and exploring the meaning of each phrase.

Hannah, aged 24

As well as praying for ourselves and for our children, we have hoped that our children will learn the value and power of praying themselves. We have tried to model to them how to pray each day over breakfast and at bedtime, as well as at other moments such as when they were anxious or unwell, or we were in the car on the way to school. Of course there were many times during their upbringing when there were grumbles and moods, and they did not want to pray. We never forced them, but simply said we would pray for them.

Over the years we have wanted to teach them the following four principles.

1. Being grateful

The first principle we have sought to pass on is to begin their prayers by saying thank you. There is always something to thank God for, however much of a struggle the day has been and whatever our feelings. Saying thank you changes our perspective and attitude. The start of a meal provides a regular opportunity to express to God our appreciation for his provision and not to take the necessities of life for granted. (We discovered that our children preferred a short 'grace'. Getting carried away, and bringing in the needs of the whole family and every front page news item, has not generally been conducive to gratitude.)

Saying thank you, as the first thing we do, prevents prayer becoming a shopping list of, 'Please do this, Lord, and please do that. And, oh, by the way, I really need an iPod, Lord. Please!'

2. Saying sorry

The second principle we have wanted to teach them is to say sorry to God when they know they have done something wrong or made a bad choice. To come clean with God every day and to ask for forgiveness sets us free both from guilt and from an abdication of responsibility.

Sila At bedtime, if there had been a particularly stormy incident earlier in the day involving something like dishonesty, unkindness or a particularly bad bout of anger, we might help them to say sorry in a prayer, such as, 'Lord, I'm so sorry for hitting Josh today and hurting him. Please forgive me,' and we would then pray for that child to know God's forgiveness and ask for his help to behave differently next time.

3. Praying for their own needs

Thirdly, we have encouraged our children to ask Jesus for his help for their own needs. We encouraged them to pray to be kind to somebody they did not really like, to be able to do their school work, to get better if they were unwell or to make right choices.

We tried to help them to see it was not wrong or selfish to pray for themselves. Rather it was part of expressing their dependence on God for all their needs, summed up in a phrase in the Lord's prayer, 'Give us today our daily bread.'

A family, who had four children and not much money, would pray together each year for a holiday and then wait to see what God would do. One of the daughters, now an adult, said it was always exciting to see what happened, and it helped to build her faith in God's provision.

4. Praying for other people

Fourthly, we have encouraged our children to pray for others: grandparents, friends, their teachers, a neighbour, people they knew who were sick, as well as those in need in other parts of the world.

Nicky When our children were teenagers, for several years we went on holiday with another family with similar aged children. Each evening before supper, two people, one from each family, would choose a verse from the Bible, say why they liked it and then tell everyone what they most wanted to be prayed for in the term or the year ahead. We then spent a few minutes praying for them. This might have involved a friend praying for a friend, an adult for

> a child, or a child for a parent.
>
> When we and our children look back on those holidays, we think of them as times of great fun and laughter, and they built a close bond of friendship between us as families.

Children who are taught to pray typically do so full of faith. In general, their trusting nature means that, while they are open to being led astray and therefore need special protection, they also more easily trust God to hear and answer their prayers. That is why Jesus says to us as adults, 'Unless you change and become like little children, you will never enter the kingdom of heaven.'[6]

Going to church

> *In my teens I hated going to church for a while and my parents were so cool about that – that made all the difference to going back again after a year.*
>
> **Tim, aged 41**

> *Going to church was such a central part of our growing up. We were encouraged to hang out with Christian friends. It was always fun.*
>
> **Chiara, aged 24**

We have tried to make going to church a normal and enjoyable activity for our children. This has meant finding a church that caters for children (and subsequently teenagers) where they could make friends among their own age group. These friendships have been very significant for them. We recognise that finding a suitable church can be difficult for many people, but we know some parents for whom finding a good, positive peer group for their children has been such a high priority that they have moved house in order to be near a suitable church.

We have not always stuck to the same Christian denomination and, even though the style of the services was less familiar to us in one church we attended, it suited us as a family as the children felt more at home. Their interest in and enjoyment of going to church has varied through the years. Each of them went through periods of complaining about having to go, that they did not learn anything in their groups and that anyway church was boring. Our answer has generally been to say that this is what we do as a family; and that, just as in our country all children go to school in order to be educated, whether they want to or not, so in our family we insist they go to church to develop their spiritual understanding.

When our children were under twelve, we all went to the same church and the same service. In their early teens, we still insisted they attended a church service but allowed them to choose where and when (within the bounds of safety for travelling).

We also encouraged them to go on youth group weekends away, or on holiday weeks organised by the church or other Christian organisations. It was the time spent with others of their own age, having great fun, as well as the teaching from the youth group leaders, which was instrumental for our children discovering a personal faith in their own time and in their own way. Having peers with similar beliefs and values has broadened their understanding of what it means to live as a Christian outside the confines of our own nuclear family.

By the time they reached sixteen, going to church on a Sunday was more or less accepted by them as being of value. Admittedly, through the remainder of their teenage years, two of them were more regular church-goers than the other two. With the latter we would occasionally remind them of the benefits of getting together with others each Sunday to worship, but we would not insist.

Allowing them to make their own choices

Of course we must recognise that our children may choose a very different path through life from the one we ourselves have taken, or the one we would have chosen for them. (We are not told in the Bible what John the Baptist's parents thought about the lifestyle choices made by their longed-for son – nor indeed about his fashion sense and diet!)[7]

When our children are old enough to live independently of us, they may adopt a different worldview or alternative lifestyle to our own and may cause us great disappointment and anxiety. If they have rejected our advice and are living in a way that we feel is detrimental to their health and well-being, all we can do is to keep loving them and praying for them in the knowledge that God loves them more than we ever could.

At the same time we can ask God to help us keep our hearts and our home open to them. The worst thing we can do is to push them away in order to make clear our disapproval. Of course, there will be some situations where parents need to put boundaries in place with an adult child. We have known families tragically pulled apart by a child who is a drug addict or an alcoholic and the parents have had to put markers in the sand and stop rescuing them. They do so to help them take responsibility for their own lives. That is love at its toughest.

Conclusion

By the time our children are eighteen, they will have had plenty of opportunities to hear and see our beliefs and values. At this point it is their choice whether or not to accept them. The parent of a twenty-year-old girl overheard her say to a friend, 'I don't know what I believe. I know there's something important in my parents' faith inside me – but right now I'm sitting on the fence.' Parents, who have children who are living recklessly and seem to have rejected their family values, can continue to hope that one day, through their love and their prayers, they will return like the prodigal son in Jesus' parable, having discovered for themselves that God loves them.

In his book, *What's So Amazing About Grace?* Philip Yancey writes a contemporary parable about the power of redeeming love:

> A young girl grows up on a cherry orchard just above Traverse City, Michigan. Her parents, a bit old-fashioned, tend to overreact to her nose ring, the music she listens to, and the length of her skirts. They ground her a few times, and she seethes inside. 'I hate you!' she screams at her father when he knocks on the door of her room after an argument, and that night she acts on a plan she has mentally rehearsed scores of times. She runs away.
>
> She has visited Detroit only once before, on a bus trip with her church youth group to watch the Tigers play. Because newspapers in Traverse City report in lurid detail the gangs, the drugs, and the

violence in downtown Detroit, she concludes that is probably the last place her parents will look for her. California, maybe, or Florida, but not Detroit.

Her second day there she meets a man who drives the biggest car she's ever seen. He offers her a ride, buys her lunch, arranges a place for her to stay. He gives her some pills that make her feel better than she's ever felt before. She was right all along, she decides: her parents were keeping her from all the fun.

The good life continues for a month, two months, a year. The man with the big car – she calls him 'Boss' – teaches her a few things that men like. Since she's underage, men pay a premium for her. She lives in a penthouse, and orders room service whenever she wants. Occasionally she thinks about the folks back home, but their lives now seem so boring and provincial that she can hardly believe she grew up there.

She has a brief scare when she sees her picture printed on the back of a milk carton with the headline 'Have you seen this child?' But by now she has blond hair, and with all the makeup and body-piercing jewellery she wears, nobody would mistake her for a child. Besides, most of her friends are runaways, and nobody squeals in Detroit.

After a year, the first sallow signs of illness appear, and it amazes her how fast the boss turns mean. 'These days, we can't mess around,' he growls, and before she knows it she's out on the street without a penny to her name. She still turns a couple of tricks a night, but they don't pay much, and all the money goes to support her habit. When winter blows in she finds herself sleeping on metal grates outside the big department store. 'Sleeping' is the wrong word – a teenage girl at night in downtown Detroit can never relax her guard. Dark bands circle her eyes. Her cough worsens.

One night as she lies awake listening for footsteps, all of a sudden everything about her life looks different. She no longer feels like a woman of the world. She feels like a little girl, lost in a cold and frightening city. She begins to whimper. Her pockets are empty and she's hungry. She needs a fix. She pulls her legs tight underneath her and shivers under the newspapers she's piled atop her coat. Something jolts a synapse of memory and a single image fills her mind: of May in Traverse City, when a million cherry trees bloom at once, with her golden retriever dashing through the rows and rows of blossoming trees in chase of a tennis ball.

God, why did I leave, she says to herself, and pain stabs at her heart. *My dog back home eats better than I do now*. She's sobbing, and she knows in a flash that more than anything in the world she wants to go home.

Three straight phone calls, three straight connections with the answering machine. She hangs up without leaving a message the first two times, but the third time she says, 'Dad, Mom, it's me. I was wondering about maybe coming home. I'm catching a bus up your way, and it'll get there about midnight tomorrow. If you're not there, well, I guess I'll just stay on the bus until it hits Canada.'

It takes about seven hours for a bus to make all the stops between Detroit and Traverse City, and during that time she realizes the flaws in her plan. What if her parents are out of town and miss the message? Shouldn't she have waited another day or so until she could talk to them? And even if they are home, they probably wrote her off as dead long ago. She should have given them some time to overcome the shock.

Her thoughts bounce back and forth between those worries and the speech she is preparing for her father. 'Dad, I'm sorry. I know I was wrong. It's not your fault; it's all mine. Dad, can you forgive me?' She says the words over and over, her throat tightening even as she rehearses them. She hasn't apologised to anyone in years.

The bus has been driving with all the lights on since Bay City. Tiny snowflakes hit the pavement rubbed worn by thousands of tyres, and the asphalt steams. She's forgotten how dark it gets at night out here. A deer darts across the road and the bus driver swerves. Every so often, a billboard. A sign posting the mileage to Traverse City. *Oh, God.*

When the bus finally rolls into the station, its air brakes hissing in protest, the driver announces in a crackly voice over the microphone, 'Fifteen minutes, folks. That's all we have here.' Fifteen minutes to decide her life. She checks herself in a compact mirror, smoothes her hair, and licks the lipstick off her teeth. She looks at the tobacco stains on her fingertips, and wonders if her parents will notice. If they're there.

She walks into the terminal not knowing what to expect. Not one of the thousand scenes that have played out in her mind prepare her for what she sees. There, in the concrete-walls-and-plastic-chairs bus terminal in Traverse City, Michigan, stands a group of forty brothers and sisters and great-aunts and uncles and cousins and a grandmother and great-grandmother to boot. They're all wearing goofy party hats and blowing noise-makers, and taped across the entire wall of the terminal is a computer-generated banner that reads 'Welcome home!'

Out of the crowd of well-wishers breaks her dad. She stares out through the tears quivering in her eyes like hot mercury and begins the memorized speech, 'Dad, I'm sorry. I know …'

He interrupts her. 'Hush, child. We've got no time for that. No time for apologies. You'll be late for the party. A banquet's waiting for you at home.'[8]

Pause and consider

Children thrive on:

- Encouragement
- Gratitude
- Boundaries
- Discipline
- Apologies
- Forgiveness
- Laughter
- Listening
- Freedom to be themselves
- Acceptance
- Trust

Children wither on:

- Criticism
- Complaining
- Legalism
- Authoritarianism
- Blame
- Fear of failure
- Intensity
- Ridicule
- Being made to conform
- Being judged
- Control

Which areas would you like to change or build on to make your home environment a place where your children can thrive?

Epilogue

I've tried everything, done everything. And being a father wins hands down.

Nick
Millionaire

Cornelia, the mother of Guacchi, once entertained a woman from Campania at her house. Since the woman made a great show of her jewels, which were among the most beautiful of the time, Cornelia detained her in conversation until her children came home from school. Then, pointing to her children, she said, 'These are my jewels.'

Valerius Maximus, 1st century

What children take from us, they give … We become people who feel more deeply, question more deeply, hurt more deeply, and love more deeply.

Sonia Taitz
Journalist and author

As the family goes, so goes the nation and so goes the whole world in which we live.

Pope John Paul II

Parenting, like white water rafting, is certainly challenging – and sometimes scary – but we should not forget to enjoy the ride. It is the journey of a lifetime. What seems overwhelming today is quite likely to blow over and seem relatively minor tomorrow. And, while it is a cliché, the time when our children are dependent on us passes so quickly and suddenly, before we know it, they are gone. The most common regret expressed by parents is that they did not spend enough time with their children: having fun, messing around, reading stories, going on outings and adventures, and taking the opportunities to talk.

Your children are a remarkable gift, and you are best placed to parent them. Wherever you are on that journey, we hope this book has provided some inspiration, some practical tools to adapt and make your own, and some ideas to think through and agree or disagree with.

Some of us, perhaps, try too hard and worry too much about how we are doing. We might become better and happier parents if we were to relax, trust our instincts and develop our own family style with its quirks and unique brand of humour. Far from being prescriptive, we hope that, within the important principles we have outlined, you feel confident to shape your own distinctive family life and parenting style.

Releasing our children

My mother has never stood between me and my life, never tried to hold me too tightly, always let me go free.

Noel Coward
Playwright

Every child has enormous potential. To see that fulfilled we may need to let go of some of our own goals for them. We may have hoped they would become doctors or play for Chelsea FC, but they prefer the arts. If so, we will need to adjust our expectations.

We may have dreamed they would be musicians or actors, but they are more interested in engineering or town planning and we need to let go of our aspirations. Our role is to create an environment in which they are free to discover their own interests, develop their own abilities and go for their own dreams. As we affirm them in their gifts and passions, we may well see them achieving greater things than we ever will.

A friend of ours, Harry Benson, who started the *Bristol Community Family Trust*, wrote about how he has sought to encourage his own children:

> I have always seen my main role as a father is to give my children a sense of mission. This doesn't mean forcing them into a box. But our problem is not too few options in life – it is too many. A sense of mission means getting them to think about what they want to do with their life, channelling them into a direction that makes sense. At home, we talk a lot

about what they are good at, what they enjoy. Even our littlest ones talk about what they would like to be when they grow up. ('Big' is the answer I like best!) We have future surgeons, sports writers, engineers and pilots in our family. Maybe. Of course it doesn't matter if the plan doesn't work out. Of course they can change direction. But having a goal to aim at provides focus, direction, confidence, opportunity, drive. And don't tell anyone, but giving the children a sense of mission gives the parent one too.[1]

The wider community

It takes a whole village to raise a child.

African proverb

Many other people besides us will help our children to fulfil their potential. Our own children's upbringing has involved lots of people who have influenced and shaped them. They include grandparents, aunts, uncles, cousins, godparents, friends, people who have lived with us, teachers who, as well as passing on knowledge, took an interest in them and inspired them, and youth group leaders who were positive role models at critical stages in their lives. We could not possibly have done our parenting alone.

Other parents, with children older than ours, acted as role models for us. They have helped us to answer positively the question that is often put to us: 'Is it possible to bring up children who are happy in themselves, who look outwards to those around them with kindness and respect, and who are motivated to make their own unique contribution in the world?'

Of course, there are no guarantees as to how any child will turn out, but we have known many children like that. They are not perfect and there have been ups and downs along the way. But we have seen that it *is* possible, and we have tried to emulate – in our own way – what their parents did.

Today as a society we tend to live isolated lives. Often we have moved far away from other members of the family. We do not know our neighbours. We encourage our children to stay indoors to keep them safe. Nick Pearce, director of the *Institute of Public Policy Research* in the UK, spoke of one of the principal reasons for the rise in antisocial behaviour by children today: 'In the past, local parents tended to look out for children in a community, deciding what behaviour was appropriate, how it should be dealt with and supporting each other in doing so. In closer knit communities, adults supervised their neighbours' children.'[2]

Family life thrives on involvement in a community. Parents have other parents for support, advice and encouragement. Part of the value of the parenting courses we run has been getting parents together. They soon discover they are not the only ones facing toddler tantrums or teenage hormones. They gain at least as much from each other as from the talks we give.

As well as our families and our friends, our church has provided a community, made up of all age groups and many different backgrounds and races. This, too, has made a profound difference to our family life. The church is, of course, open to all. Some have been Christians all their lives, while others are exploring faith. Some are drawn in by the worship or the teaching, while others are attracted by the network of relationships.

The church is designed to be a place of love, a place for growth and a place where we can be inspired by watching the way other people (including parents and children) relate to each other. We have been grateful for the way our children, growing up in this community, have had the opportunity to be part of a group of close friends, who support and influence each other for the good.

However, nothing is more important for our children's future than the family in which they grow up. At the end of the day, their own family is the place where they learn to relate.

Foundations for life

> *What family means to me is knowing what it means to my sister, brothers and parents. All else stems from this; a rooting that gives value to all other sentiments. It is the assurance that what is important to me is important to them. It is the assurance that my love for them matters to them, and, most importantly, that they unconditionally reciprocate that love.*
>
> *There is a wonderful sense of identity and belonging in knowing that whatever you do or pretend to be there is a group of people who will always know exactly who you are and love you unflinchingly. I once pretended to be an historian, but they knew I wasn't really and loved me anyway. I also pretended at the age of six to be Lawrence of Arabia, but I suspect that's beside the point.*
>
> **Barny, aged 23**

Nothing will equip children for life better than experiencing unconditional love within their family.

"There's nothing my son can do to make me love him more.....

but flowers would help occasionally"

Philip Yancey wrote about God's love, 'There's nothing we can do to make God love us more, and there's nothing we can do to make God love us less.'[3] That is the type of love our children need to know, first from us and ultimately from God. And that is the type of love we can all give, whatever our own family situation and whatever trials and heartache we may face along the way.

Recently we attended the funeral service of a friend, called Ify, who died of cancer at the age of forty, leaving her husband, Agu, and their two children, JJ, aged twelve, and Nonye, aged ten. Agu spoke at the service of their close family life, 'We have laughed a lot together. We laughed with each other and at each other. We laughed at other people and with other people. There has always been a lot of laughter in our home.' At the same service a recorded message by each of the children was played. This is what Nonye said:

> Dear Mum,
> You were a great mother, the best I could wish for. For the eleven years and five months I have known you (including the time in your tummy), you have always been there for me and cared for me; even when I was bad and did something really wrong you never stopped loving me and that I am grateful for. When I cried you picked me up and made me keep going.
>
> You helped me with my homework when I didn't understand and gave me advice for all my problems in school. You taught me to look at problems from both perspectives, and to always

stick to my Christian morals. You gave me great logical thinking skills which have come in handy a lot of times.

I remember our intense conversations or when I used to climb into your bed and ask, 'How was your day?' and you would ask me in return. You always had something interesting to tell or a lesson to learn and made a boring day sound really exciting. We used to cuddle up close and just talk about anything and everything as random and abstract as it may have been. I never had trouble talking to you because you always understood and never judged me.

Now I have to come to a close, but Mum, you were the best mum I could ever have. I love you and hope to see you again, not too soon though! Enjoy your time with God.

Nonye XXX

Endnotes

Chapter 1

1. *Focus on the Family* magazine, November 1991
2. Ross Campbell, *How to really love your child* (Scripture Press, 1977), p. 38
3. *The Marriage Course* is designed for any couple to strengthen their relationship whether or not they are married. (See 'Other useful resources' at the back for more information)
4. Kay Warren, AIDS awareness campaigner and author of *Dangerous Surrender* (Zondervan, 2007)

Chapter 2

1. Sarah Womack, The *Daily Telegraph*, 9 November 2006
2. Stephen Covey, The *7 Habits of Highly Effective Families* (Simon & Schuster UK, 1997) p. 115
3. Proverbs 31:15, 16, 18, 24, 25
4. Sue Palmer, *Toxic Childhood* (Orion Books, 2006) p. 174
5. Sue Palmer, *Toxic Childhood* (Orion Books, 2006) pp. 140–1
6. In the USA, MOPS (Mothers of Pre-Schoolers) provides similar help
7. Stephanie Condron, The *Daily Telegraph*, 13 November 2006, p. 3
8. Mental Health Foundation, *Bright Futures: Promoting Children and Young People's Mental Health*, 1999
9. 'The obsession that can end marriages', The *Daily Mail*, 21 May 1998
10. Raymond Blanc, quoted in 'Let's eat en famille!' The *Daily Mail*, 4 January 2007
11. Susan Jebb, quoted in Sue Palmer, *Toxic Childhood* (Orion Books, 2006) p. 36
12. The table on recommended hours of sleep for children under 12 is taken from Sue Palmer, *Toxic Childhood* (Orion Books, 2006) p. 80 and for adolescents from www.kidshealth.org/parent/general/sleep/sleep.html
13. Sue Palmer, *Toxic Childhood* (Orion Books, 2006) p. 187

Chapter 3

1. We have written in more detail about this in *The Marriage Book* (Alpha International, 2009 reprint), from p. 33
2. Rob Parsons, *The Sixty Minute Father* (Hodder and Stoughton, 1995) p. 15

Chapter 4

1. Pat Spungin and Victoria Richardson, *The Parentalk Guide to Brothers and Sisters* (Hodder and Stoughton, 2002) p. 81. The book has two chapters entitled 'Preparing for the new arrival' and 'Home at last', which have practical and helpful suggestions on how to make the arrival of a new baby as easy as possible for an older sibling
2. Penny Palmano, *Yes, Please. Whatever!* (Harper Thorsons, 2005) p. 227
3. Pat Spungin and Victoria Richardson, *The Parentalk Guide to Brothers and Sisters* (Hodder and Stoughton, 2002) p. 83
4. Linda Blair, *The Times*, 5 December 2007, p. 8

Chapter 5

1. Tom Marshall, *Right Relationships* (Sovereign World, 1992) p. 39
2. Gary Chapman, author of *The Five Love Languages* (Northfield Publishing, 1992). For a fuller understanding of these helpful insights for all relationships, we would recommend reading this together with Gary Chapman and Ross Campbell, *The Five Love Languages of Children* (Moody Press, 1997) and Gary Chapman, *The Five Love Languages of Teenagers* (Northfield Publishing, 2000)
3. Gary Chapman has a chapter in his book *The Five Love Languages of Children* written particularly for single parents
4. Gary Chapman and Ross Campbell, *The Five Love Languages of Children* (Moody Press, 1997) pp. 140–1

Chapter 6

1. Lester Middlehurst interview with Dawn French, *Daily Mail Weekend*, 4 May 1996, pp. 6–7
2. Sam McBratney and Anita Jeram, *Guess how much I love you* (Walker Books Ltd., 1996). We read a page with a child and then say, 'That's what I feel about you.' If we do this on a daily basis, using affirming words to express our love will

start to come more spontaneously

3. Steve Chalke, *How to succeed as a parent* (Hodder and Stoughton, 1997) p. 80
4. *Care for the Family Magazine* (Autumn 2006)

Chapter 7

1. Ross Campbell, *How to Really Love your Child* (Scripture Press, 1977), p. 67
2. Stephen Covey, *Living The 7 Habits: Stories of Courage and Inspiration* (Simon and Schuster, 1999) pp. 61–62
3. Rob Parsons, *The Heart of Success* (Hodder and Stoughton, 2002) pp. 147–150

Chapter 8

1. Rick Reilly, 'Meltdown at Augusta', *Sports Illustrated*, Vol. 85, Issue 27, 30 December 1996
2. Paul Scott-Evans, *Preparing to Parent Teenagers* (Authentic Media, 2000), p. 68
3. Gary Chapman and Ross Campbell, *The Five Love Languages of Children* (Alpha, 1998), pp. 83–84
4. Rob Parsons, *Care for the Family Magazine* (Autumn 2006)

Chapter 9

1. Damian Whitworth, 'Just Say No,' *The Times*, 20 July 2007, p. 4
2. *Ibid*
3. Hebrews 12:11
4. Proverbs 13:24
5. Credited to Erma Bombech. A number of variations to this poem exist
6. Sue Palmer, *Toxic Childhood* (Orion Books, 2006) pp. 281–282
7. Adapted from Sue Palmer, *Toxic Childhood* (Orion Books, 2006) pp. 282–284
8. *Ibid*, p. 282
9. Adapted from Anita Gurian, 'Parenting Styles/Children's Temperaments: The Match', www.AboutOurKids.org
10. Damian Whitworth, 'Just Say No,' *The Times* 20 July 2007, p. 4
11. *Ibid*

Chapter 10

1. Proverbs 22:6
2. Tessa Livingstone, *Child of our Time* (Bantam Press, 2005) p. 205
3. Dr Dorothy Einon quoted in 'How to Cope with Toddler Tantrums' by Louise Atkinson, *The Times*, 12 December 2000, p. 8
4. Thomas W. Phelan, *1-2-3 Magic* (Parent Magic, 2003), p. 27. This book has a number of helpful insights and practical ideas for imposing boundaries
5. Interview with Jan Parker and Julie Myerson, *Red magazine*, (1999) pp. 95–98
6. A medical condition such as autism or ADD (Attention Deficit Disorder) will require specialised advice on how to set proper expectations for your child's behaviour and how to handle disobedience

Chapter 11

1. Rob Parsons, *The Sixty Minute Father* (Hodder and Stoughton, 1995), p. 83

Chapter 12

1. Adapted from Tim Smith, *Almost Cool* (Moody Press, 1997) p. 33
2. Penelope Leach, 'Bringing up today's child' Part 3, *Sunday Mirror*, supplement, 25 April 1999, p. 5
3. Judith Wilson, 'Welcome to my space', The *Daily Telegraph* 14 July 2007, p. 66
4. Libby Purves, *Nature's Masterpiece* (Hodder and Stoughton, 2000) p. 208

Chapter 13

1. Haim Ginott, quoted in Tim Smith, *Almost Cool* (Moody Press, 1997) p. 75
2. Libby Purves, *Nature's Masterpiece* (Hodder and Stoughton, 2000) pp. 187–188
3. Daniel Hahn, quoted in Tim Smith, *Almost Cool* (Moody Press, 1997) pp. 64–65
4. Duncan Graham-Rowe 'Teen angst rooted in busy brain', *New Scientist*, 19 October 2002, Issue 2365 which cites

research on 'Cognitive efficiency on a match to sample task decreases at the onset of puberty in children' by Robert F. McGivern, Julie Andersen, Desiree Byrd, Kandis L. Mutter and Judy Reilly, *Brain and Cognition*, Volume 50, Issue 1, October 2002, pp. 73–89
5. Tim Smith, *Almost Cool* (Moody Press, 1997) pp. 150–151
6. Wayne Rice, *'Help! There's a teenager in my house'* edited by Wayne Rice (InterVarsity Press, 2005) p. 101
7. Penny Palmano, *Yes, Please. Whatever!* (Harper Thorsons, 2005) p. 248
8. Tony Campolo, *Following Jesus without embarrassing God* (Word Publishing, 1997) p. 205

Chapter 14

1. Rob Parsons, *Loving against the odds* (Hodder and Stoughton, 1998) p. 6
2. Simon Carr, 'A Boys World – Tears and All', The *Daily Telegraph*, 3 December 1998, p. 28
3. We will not adjudicate on whether smacking (termed 'spanking' in the USA) when the parent is in control of him or herself is ever right. In some countries it is illegal. In the UK, the current law allows a reasonable level or chastisement as long as it does not leave a mark on the child. Most child development experts are against smacking. All we would urge here is that it is better for a parent not to smack their child at all if he or she is in danger of doing so out of anger
4. David Ferguson, *Parenting with Intimacy* workshop tapes (Center for Marriage and Family Intimacy)
5. Colossians 3:13
6. Adapted from Beth Moore, *Praying God's Word* (Nashville: Broadman & Holman, 2000, 2003) pp. 220–223
7. Ross Campbell with Carole Sanderson Streeter, *Kids in Danger* (Alpha Publication, 1995), pp. 84–86

Chapter 15

1. Ross Campbell with Rob Suggs, *How to Really Parent Your Teenager: Raising Balanced Teens in an Unbalanced World* (W Publishing Group, 2006) p. 168
2. Leah Hardy, 'Ready, mummy? Maybe, baby.' *The Times*, 14 April 2007

3. Dr Hugh Jolly, paediatrician and author, puts forward this concept of the 'good enough parent'
4. Philippians 4:6
5. Taken from *Care for the Family Support Net* website www.careforthefamily.org.uk
6. Taken from kidshealth.org and www.mayoclinic.com
7. Combination of kidshealth.org and Ellis P. Copeland 'Stress in children: Strategies for Parents and Educators' (National Association of School Psychologists, 2004)
8. Taken from kidshealth.org
9. Maureen Rice 'The High Price of Success', The *Daily Mail* 22 August 2004, *You* magazine
10. Adapted from advice given by Lynette on *Parenting Café* website (www.parentingcafe.co.uk) and by the vice-principal of a Sixth Form college
11. There is a fourth group referred to as EDNOS (Eating Disorders Not Otherwise Specified) for people who do not have the classic symptoms of anorexia, bulimia or compulsive overeating, but still have very disordered eating and thinking
12. Nancy Alcorn, *Mercy for Eating Disorders* (Providence House Publishers, 2003), p. 137

Chapter 16

1. John Clare, 'Parents abandon sex education role', The *Daily Telegraph*, 30 April 2002
2. Jan Parker, 'Teenagers: Not Quite so Bad as They're Painted?', *The Times*, 25th October 2003, p. 12 and '*Everyday Conversations* Every Day' report commissioned as part of the Department for Children, Schools and Families 'Time to Talk' campaign (June 2008)
3. The *Week*, 13 October 2000. Paraphrase from Yasmin Alibhai-Brown's article 'Victims of a culture that won't let our young people say no to sex' The *Independent*, 11 October 2000
4. Dr Tanya Byron, 'How do I stop her having sex at 13?' *The Times*, 13 August 2007
5. Philip Yancey, *Rumours of Another World* (Zondervan, 2003) p. 92
6. Contraceptive failure rate for male condoms by inexperienced users recorded as 17.4 per cent by Guttmacher Institute in 'Facts of contraceptive use' at www.guttmacher.org/pubs/fb_contr_use.html.

See the table for 'First-year contraceptive failure rates'. For information on the levels of effectiveness of condoms in preventing different sexually transmitted diseases, see the Medical Institute, 'Sexual health for life', at www.medinstitute.org/public/department40.cfm

7. Kiernan, K., 1999, 'Childbearing outside marriage in Western Europe', *Population Trends*, Vol. 98, pp. 11–20
8. We are grateful to Lin Button, a counsellor in London, UK, who runs healing conferences, for her input into this section on the roles of mother and father
9. Penny Palmano, *Yes, Please. Whatever!* (Harper Thorsons, 2005) p. 164
10. See the report by the Health Protection Agency 'Sexually transmitted infections and young people in the United Kingdom: 2008 report', www.hpa.org.uk
11. There are more than a hundred crisis pregnancy advice centres around the UK run by CARE www.careconfidential.com
12. Information about the effects of having an abortion can be found at www.abortionrisks.org
13. Nicky and Sila Lee, *The Marriage Book* (Alpha International, 2000) p. 303

Chapter 17

1. Anon., 'Teen voices', The *Independent on Sunday*, 5 November 2006, p. 25
2. Barbara Green, The *Daily Telegraph*, 2 April 2007, p. 24
3. *Ibid*
4. Michael Shelden, 'I drank so that I felt as if I belonged', The *Daily Telegraph*, 26 February 2007, p. 27
5. Linda Blair, 'We don't do drugs', *The Times*, 11 June 2007
6. Michael Shelden, 'I drank so that I felt as if I belonged', The *Daily Telegraph*, 26 February 2007, p. 27
7. 'Discussing drinking with your children' published by The Portman Group Trust
8. *Ibid*
9. 'Sorry I never touch a drop', *The Times*, 17 November 2000 p. 5
10. Jonathan Leake, 'Steady, folks, you may turn teens to drink' The *Sunday Times*, 28 September 2008, p. 13
11. Anon., 'Children who drink at home "less likely to binge drink" ', The *Daily Mail*, 11 May 2007

12. Kate Summers, 'Skunk killed my beloved son', The *Daily Telegraph*, 26 March 2007, p. 27
13. Barbara Green, *The Daily Telegraph*, 2 April 2007, p. 24
14. Linda Blair, 'We don't do drugs', *The Times*, 11 June 2007
15. Leah Hardy, 'Cocaine: Another line, dear?', *The Times*, 7 December 2003, p. 42
16. *Ibid*
17. *Ibid*
18. Adapted from *Care for the Family*, 'How to drug proof your kids', www.careforthefamily.org.uk and Linda Blair, 'How can parents turn their teenagers away from drugs', *The Times*, 11 June 2007
19. To contact FRANK within the UK, ring 0800 776600, or go to www.talktofrank.com

Chapter 18

1. Mark Hooper, 'Old before their time', The *Independent on Sunday*, 5 November 2006, p. 16
2. Lee Glendinning, 'Psychologists tame these teenage terrors by taking away their television (But guess what... it was all an experiment for TV)', *Evening Standard*, 14 March 2005, p. 21
3. Bruce Stockler, 'No PlayStation, kids. Get ready to be social outcasts', *The Times*, 6 February 2007
4. The children on the sponsoring family may send presents and photos, write letters and pray for the sponsored child. We recommend the work of Compassion – www.compassionuk.org
5. Laura Clark, 'The 15 ways in which too much TV wrecks your child's health', The *Daily Mail*, 19 February 2007
6. Aric Sigman, 'Visual voodoo: the biological impact of watching TV', The *Biologist*, Volume 54, No.1, February 2007, pp. 12–17
7. Dave Veerman, *'Help! There's a teenager in my house'*, edited by Wayne Rice (Inter Varsity Press, 2005) p. 146
8. Rosemary Behan, 'My name is Rosemary. I'm an internet addict …' *The Times*, 26 February 2007
9. Paul Lewis, 'Teenage networking websites face anti-paedophile investigation', The *Guardian*, 3 July 2006
10. Celia Dodd, 'Is it really spying if you love them?', *The Times*, 28 April 2007, p. 9

Chapter 19

1. Tony Campolo, *Following Jesus without embarrassing God* (Word Publishing, 1997), p. 258
2. *Ibid*, p. 258
3. *Ibid*, p. 259

Chapter 20

1. Emma Cook, 'Bad News Bunnies', *The Times*, 16 April 2005, p. 18
2. Interview with Sir Paul Smith, *Easy Living*, June 2005, p. 216
3. The Alpha Course offers the opportunity to hear and discuss the relevance and truth of the Christian message. (See 'Other useful resources' at the back for more information)
4. Proverbs 22:6
5. John 15:12
6. Emma Cook, 'Bad News Bunnies', *The Times*, 16 April 2005, p. 18

Chapter 21

1. Ephesians 6:4
2. Deuteronomy 6:4–7
3. Luke 1:41
4. Galatians 5:22–23
5. Psalm 138:8
6. Matthew 18:3
7. Matthew 3:4
8. Philip Yancey, *What's so Amazing about Grace?* (Zondervan, 1997), pp. 49–51

Epilogue

1. Harry Benson, BCFT newsletter (www.bcft.co.uk), July/August 2008
2. Nick Pearce, *Freedom's Orphans: Raising youth in a changing world* (Institute for Public Policy Research, 2006)
3. Philip Yancey, *What's so Amazing about Grace?* (Zondervan, 1997) p. 71

Index

Other useful resources

General

raisingkids.co.uk – a general parenting website offering help on most of the issues below

Support for single and step-parents

careforthefamily.org.uk – Care for the Family is a national UK charity that provides resources for all areas of family life, including support for single and step-parents and those who are bereaved. Organises residential breaks in the UK for single parents and their children

Support for couples

- *The Marriage Book* by Nicky and Sila Lee (Alpha International, 2000) is easy to read and is designed to prepare, build and even mend marriages
- **themarriagecourse.org** – *The Marriage Course* is designed for any couple to strengthen their relationship whether or not they are married. Started by Nicky and Sila Lee in London, UK, it is now being run in thousands of locations around the world with DVDs or live talks. Over seven sessions the course covers the essential tools for a healthy, lasting relationship and is applicable to couples who have a strong relationship and to those who are struggling. The talks are interspersed with opportunities for each couple to discuss how the topic affects them and to work through their differences. Their conversations are private and there is no groupwork. See the website for more information and a directory of courses running around the world

Outdoor activity centres

- **goape.co.uk** – physically and mentally challenging fun, laughter and adventure high up in the trees. High wire adventure courses in outdoor activity centres in different forests around the UK

Post-natal depression

- **nctpregnancyandbabycare.com** – the National Childbirth Trust provides information on many aspects of pregnancy, birth and early parenthood, and offers support to those experiencing post-natal depression
- **apni.org** – the Association for Post-Natal Illness provides information and advice about post-natal depression, and offers telephone support from women who have experienced and recovered from the condition

Stress and depression in children

- **youngminds.org.uk** – Young minds is a national UK charity helping with children and young peoples' mental health. It provides information and advice to both sufferers and parents

Handling anger

- Further help for parents to understand and handle their anger: *Anger: Handling a Powerful Emotion in a Healthy Way* by Gary Chapman (Northfield Publishing, 2007)
- Further insights to train children to handle their anger: *How to Really Love Your Angry Child* by Ross Campbell (David C. Cook, 2004)

Drugs and alcohol

- **dpyk.org.uk** – *How to drug proof your kids* is a resource of *Care for the Family*. They run a six-session course in different locations around the UK to help educate and provide skills to parents and carers concerned about drugs

- **talktofrank.com** – a national UK drugs advice helpline with useful 'need help' section that lists all local agencies, clinics and support groups
- **addaction.co.uk** – *Addaction* is the UK's largest drug and alcohol treatment charity and has a guide for parents that gives advice on how to broach the subject of drug use with teenagers
- **knowcannabis.org.uk** – a website for cannabis users, providing information on the physical and mental effects of cannabis and the risk of dependency, alongside resources for those who wish
to assess their own use or to stop

Debt counselling

- **creditaction.org.uk** – *Credit Action* is a national UK charity which offers debt counselling and advice on management of resources to help people manage their finances
- **capuk.org** – *Christians Against Poverty* is a debt counselling and management charity with a national network of centres operated by local churches

Eating disorders

- **b-eat.co.uk** – the *Eating Disorders Association* offers help to people with eating disorders and their families. They provide information, a helpline and a network of self-help groups around the UK. Their website has a facility for searching for services available locally
- **b-eat.co.uk/YoungPeople/Home** – created with the help of young people for those with an eating disorder or worried about a friend
- **careforthefamily.org.uk/supportnet** – the *Care for the Family Support Net* website has helpful articles on a variety of subjects including information on eating disorders
- *The Golden Cage: The Enigma of Anorexia Nervosa* by Hilde Bruch (Harvard University Press, paperback edition 2001)

- *A Way Out of Despair* (CWR Publishing, 1995) by Helena Wilkinson
- *Love Hunger – Recovery from Food Addiction* (Guideposts, 1989) by Dr. Frank Minirth, Dr. Paul Meier, Dr. Robert Hemfelt & Dr. Sharon Sneed

Talking about sex with children

- *Who made me?* by Malcolm and Meryl Doney and illustrated by Nick Butterworth and Mick Inkpen (Candle Books, 2006). Illustrated book to explain the facts of life to young children
- *What is God's design for my body?* by Susan Horner (Moody Publishers, 2004). An explanation of the reasons for sexual boundaries written for pre-teens and young teenagers using biblical references and personal stories
- For other resources to help children and teenagers maintain appropriate sexual boundaries, see *Focus on the Family* website at www.focusonthefamily.com/parenting/sexuality/talking_about_sex.aspx

Crisis pregnancy advice

- **careconfidential.com** – *Care Confidential* offers crisis pregnancy advice, information and support via their helpline and online advisors. *Care Confidential* also provides links to a national UK network of independent local advice centres offering free and confidential help
- **abortionrisks.org** – information on the risks and long term harm associated with abortion

Addressing sexual abuse

- **nspcc.org.uk** – gives advice and support to adults and children, including free and confidential telephone counselling for children through *ChildLine*. See contact details at www.childline.org.uk
- **intothelight.org.uk** – offers practical and spiritual support, information and resources for those who have been sexually abused and those who support

them. Parents who have been abused will find it harder to talk to their children about sexual boundaries unless they have addressed their own past

- *The Wounded Heart: Hope for Adult Victims of Childhood Sexual Abuse* by Dan B Allender (NavPress Publishing Group,1995)
- *The Sexual Healing Journey: A Guide for Survivors of Sexual Abuse* by Wendy Maltz (Harper Perennial, revised edition 2001)

Exploring beliefs and values

- **alpha.org** – the Alpha course offers the opportunity to hear and discuss the truth and relevance of Christianity. It has helped many parents to explore their own beliefs and to know what they want to pass on to their children. It is currently being run in over 7,000 churches in the UK and over 30,000 churches world-wide. The website has a 'find a course near you' facility

Children's Bibles

- *Baby Bible for Boys* and *Baby Bible for Girls* (Lion Publishing, 2006) and *Baby Prayers* (Lion Publishing, 2007) by Sarah Toulmin – an ideal first Bible to read with young children
- *The Children's Bible* in 365 Stories by Pat Alexander (Lion Publishing, 2001) – to read with children aged five and upwards. Each day has a story of a suitable length for bedtime with imaginative pictures and in language that is well-written and easily understood
- *New Century Version Youth Bible* (Authentic Media, 2007) – designed for teenagers with relevant comments around the text

Addressing death and dying

For children up to seven:

- *Badger's Parting Gifts* by Susan Varley (Picture Lions, 1994)
- *Granpa* by John Burningham (Red Fox, 2003)

- *Waterbugs and Dragonflies: Explaining Death to Young Children* by Doris Stickney (Continuum International Publishing, 2002)
- *Remembering Mum* by Ginny Perkins and Leon Morris (A & C Black Publishers Ltd, 1996)

For children aged eight to thirteen:

- *What on Earth do you do when Someone Dies?* by Trevor Romain (Free Spirit Publishing, 2003)

For teenagers/young adults:

- *Facing Grief: Bereavement and the Young Adult* by Susan Wallbank (Lutterworth Press, 1991)
- *My Father Died and My Mother Died* by Susan Wallbank (Cruse, 1998)

Other resources available from Family Life and Relationships at Alpha International

The Marriage Preparation Course

Five sessions designed to help engaged couples develop strong foundations for a lasting marriage, covering:

1. Communication
2. Commitment
3. Resolving Conflict
4. Keeping Love Alive
5. Shared Goals and Values

The Marriage Preparation Course **DVD**
Code MPDVD05 / £40
Guest Manual
Code 978 1904074 39 7 / £2
Leaders' and Support Couples' Guide
Code 978 1904074 75 5 / £2
The Marriage Preparation Course Leaders' Toolkit **DVD with CD-Rom**
Code MPCTKDVD / £30
Ready for Marriage? **Booklet**
Code 978 1905887 02 6 / £1

See alphashop.org for more resources to support the running of this course.

The Marriage Course

Seven sessions offering any married couple the tools to build a strong and healthy relationship that lasts a lifetime. During each evening couples talk about important issues that can get swept under the carpet in the rush of daily life. Topics covered are:

1. **Building Strong Foundations**
2. **The Art of Communication**
3. **Resolving Conflict**
4. **The Power of Forgiveness**
5. **The Impact of Family - Past and Present**
6. **Good Sex**
7. **Love in Action**

The Marriage Course Party (an opportunity for guests to invite frends to hear about the course)

Extra Session: **Coping with Times of Separation**

The Marriage Course **DVD**
MCDVD09 / £50.00
Guest Manual
978 1 902750 27 9 / £2.00
Leaders' Guide
978 1 904074 69 4 / £1.50
The Marriage Course Leaders' Toolkit **DVD & CD-Rom set**
MCTKDVD / £35.00

See alphashop.org for more resources to support the running of this course.

While both courses are based on Christian principles, they are designed for couples with or without a church background.

Discounted Starter Packs containing everything you need to run a course are available for both *The Marriage Preparation Course* and *The Marriage Course* – see alphashop.org for more details.

Also from Alpha International

Is God a Delusion? by Nicky Gumbel
Drawing upon his experience as a barrister, Nicky Gumbel addresses the biggest issue of our age: does God exist?

(Book/Code 9781905887194/£4.99)

Alpha – Questions of Life by Nicky Gumbel
The Alpha course talks in book form.
Over 1.3 million copies sold.

(Book/Code HTB04/Trade Code 9781842911648/£6.99)

Searching Issues by Nicky Gumbel
Tackles the seven most common objections to the Christian faith.

(Book/Code HTB05/Trade Code 9780854767397/£6.99)

Challenging Lifestyle by Nicky Gumbel
Examines the Sermon on the Mount and presents us with some radical alternatives for how to live in the 21st century. A small group DVD and manuals for guests also available.

(Book/Code HTB46/Trade Code 9780854767427/£6.99)

How to Run The Alpha Course – Telling Others by Nicky Gumbel
A useful 'how to' book that includes material from the Alpha conference and Alpha leaders' training.

(Book/Code HTB20/Trade Code 9781842911723/£6.99)

30 Days by Nicky Gumbel
An excellent introduction to reading the Bible, designed to be read over thirty days.

(Booklet/Code 9781902750811/£2.50)

A Life Worth Living by Nicky Gumbel
Based on Paul's letter to the Philippians, this book offers a practical and positive guide to achieving exactly this.

(Book/Code HTB09/Trade Code 9780854767403/£6.99)

Why Jesus? by Nicky Gumbel
An evangelistic booklet for those having their first thoughts about the Christian faith. Designed to be given away. Christmas and Easter versions of *Why Jesus?* are also available, see alphashop.org for more details.

(Booklet/Code 9781904074571/£0.50 Large Print Booklet/Code 9781905887156/£0.50)

God at Work by Ken Costa
Countering the widespread view that God and business just do not mix, investment banker Ken Costa argues that the God who created and sustains the world is also the God of the workplace.

Published in association with Continuum
(Book/Code 978 0826496 35 5/£7.99)

From Vision to Action by Tricia Neill
Drawing on more than 12 years experience as Executive Director at Holy Trinity Brompton, Tricia offers valuable insights for churches of all sizes. A 'how to' for turning vision into reality.

(Book/Code 978 190407 487 8/£5.99)

Café Theology by Michael Lloyd
Whether we've been on the Christian journey our whole life, we're just starting out or we haven't even bought a ticket, this extraordinary book is applicable to our ordinary lives. This new edition has been updated and revised.

(Book/Code 978 1 905887354 7/£7.99)

Also by Nicky and Sila Lee

The Marriage Book

- How can we be happily married to one person for the whole of our lives?
- How do we resolve conflict?
- How can we discover and rediscover sexual intimacy?

ISBN 978 1904074 55 7
Price £7.99

Other titles from Alpha International available from alphashop.org

Nicky and Sila Lee with their four children, Barny, Kirsty, Josh and Benj and their son-in-law Rick, and daughter-in-law Tamsin.